Advance Praise for *American Cider*

"Sommelier Pucci and food journalist Cavallo impress in this deeply researched account of the history of apple cider. . . . This fascinating guide will appeal to history buffs and imbibers alike."

—*Publishers Weekly*

"*American Cider* is not just a thorough guide to the history of apples and cider in this country; it is an inspiring survey of the orchardists and cidermakers alive today who are devoting their lives to pomaceous diversity, agricultural sustainability, and a fairer food system for all."

—ALICE WATERS, owner of Chez Panisse, founder of The Edible Schoolyard Project

"Starting five hundred million years ago and continuing through to the tasting rooms of today, *American Cider* meticulously explores each branch of cider's family tree. Pucci and Cavallo are thorough and enthusiastic chroniclers, who celebrate cider's pomologists and pioneers with infectious curiosity and passion."

—BIANCA BOSKER, *New York Times* bestselling author of *Cork Dork*

"For years, American craft cider has been one of the most dynamic players on the contemporary beverage scene, a delicious and distinctive drink seemingly appearing from nowhere, but as Dan

Pucci and Craig Cavallo show, cider and America have been deeply entwined for more than four hundred years. Until now, we've had only glimpses of this story, but *American Cider* puts it all together, weaving history, botany, anthropology, and insight into the first comprehensive account of what American cider is and how it got that way. This is an essential volume for anyone wishing to navigate the extraordinarily diverse landscape of contemporary cider, but it is much more than that. By tracing the human and natural forces at work over four centuries, Pucci and Cavallo provide a new context for understanding how America has shaped cider—and, in so doing, a new way for understanding America."

—ROWAN JACOBSEN, author of
Apples of Uncommon Character and *A Geography of Oysters*

"Pucci and Cavallo survey the American cider landscape with a compass both diplomatic and passionate. It's a far-reaching scene, dotted with tidbits and profound with consequence, but our guides are skilled artisans; the painting is both intimate with detail and bucolic in its sum."

—ANDY BRENNAN, cider maker,
apple grower, and author of *Uncultivated*

"Whenever I've had questions about cider, Dan Pucci has long been my first stop for expertise. Now he can be everyone's go-to expert, thanks to this thorough, comprehensive guide on ciders and the apples used to make them."

—KARA NEWMAN, author of *Cocktails with a Twist*
and spirits editor, *Wine Enthusiast* magazine

"*American Cider* is a deeply researched road map to modern cider's revival, reminding readers why well-made cider should always be the apple of drinkers' eyes. All too often, cider is seen as the sugary stuff that's sold by the juice box. Cider evangelists Pucci and Cavallo take readers on a centuries-spanning journey from colonial

America's historic orchards to today's visionary makers that are spearheading the juiced-up cider revival. After reading *American Cider*, you'll never eye an apple the same way again."

—JOSHUA M. BERNSTEIN, author of
The Complete Beer Course and *Drink Better Beer*

"*American Cider* offers a multilayered narrative that will appeal to anyone curious about the past, present, and future of this iconic beverage, which is as rich and diverse as America itself. Dan Pucci and Craig Cavallo delve into the social, political, and geographic history behind cider's rise, decline, and rebirth in this country, and profile many of the influential figures on the contemporary cider scene. Highly recommended for ciderphiles and history buffs alike."

—BEN WATSON, author of *Cider, Hard and Sweet*

"A welcomed and informed deep dive into our little, growing industry—shedding a much needed light on what we're really made of: interesting people, from all walks of life, trying to get the best from the fruit we exalt."

—RYAN JAMES BURK, head cidermaker, Angry Orchard

AMERICAN
CIDER

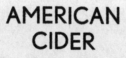

BALLANTINE BOOKS | NEW YORK

AMERICAN CIDER

A Modern Guide to a Historic Beverage

Dan Pucci
and Craig Cavallo

For Lucy and Sylvie

———

For Jenny, the roots that keep me standing.

CONTENTS

AMERICAN
CIDER

INTRODUCTION

Welcome to the emerging and dynamic world of cider in the United States of America. While this book can steer you to great bottles, amazing orchards, and unforgettable experiences, it can also serve as your guide to the changing tides of this country, its farmers, fermenters, and imbibers. American cider is standing at the precipice of a new era, with contributions drawn from around the world to create a unique American chorus filled with voices big and small, established and rising, revolutionary and reactionary.

When we embarked on this project, we were committed to outlining for cider drinkers of all experiences how cider and apples vary throughout the United States. We talked to growers, pomologists, cidermakers, and orchardists from all over the country, and explored the historical significance of apples and cider throughout the nation's development. We believe that by sharing these differences, we can help the reader better understand the industry and become an informed cider drinker—provided with the knowledge and foundation to comprehend what has been a boom in apple growing, cidermaking, and cider drinking in the United States.

American cidermakers, along with cidermakers around the globe, are adapting contemporary techniques from agriculture, brewing, winemaking, and marketing to breathe new life into this historic beverage. Cider, like wine, is not a monolith. It is a category with a diverse range of options that can satisfy nearly every drinker without compromise. With nearly a thousand cider producers across America as of 2020, as well as a wide array of different styles and formats, the beverage can be intimidating to the newcomer. But it's important to remember that cider is about exploration, from the drinker who is willing to push their palate and expectations to the producer who betters their technique and understanding of their craft year after year. This budding collection of beverages is poised to build a unique and definitive American identity that is shaped by its community, history, and geography, as cidermakers and consumers learn more about the potential of the land around them and the apples among us.

Diane Flynt, of the late Foggy Ridge Cider in Dugspur, Virginia, was the first phone interview we conducted for the book. She is an advocate for Dan and his passionate work in New York City on (coincidentally) Orchard Street at the since-closed cider bar Wassail. Flynt's own passion and depth of knowledge, we thought, would be the perfect place to dive in.

Flynt, who is known within the cider community for her spirited opinions, was quick to caution us against the many tropes surrounding apple and cider cultures. In reflecting on what this project became, how it took its own course, we go back to that first phone call with her. "I'm not so sure there *are* any regional differences in the ciders," she said. "I think you need to be very careful about examining that idea."

She was right. Throughout our research and interviews, we found more similarities than differences in the country's multitude of apple and cider cultures. The few differences we did find— climate, geography, and fermentation styles—were overshadowed by similar obstacles, pressures, and limitations deeply entwined with today's culture. Apple growers, orchardists, academic researchers, fermentation enthusiasts, industry giants, home growers, farmers, and pomologists all face a near identical set of problems.

Orchardists struggle with limited resources while trying to sell a valuable product at low prices. We learned that all anyone needs to be convinced of climate change is to talk to a farmer for five minutes. People want to make cider, but the fruit to make cider is not available, because the people who need to grow the fruit do not have the information needed to plant the right apples, because the people they need to do the research are tied up in bigger agriculture. In this country, agriculture big and small is built upon white supremacy and a legacy of exploitation—of both people and land. Despite cider being a comparatively inclusive industry, reverberations of this legacy remain.

When people talk about cider, they often begin with American cider's glory days, when the drink was more American than apple pie and was drunk with abandon by urban merchants, landed gentry, and poor journeymen alike. This incomplete history focuses on the apple preferences of the aristocratic, educated, wealthy, and Christian white elites who became the nation's founding fathers. But little has been written about the country's regional cultures and farm systems, and contributions to apple growing and cider-making from Indigenous and slave communities have been all but forgotten.

Apples and cider played an inestimable role in the creation of the United States beyond its privileged culture. These pages merely scratch the surface, but in them we've made a concentrated effort to tell the history of the United States through the apple's lens. The where, why, and how of apple planting, who was growing them, and the motives of the federal government are vital pieces consistently missing from the puzzle. With these pieces, we see American cider as a story not solely of aristocrats, but of farming, of individuals who struggle and those who find opportunity, of rural and urban lifestyles, of producers, workers, and consumers.

We hope this book does justice to the generations—whether first, fifth, or tenth—of workers faced with the daunting task of educating the populace. We were never concerned with describing the differences in flavor between a Golden Russet apple from Virginia versus one from New Mexico, because cider's true beauty does not start when it hits our lips. It begins with the intentions and agricultural principles that guide this fledgling community. While we express the basics of regional apple characteristics, we sought to more thoroughly root around in the annals of history, dust off the analog and digital archives, connect with people, and bring information to light in book form in a way no one has yet done.

And so, with this book, we hope to join a nation of laborers working with apples as their compass. Like the laborers of the First Transcontinental Railroad, set on an ambiguous path to meet at a later point in life and geography, today's cider community works on the same path, eager to navigate it but unsure of where it will end up. The regional differences in cider are details that tell us a story about the character of North America. We want to help guide the rails to a central point, from which we can all share a perspective, come to understand history through the apple's lens, and see the work that has gone into clearing the way from footpath to intercontinental superhighway.

And of course, we want more people to enjoy (and drink more) cider, so we also hope to help the reader feel informed and empowered to make choices about cider that bring them joy and foster community.

As we enjoy this wonderfully complex yet perfectly simple beverage, we can both reflect on the past and look forward to the future. We do not aim for this book to be about a niche community, but instead to be a new voice in the ongoing, 400-year-old national conversation that is the history of the United States of America.

Cider today is fueled by a quest to embrace something better, to change our relationship with consumption and return to values of farming, clean food, and community. The local food movement in North America—the desire to support localized, small-scale, sustainable efforts in agriculture—is partly a reaction to the ills of the industrial food system. There is perhaps no greater symbol of that system's perversity than the glossy, beaming-but-flavorless Red Delicious apple, bred for appearance and not taste. Consumers' values have shifted from food as sustenance to food with meaning, quality, and distinction. The future of great cider lies in its story of community and place, empowering drinkers to find meaning and expectation within their beverages.

As Americans, we each have an alluring, albeit indescribable, relationship with the apple. Call it a symbol of this country. But the table apple as we know it is a relatively recent arrival to the United States. Like the settlers who came to the Atlantic shores and established roots for a new life, the apple first had to cross the ocean. Upon setting out for new land, many people brought cultural relics from their old home, unsure and hopeful of what would prove fruitful. Among them were apple seeds. Not all of them survived, but, through perseverance and luck, some have been fortunate enough to reap the bounty sown into the soils of history.

A Short History of Cider

The earliest records of cidermaking are often credited to Greco-Roman geographer Strabo (64 or 62 BC – AD 24) and Roman philosopher Pliny the Elder (AD 23 or 24 – AD 79). But their accounts are not explicit, and it is likely that older generations merely ascribed cider to their writings. Cider expert Eduardo Coto claims the *Ego Faliko*, a will of sorts written in 803 in Asturias in northern Spain, which designates orchards there for making cider, is the earliest literature to cite cider specifically. In the eighth and ninth centuries, Charlemagne, the Frankish king, supported cidermaking in his domain, and Norman conquerors most likely brought the craft to England after the invasion of 1066.

Even in medieval times, wine was traded internationally, but cider remained a local beverage. Distinctive regional cider cultures emerged from this relative isolation, with individual cider traditions, styles, and perspectives growing out of local resources and demand. These cidermaking regions were often poorly suited for grapes or barley, making apples the most prolific source of alcohol.

Cider was once very popular in North America, as well, beginning in the seventeenth century, when most apples were grown from seed—their vast diversity of genetics celebrated and fermented—before commercial orcharding and fruit breeding for fresh eating. But cider was unable to keep pace with the changing markets, customs, and cultures of a nation quickly developing its urban centers, and its popularity waned by the mid-nineteenth century. A summary from a 1900 Connecticut Pomological Society meeting addresses the change:

> From the earliest settlement of the state, fruit-growing for the family home-supply has been a prominent feature of Connecticut agriculture, the apple being a main reliance. The old seedling trees scattered over all our farms today are plain evidence that our ancestors took their apple-juice through the spigot of the cider-barrel rather than fresh from the pulp of the ripe fruit of some finer variety. A hundred years ago every farmhouse cellar wintered from thirty to fifty barrels of cider, while today it is hardly respectable to have any, and probably not one family in ten now has even one single barrel on tap as a beverage.

Cider was never entirely snuffed out of existence, but as the mainstream moved off the farm and into cities, cider did not follow. Agriculture shifted from small, self-supporting farms to large operations functioning as links in a supply chain, and cider did not keep up. Cider today is testing the limits of that supply chain by tapping into it for materials—or by casting it aside to create something different.

Contemporary cider has not simply appeared from thin air. It has grown slowly over the course of decades. In 1991, there were ten cideries in the United States, and that number would see only marginal growth for twenty years. It was not until 2009 that the total exceeded a hundred. But the ensuing decade saw a tenfold increase. Cider is now made in all fifty states and continues to take up more and more space in bars, restaurants, bottle shops, and convenience stores. The thousand producers of cider across the country are now an ingrained part of the beverage and farming community. These producers, and their products, have the power to repair a broken agricultural system that has been fighting to get by for multiple generations.

Cider is often viewed by drinkers as somewhere between beer and wine, but all three developed along very different paths in the United States. Both wine and beer were framed as European beverages in the beginning, as European culture took root in North America. In the twentieth century, as wine and beer went mainstream, cider took its own less commercial-minded path. It took generations for American wine and beer—very popular in-country—to find their unique identities on the global stage, but cider today is moving at a meteoric rate, and the rest of the world is looking toward the United States for inspiration.

The Origin of Apples

To understand cider, you must understand apples. The domesticated apple originated in Central Asia, in the mountains of southern Kazakhstan along the border with Kyrgyzstan. Forests of wild apples overlook the Kazakh city of Almaty, which translates to "full of apples." Rugged, inaccessible mountains there are home to bands of wild horses that, along with other animals, feast on the apples. If

Mesopotamia is the breadbasket of the world, then Central Asia is the orchard, with many ancestors of contemporary fruit and nut trees first growing along its hillsides. Seeds were spread by animals, weather, and humans as populations shifted, migrated, and traded. So began the apple's journey from wilderness to orchard. It took thousands of years, hundreds of miles, and persistent nudging by the animals and people who have found pleasure in its fruit. These apples emerged from the western migration of Central Asia's *Malus sieversii* (wild apple) and hybridized with Europe's native crab *Malus sylvestris* (forest apple), giving rise to the species *Malus domestica/ pumila*, which consists of tens of thousands of varietals and claims the vast majority of today's wild and cultivated apples. There are dozens of other species, as well, including several native to North America.

One of the reasons apples are such a successful species is because each seed has the genetic material to produce an entirely different apple. Apples contain fifty-seven thousand genes (compared to the thirty thousand or so found in humans) that have spread, reorganized, and evolved over the fruit's journey to North America. They are extreme heterozygotes, meaning that rather than inheriting the exact characteristics of their parents, apples may exhibit a wide combination of unique traits. These unique and infinite combinations of traits enable apples to thrive and adapt in different environments, cultures, and pressures.

Generally, each apple contains five seeds, each capable of growing into its own distinctive tree, unique from its parent. When you plant a Golden Delicious seed, that does not mean the tree will grow to produce Golden Delicious apples. The fruit may resemble its parent, sometimes significantly, but will more often than not be dramatically different. They may be sour, bitter, and astringent—ideal for cider—or sweet, more suited to fresh eating. These seedling trees do not need much human intervention to thrive. They are able to grow in unusual terrain like ditches and streams and along fence lines, and they survive based on hardy traits that have evolved over decades. Herein lies the apple's superpower.

GRAFTING

For consistency's sake, orchardists turn to grafting in order to grow a desired variety. Grafting is a simple but magic-like process in which a living piece of a donor tree—known as the scion or budwood, and about the size of a chopstick—is attached to a rootstock, which is an established root system on a tree that can be young and small or old and big. The single tree is now made up of two genetic parts: the roots of one plant with the fruit and limbs of another. The apples that grow from that point forward will resemble the ones from the donor tree, and they will be supported by the root system of the original. Grafting brings control to orchards and allows growers to choose not only the type of fruit but also the size of the tree. Grafting has been a part of orchards since the inception of orcharding millennia ago, but for most of human agricultural history, trees were often planted from seed.

And so, the first generations of American apples came across the ocean as seeds, with American colonists who left behind established apple orchards and communities of cidermaking know-how. The apple seeds faced a climate radically different from their European cousins', and the seedlings they grew into became the basis for a vast range of uniquely American apples. Humans and animals alike have carried the apple and its seeds throughout history, west from the Central Asian highlands to Europe and on to North America, as the first seeds of globalization and today's apple culture took root.

ROOTSTOCK

Rootstock comes in a variety of sizes, including dwarfing, semi-dwarf, semi-standard, and standard. Well into the twentieth century, apple trees were planted only on standard rootstock, meaning root systems that allow trees to grow to their full height and potential. Variations to rootstocks developed in the twentieth century shrank the size of trees, making them easier to manage without special equipment while increasing the amount of trees per acre and thus the total yield.

Dwarfing rootstock produces trees that are roughly eight feet tall. The root systems are not as strong or deep as semi-dwarf, semi-standard, or standard trees, and they need to be secured to upright support systems. The upside is that the trees yield fruit in about three years, which is significantly faster than semi-standard and standard trees. Most modern orchards are planted with dwarfing rootstock. The initial cost to establish such orchards is higher, but the return— first crop—comes in faster, and larger per acre. Because of the root system's marginal strength, though, dwarfing rootstock trees have a short life-span and need to be replaced after ten or twelve years.

Semi-dwarf trees are between twelve and fifteen feet tall, and semi-standard trees are between fifteen and twenty. Both produce their first harvest in five to seven years. These trees are more resistant to disease than trees on dwarfing rootstock, and they enjoy decades-long production.

Standard trees ultimately reach thirty feet or higher and take upwards of ten years to produce apples. Some standard trees that were planted as long ago as the eighteenth century are still in production. Root systems of standard trees are widespread, reaching farther across the land than down into it. This creates remarkably sturdy trees, and many argue that fruit from old, vigorous standard trees is unrivaled—more complex and delicious than fruit from young trees on dwarfing rootstocks.

Apples for Cider

Over 15,000 apple varieties have been grown in North America since the arrival of Europeans, and cidermakers call on all types.

Most American ciders are made from apples grown with multiple intended purposes, whether they be Red Delicious grown for the fresh market, Northern Spy for pies, or Rhode Island Greening for applesauce. Some of these apples, like Red Delicious, make dreadfully neutral and boring cider, while others like Northern Spy and Rhode Island Greening can make exceptional cider.

Apples with great cider potential in addition to other uses (cooking, eating, drying, baking) are generally called dual-purpose apples, but nodding to their greater versatility, we will refer to them instead as multipurpose. These apples, along with eating apples intended to be eaten fresh, or out-of-hand, form the backbone of American cider. They are part of a centuries-old supply chain that has long serviced farmers' markets, grocery stores, and applesauce processors.

More often than not, multipurpose apples are older varieties, historically grown to support the vast needs and demands of small subsistence farmers—who produced nearly everything needed to feed themselves and their family—and early settlers looking for varieties that tasted good fresh and could be dried, baked, juiced, and cooked down for applesauce or apple butter. These apples were cultivated before the advent of modern farming and immense supply chains. Because of their age, older apples like Black Twig, Newtown Pippin, and Rome Beauty are often called heirloom varieties. But that is a particularly fluid term, as Cortland, introduced in 1915, is sometimes called an heirloom just the same as Newtown Pippin, first discovered early in the eighteenth century.

Cull apples, or culls, is a blanket term for the apples of any category that are considered unfit for their intended market. They are generally deemed culls if they are undesirable in size, shape, or color or have cosmetic issues, including discoloration and apple scab—rough dark bumps on the skin.

Any apple, culls included, can be pressed and fermented into cider, but that does not mean that any apple pressed and fermented into cider will be excellent. Look at the wine industry: we do not buy Merlot grapes in the grocery store just as we do not make fine wine out of Thompson seedless grapes.

So while all apples can make cider, some apples excel at it, and some apples are developed, cared for, and grown exclusively for the production of cider. Cider apples are highly valued because, in addition to the alcohol and carbon dioxide that result from a few simple sugars fermenting, they have potential to build thousands of unique compounds, flavors, aromas, and textures during alcoholic fermentation.

Now comes the seemingly obvious question: How do we discuss the taste of different apples? Of the myriad characteristics and descriptive methods one might use to approach an answer, where should we begin?

One feature of many of these cider apples is tannins. Tannins give cider body, texture, and weight, and they bind with proteins in the drinker's mouth in ways that can make the palate salivate or leave it feeling dry and bitter. Tannin is a complex topic, and its relationship with apples and cider is yet to be fully understood. Grapes primarily have tannins in their skins and seeds—hence red wine, which is made with the skins, has tannins, while white wine, made without skins, does not. On the other hand, many cider apples are tannic throughout the fruit, from the skin to the flesh, and most of the tannin accessible during fermentation is actually in the flesh of the apples. While apple skin does have tannin, little of it is absorbed by the cider.

Tannin comes in many shapes and expressions. A drinker will find the soft elegant tannins of Yarlington Mill cider very different from the astringent, spicy tannins found in crab and wild apples. Cidermakers around the world may spend decades arguing over the details and merits of these apples, but as drinkers, we must understand that each brings its own voice to the glass. While tannins can offer complexity, they are not a necessity for great cider.

Acid, however, is crucial to all ciders. Malic (derived from *Malus*, the botanical genus under which apple trees fall) is the primary acid found in apples. While there are also traces of ascorbic acid (aka vitamin C), apples do not benefit from the abundance of other acids that are found in grapes, like citric and tartaric. Celebrating cider's acidity is the ultimate balancing act for cidermakers. The ability to fold cider's tannin, sugar, weight, and alcohol into a tidy sip can create a deep and nuanced experience. Malic acid can at times be converted into lactic acid (derived from lactose but dairy-free) in a process called malolactic fermentation. In this scenario, crisp malic acid gives way to rich and round lactic cider, trading tart green apple and fruit flavors for butter and wool-like characteristics. Many (but not all) cidermakers tend to avoid this during their process because of the freshness and acidity that is sacrificed, though a lactic cider can remain vibrant and balanced, taking on creamy, nuanced characteristics.

The marriage of acid and tannin with complexity of flavor is not random; it is the result of generations of breeding, trials, testing, and hard work on the part of thousands of known and unknown breeders, hobbyists, scientists, and professionals. In a Latin treatise of wine and cider from 1588, believed to be the first known book on cider, Julien le Paulmier de Grantemesnil wrote from Normandy, France, and mentioned over a hundred different varietals used in cidermaking. In the mid-seventeenth century, the English began reexamining their own apples and ciders and developed sparkling methods in bottle fermentation decades before the technique was adopted in Champagne.

In 1903, the Long Ashton Research Station (LARS) was founded outside of Bristol, England, to better study and develop cider and its apples. Professor B.T.P. Barker, its first director, developed a scale to clarify communication. His scale makes no mention of sugar, which, like all of the other values, can dramatically swing depending on where and how the apple is grown. But for over one hundred years, his chart has been the basis for talking about cider apples in the English-speaking world.

BITTERSWEET: high tannin, low acid	BITTERSHARP: high tannin, high acid
SWEET: low tannin, low acid	SHARP: low tannin, high acid

These four broad categories of apples are helpful, but they can miss the nuances that make up the excess of fifteen thousand different apples grown in North America. Bittersweets and bittersharps, also called "spitters," have little value outside of cider and therefore have never been a large part of contemporary American orchards. True sweet apples, like Tolman Sweet and Pound Sweet, were popular in the nineteenth and early twentieth centuries as cooking apples, but have mostly been relegated to horticultural oddity and are rarely grown commercially. Their sweet, rich, and often soft texture is incongruent with the snap or acid of American apple expectations. Sharp apples may be as mild as Gala or as abrasively acidic as Foxwhelp, but both apples have a place in the American cidermaking conversation. The quadrant system fails to capture the diversity and range of apples in the United States, as the vast majority of apples fall somewhere between sharp and sweet.

Most domestic apples were planted not with cider in mind but for a variety of other purposes, the most common of which is fresh eating. But these apples have since been adapted to cidermaking, and the practice has become a foundational pillar of contemporary American cider. That is changing, however, as more and more cider-specific orchards are being planted around the country. The relative absence of tannic and bitter fruit in North America means that only a minority of ciders in the United States are made from those apples.

Many cider apples grown today, in both Europe and North America, entered into cultivation during the nineteenth century. European varieties grew up well suited to their climate, whether that meant the Atlantic coast in Brittany, France, or the hills of Asturias,

Spain. While cider apples were studied and developed in Europe, there was little interest or market for such research in North America. But today's growing interest in cider has created a changing orchard landscape.

EUROPEAN CIDER APPLES

With their roots in European cider-growing regions, these apples have been introduced and adapted to the American orchard, growing for the first time in a totally new climate, terroir, and conditions.

Dabinett, Yarlington Mill, and Harry Masters Jersey (a possible seedling of Yarlington Mill) are among the most coveted European bittersweet cider varieties. The tannic characteristics these apples deliver in cider, as well as the trees' general resilience in the orchard, make the varieties all-stars in the eyes of orchardists and cidermakers alike. European bittersharps like Porter's Perfection and Ellis Bitter have found fast favor in the States, and Kingston Black has become the poster child for single-varietal cider, with its high tannin and high acid. Multipurpose apples native to Europe, like Ashmead's Kernel and Cox's Orange Pippin, have likewise found a favorable new home in orchards and cideries throughout the United States, particularly in the Northeast and Michigan, where comparable continental climates maintain the apple's famed quality.

The fact that these varieties are grown in a commercial setting in Europe shows promise for the American cider industry, and their stateside popularity suggests that the path forward will certainly be paved, at least partially, with European cider varieties adapted to U.S. soils, climates, and cultures.

AMERICAN CIDER APPLES

Planting and propagating cider apples commercially is a recent phenomenon in the United States. While most cider varieties today come from Europe, an increasing number have their origins in North America. With a growing interest in cider, wild and abandoned trees are being found in the country's national forests, next to stone walls, and along old fence lines. Cidermakers are naming these apples and propagating them to be dispersed among an increasingly interested national community. Some apples, like Harrison, were rediscovered after centuries of obscurity in the suburbs. Others, like Denniston Red, were just hiding in the woods waiting to be uncovered.

THE CIDER SURGE

Apple growers in the later half of the twentieth century became so efficient at their job that overproduction drove the price of apples down. The coup de grâce for the industry came in the 1980s, when China entered the apple business, sending already depressed prices into free fall. With rock-bottom prices and bleak future potential, orchards began looking for alternative uses for their apples. Cider became a viable option once existing fruit avenues had been exhausted. In 1990, there were ten cideries in the United States. That number jumped to thirty-four in 2000, and close to a thousand in 2020, with collective annual sales of $1.2 billion. Cider offers opportunity, creativity, and success for the next generation of orchardists. With the promise of cider, family farms have an opportunity to continue with new excitement and drive.

The development of cider also means a shift in how fruit is grown, treated, and planted. Apples like Fuji and Gala that are grown for the fresh market need to look as good as they taste. Imperfections, blemishes, and asymmetries may mean the difference between fruit going to market or being left on the ground. Growing apples for processing is about sugar, with flavor taking a backseat to increasing yields. But growing for cider is about flavor and ripeness, so pesticides, fungicides, and other chemical additions can be applied with less frequency, since the apple's appearance means nothing by the time it's in the bottle.

How Cider Is Made

All cider starts with apples, of course. Whether it is from concentrate or from meticulously grown estate fruit, there is no single formula from apple to glass (or can or keg). America's orchards contain thousands of varieties, and cidermakers all make different choices, from farming practices to fermentation techniques, so cidermaking variations abound.

HARVEST

Apples have a surprisingly long harvest season, with some apples being harvested as early as July, shortly after the summer solstice, and others holding on to the tree long after the arrival of snow. When apples are harvested plays a crucial role in the final cider. Each day an apple remains on the tree is another chance for it to develop and reach its full ripening potential. Most apples fall to the ground as they become fully ripe.

Ground apples can make excellent cider, and some cidermakers insist on using ground apples for maximized ripeness. The vast majority of apples in the United States are harvested by hand from the tree, long before they have reached their peak ripeness; headed for the market, they need to last an extended stay in controlled storage. But that process greatly stifles the apple's potential. Picked early, apples have not fully developed, and sugar, a crucial element for fermentation, is outweighed by gluey starches.

Some cidermakers choose to sweat their apples, a process whereby the fruit is left to sit after being harvested. The idea is to concentrate the sugars by allowing water to evaporate. In colder climates, where apples do not develop high sugars due to shorter growing seasons and a lack of hot days, this process ultimately produces cider of higher alcohol content.

GRINDING, PRESSING, AND EXTRACTING

Unlike beer, cider is never brewed. Brewing is a process of heating grains (usually barley) to extract their sugars into water, since sugar is necessary to make alcohol. Cidermaking is more analogous to winemaking, relying only on a seasonal harvest and then fermentation. But while grapes are delicate enough to be crushed directly, either with a press, by hand, or underfoot, apples need more coercive methods to yield juice. After the apples are harvested, the first step in cidermaking is generally to rinse the fruit, since unwanted bacteria can spoil entire fermentations and dirty equipment.

After the fruit is rinsed, it is milled into a pulp (seeds and stray stems included) via various methods of grinding and smashing. Historically, apples were crushed under an upright millstone drawn by horse or ox. The animal walked the stone around a circular trough filled with apples, and the juice was collected from a notch in the trough. Today, most crushing and pressing has been mechanized. Before pressing, some cidermakers let their pulp, or pomace, sit for a bit in order to give the liquids and solids a chance to meld, a process known as maceration. Some argue that the added oxygen exposure from macerating leads to more aromatics, better color, and a higher yield of juice, but it does decrease tannin.

When it comes time to press, there are a handful of options, each with its advantages and drawbacks, but the two most common are the rack and cloth press and the bladder press. The more traditional rack and cloth presses work on a hydraulic, or screw, mechanism that applies pressure to the crushed fruit. These powerful machines have a base on which apple pomace is stacked in multiple rack and cloth layers. Today, most cidermakers use nylon or other fabric that keeps solids from spewing while allowing liquid to escape, but in the early nineteenth century, rural cidermakers used burlap and even hay to contain their apples. Once the press is full, a large top plate is slowly lowered to gently press the liquid from the pomace. Large rack and cloth presses are able to handle significant volumes at a time, but they require multiple people to operate them efficiently.

Many of the country's smaller cidermakers opt for the more manageable—and cheaper—bladder press. These presses collect pomace in a tall cylinder made of perforated walls, at the center of which is a rubber bladder. This bladder is connected to a water or air supply and slowly filled like a balloon. As the bladder inflates, it gently presses the pomace up against the perforated walls. This keeps the pomace inside the press while allowing the juice to escape, fall, and collect in a notched trough. These presses are generally easier to operate and require fewer people; their downside is that they can handle only a fraction of the amount of apples that larger rack and cloth presses can.

ALCOHOL FERMENTATION

The next step in the process is alcohol fermentation, whereby yeasts convert sugar to alcohol. Yeasts are naturally occurring microorganisms that metabolize sugar anaerobically, meaning in the absence of oxygen. As long as there is enough sugar and sufficient nutrients in apple juice, it will begin to ferment naturally within a week to ten days thanks to naturally occurring yeasts in the solution. Cidermakers have the option to jump-start this process, by adding—or "pitching"—yeast, thus creating endless opportunity for variation because of the bounty of commercial yeasts available. Whether a cidermaker relies on wild or commercial yeast is a very differentiating philosophy within the cider (and wine) community.

Carbon dioxide (bubbles) and ethanol (alcohol) are natural byproducts of fermentation and the reason most cider is sparkling. In order to produce a still (not sparkling) cider, the CO_2 must be given time to completely leave the liquid. In the traditional or classic method of producing sparkling cider, the cider is first fermented to dry, meaning the yeasts are left to consume all of the sugar. Then, sugar—in the form of honey, maple syrup, apple juice, or just granulated sugar—may be added back into the solution before being bottled, so that a secondary fermentation will take place in the bottle, creating more bubbles. If the lees—dead yeast cells that result from fermentation—are disgorged, or removed, the process is known as the Champagne method, or *méthode champenoise*. The Charmat—or tank—method, commonly used for Prosecco, is also used for cider. Rather than the secondary fermentation happening in each bottle, the fermentation takes place in large tanks, and the liquid is subsequently bottled under pressure. Cider can also be force-carbonated—like most beer—in which case a cidermaker will force CO_2 back into the solution. Each of these techniques yields its own unique bubble profile, size, and duration.

What to do with lees is another piece of the cider puzzle. Cidermakers in New York State's Finger Lakes are experimenting with extended lees and aging ciders to better understand the effects that both the gross lees (primary fermentation lees) and fine lees (yeast that falls out of solution) can have on cider. Some cidermakers prefer to rack, or siphon off, their juice from the gross lees a few weeks after fermentation starts. This leads to a finer, cleaner solution and a cider with fewer particulates and suspended solids, but perhaps less texture.

Racking is often done during the final stages of cidermaking. In order to bottle the final product, gas-powered or gravity pumps (another decision!) transfer cider from tank or barrel or drum to a bottling machine, which will gently fill whatever size vessel is desired. Traditionally, cider was consumed right from the barrel, but glass bottles became the norm in the late eighteenth and nineteenth centuries, as materials, production, and transportation became available.

FERMENTATION VESSELS

The containers in which fresh apple juice is placed while it undergoes fermentation also have an impact on the final product, based on both size and material. Glass (carboys and demijohns), oak (barrels), steel (tanks), and plastic (bins or drums) are the most common materials used in cidermaking. Once the vessel is chosen and the fermentation is under way, it will take anywhere from three months to a year for the juice to ferment to dry. Of course, there is the option to arrest, or stop, fermentation and bottle the cider with residual sugar, which gives a more fruit-forward, semi- or off-dry product.

PACKAGING

Nothing has defined American craft beverages in the second decade of the twenty-first century like cans. Accessible, portable, and scalable, canning lines are too costly for many cidermakers to own, but mobile canning companies have recently started taking their setup directly to a cidery, charging a fee for their service. Because of this easier access to canning, some of the best ciders being made anywhere are found in cans. This format continues to be the fastest-growing segment of the cider community. As cider continues to borrow from the beer world, with adjunct products, flavors, and fruits being added to juice or concentrate, more and more cideries have chosen to can their product in order to reach a wider audience.

At the same time, many cidermakers nationwide are wrestling against the urge to can, claiming that it detracts value from the final product. It remains common for cider to be bottled in 750-milliliter glass bottles, like wine, and the argument for doing so is often that this format better represents the labor, agriculture, and seasonal cycle in which orchard-based cider is made.

Depending on the cider, be it still, traditional, or Champagne method, bottled ciders can be capped like beer or corked like wine or Champagne (with a metal cage). Today, 750-milliliter glass bottles are the preferred method among cidermakers using multipurpose, heirloom, and cider-specific apple varieties in their ciders. For many of them, it is the best way to celebrate and highlight the cider's characteristics, as well as the decisions made in the orchard and the cellar. And, like a bottle of wine, it also warrants and connotes a more festive, celebratory, and special moment to open a bottle and share it (or not) with friends, family, and loved ones.

How to Taste Cider

How can all the variations and decisions made by cidermakers throughout the process be detected, understood, and appreciated? Sipping a glass of cider is far from a challenge. But each cidermaker's process is unique, so many ciders on the market have enough nuance, complexity, and variation to warrant contemplation while drinking them. Still, it's important to remember that cider is a beverage meant to be enjoyed!

Consumption can be as simple as open and drink. Or, you can smell, sip, savor, and repeat. During fermentation, dozens of flavor components within the apple develop into thousands of esters and compounds that all lend complexity to the final cider. But how do these complexities that start in the orchard and are fortified in the cellar translate to the bottle, and into your glass? What should you look for when drinking cider? How many kinds of cider are there? What apples are best for cider, and how do you know what apples went into the cider you are buying and drinking?

To start, before opening your next bottle of cider, think about how temperature affects flavor. Tannin, acid, body, and weight should all be considered when deciding the ideal temperature to store and serve your cider. Between 42 and 50 degrees Fahrenheit is ideal for ciders made from eating apples that are light in body with primary fruit characteristics, little tannin, and under 7 percent alcohol by volume (ABV). For a richer cider with more body, weight, and texture, 48 to 55 degrees Fahrenheit is optimum. These ciders may contain some tannic fruit along with multipurpose varieties like Northern Spy or Newtown Pippin, and they will often exceed 7 percent ABV. For ciders made using a large amount of bittersweet, tannic fruit, usually European varieties, anywhere from 50 to 60 degrees Fahrenheit will most effectively accentuate the cider's layered characteristics.

THE LANGUAGE OF CIDER

Finding words to describe the limitless potential of cider is no small feat. The American Cider Association develops and revises its lexicon and style guidelines almost annually as the industry struggles to find a vocabulary that everyone can agree upon. Having a shared vocabulary is important for the future of cider as consumers and producers alike attempt to get on the same page with cider expectations.

One strong consideration looks to the wine world and its use of the terms "grape juice" and "wine." Cider and apples should be no different, in that the fresh-pressed apple juice that is ubiquitous during fall in grocery stores and farm stands nationwide should be sold as apple juice, not cider. Cider is the fermented by-product that contains alcohol. The common use of prefacing cider with the word "hard" to denote a fermented product is thus redundant—or at least, it should be!

Being able to describe what a glass of cider tastes like and why you like it is critical to communicating your love of cider to others. But describing taste is like an expedition into the conscious and unconscious mind, as our brain draws connections between the beverage on the tongue and our past experiences. And so we need an interpretive lexicon that can be used to better talk about what is in the glass and on the palate.

Sweet and **dry** are two of the most common adjectives

consumers use in an attempt to understand cider. The misconception that all cider is sweet stems in large part from early, nationally distributed ciders that were crafted to compete with wine coolers and alcopops. Because of that reputation, many cider conversations begin and end with the dichotomy of sweetness.

From a production standpoint, **residual sugar** is the term used to describe how much sugar is left once the fermentation is stopped. Higher levels of residual sugar translate to sensations of sweetness, but by no means does this automatically equate to a "sweet" cider. Sugar can offset or balance acid and tannin levels, or it can serve to incite salivation sensations on the palate, as is the case with semidry ciders, which are great as an aperitif.

Off-dry, **semidry**, and **semisweet** are sometimes used to denote levels of residual sugar and perceived sweetness, and while this is ultimately a subjective experience, some cidermaking regions have begun to qualify the language through a sweetness scale. In New York, for example, the Orchard-Based Cider Dryness Scale measures sugar, acid, and tannin and uses a range of 1 (dry) to 4 (sweet), which is indicated on the back of each bottle. It is applicable only to cider made entirely from apples and, because of its limited range, has not been widely adapted outside of the Northeast.

One of the beauties of fermentation is that cider can have the sensation of sugar without containing any. Perfumed and honeyed McIntosh cider can taste sweet even if it has totally fermented. On the other hand, massive tannins or striking acidity can easily mask a cider's sugar. Finding the proper balance is a challenge for any great cidermaker.

Regional uniqueness can also make descriptions difficult, as certain communities are used to certain agricultural products. In Maine and Michigan, for example, sour and tart apples, cherries, and blueberries have shaped people's expectations and acceptance of certain flavor profiles. In other words, "sweet" to a New Englander might be perceived as "dry" to those in other parts of the country without such high-acid, tart foodstuffs.

Fruit is the building block of cider, and cider is an extension of said fruit's profile—especially in North America, where many of the apples exemplify freshness. When apples are fermented, they release thousands of esters that come together in new and unique combinations to create compelling and exciting flavors and sensations. Fruit can be the dominant flavor profile, or it can be only one in a chorus supported by other elements. Sometimes the fruit sings out from across the table, screaming *cherries* or *lychee;* other times the fruit is more subtle, mixed, and muddled.

Describing the **fruitiness** of cider, or calling a cider "fruity," can be in reference to pomaceous fruit (think green apple flavors), as well as tropical fruit (pineapple), citrus (lime), berries (fresh or dried black fruits or red fruits), or stone fruit (peaches and plums).

While notes of pear, melon, and cherry are ubiquitous cider flavor descriptions, it is important to go deeper and think about how that fruit presents itself. Tree-ripened peaches and gummy peach rings, for example, share a passing resemblance but would not be confused for each other. Fruit can come across in cider as underripe, ripe, overripe, candied, dried, stewed, or even rancid. Together, these notes help craft an individual identity for the cider, allowing a level of detail that speaks to the regional differences of cider around the country. Today, the global commercial fruit network brings a world of fruits to every corner and grocery store, and with it an unprecedented vocabulary for fruit.

Nonfruit descriptors often include organic flavors like flowers, nuts, herbs, and mushrooms. These more tertiary and savory flavors are more often found in cider apples than fresh-eating ones. **Herbaceous** flavor profiles often reference green culinary herbs like mint, tarragon, and parsley. Varieties like Gravenstein can be loaded with dried oregano aromas. Some apples, like Wickson, are immensely floral and produce cider that is suggestively rose scented.

As with wine, talking about **minerality** can be complicated, but minerality generally comes across as the sensation of stones and earth in the beverage. Cider may be slaty and stony, like some from New York's Finger Lakes, or it may present as dried and dusty, like certain bottles from California's central coast.

Barnyard is a term often used to describe flavors or smells that fall somewhere between a horse blanket and manure—neither of which are particularly helpful to contextualize now that most people do not live on or near farms. "Barnyardy" ciders' aromas lean more savory and earthy rather than fruit-forward. Processes like keeving (which we'll describe later) can often lead to this profile. Bittersweets, especially those not fermented cool enough, can easily develop their own animal aromas.

Umami, the so-called "fifth taste," refers to savory flavors that can present as mushroom, soy, or even cured meat. Cider apples, especially those from western England like Yarlington Mill and Harry Masters Jersey, can develop a meaty, shiitake-broth character that lingers on the palate.

Funky is easily one of the most controversial terms in the contemporary beverage community. Funk is hard to classify but easy to identify, and whether funky is a positive or negative description depends on the product and the taste of the drinker. A spectrum exists—it could be reminiscent of anything from blue cheese to compost or cured meat to potting soil—but not everyone has the same preferences or tolerance. Funk can be a great quality that builds savory complexity and character, but it can just as easily overwhelm the rest of the cider, failing to integrate with the other flavors in the glass.

Depending on a cidermaker's decision-making and fermentation process, cider can also end up with a slew of flavors that result from the production process. Oak barrels have the potential to play either a subtle or dominant role in a cider, based on their usage. Typically, cider made in barrels has notes of vanilla, cinnamon, and allspice. Used spirits barrels are very popular among cidermakers because of their high flavor and low cost. The former occupant of the barrel, be it bourbon or brandy, can make an appearance in the subsequent ciders. Wine barrels generally have less of an effect than do their spirit counterparts.

Hops, the flowers of a perennial vine that have been used in brewing for over a thousand years, are increasingly added to contemporary cider. Before IPAs, hops were used to prevent beer from spoiling, but they provide little stability benefit to cider. Cidermakers use hops mostly for flavor, and, with the increased awareness of particular hop strains thanks to the craft beer world, cidermakers in parts of the United States are finding success with hopped cider. As with apples, hops have different aromatics and flavors depending on the variety, and cider—with its high acid and delicate profiles—can showcase the full hop profile in a different way than its malt counterpart.

Cofermenting, also increasingly popular, combines apples or pears with other things during fermentation. This results in a widely different beverage that resembles cider but often takes on its own personality. Wine grapes, stone fruit, berries, and even ginger are popular mediums for experimentation. There is a growing trend to ferment apple juice with red wine grapes, producing a rose-colored product that may carry nuances of both apples and grapes. But the fruit added may not always be recognizable because fermentation can dramatically change its flavor.

Adjunct cider typically refers to cider to which flavoring has been added after fermentation has stopped. Fruits, spices, botanicals, even peanuts have been used to flavor adjunct ciders. Unlike their cofermented counterparts, these ciders generally taste like their additions.

Acid is the backbone of many ciders. It lingers from the tip of the tongue to the back of the palate and reacts with food in pleasurable ways. Acid can be described in different ways, based on the sensation of how it tastes and feels on the palate. **Tart** often refers to a sharp, piercing sensation and is commonly the dominant flavor in the glass, usually in conjunction with equally fruity flavors. **Sour** is generally used to describe cider that has a strong, citrus-like acid profile. And other, fattier lactic acids, usually with notes of clotted cream and a roundness of texture, are the result of cider that has gone through malolactic fermentation.

Though cider is, of course, a liquid, you can better understand it by considering its varying textures and the so-called **weight** of the drink. **Bright** can refer to a clean-tasting cider with open, generous fruit notes and lean acidity. **Brilliant** surpasses bright, with intense clarity of fruit and high minerality. **Rich** is ascribed to full-bodied cider that marries alcohol with tannins and is particularly mouth-filling. **Light**, the opposing term, is designated for those ciders that are comparatively weightless on the palate, that feel lifted, in a sense, with few tannins and lower levels of acidity.

The interplay of acid and **tannin**, which we have seen is a complicated relationship within the cider community, works together to build complexity and accentuate the fruit and non-fruit flavors in cider. Tannins can both attack and linger on different parts of the palate, lending considerable texture and weight to the cider and allowing it to hold up to fatty and rich food, all while remaining refreshing. Other techniques in the cellar, including fermentations, vessels, and aging can all have an impact on the final weight of the cider.

CIDER TERROIR

Collectively, these singular nuances that we attempt to define and comprehend through language can all fall under **terroir**, the sum total of the environmental, geologic, and cultural conditions of a product. *Terroir*, the French word for "earth" or "land," is the distillation of a place into a product. This means more than the fact that cider made in California tends to have more tannin and alcohol than its Vermont counterpart. The communities, resources, traditions, and people surrounding the apples have a direct effect on the beverage. Cider's terroir extends beyond how the apples grow and taste, and into decisions of the producer, the style of cider they choose to make, and what their community wants to drink. In the United States, varieties, orchard techniques, and uses for the fruit were mapped out decades—if not centuries—ago, and makers are blending traditional knowledge with modern insights to forge a new and unique path for cider.

STORING CIDER

Like most beer and wine, the majority of cider is meant to be drunk soon after it is released by the producer. Some cider does have the potential to age gracefully for years, though, depending on its structure—the combination of acid, tannin, sugar, and alcohol. There is no single formula for age-worthy cider, but tannic apples can be an important part of the aging process, since they can lend a certain weight, concentration, and bitterness. Sugar and the alcohol that results from fermentation are also important components. The higher the starting brix (sugar content) in an apple, the higher the ABV in the final cider; this alcohol will act as a stabilizer and fortifier that protects the cider against oxidation and other ill effects of aging. The structure provided by naturally occurring sugar can also allow cider to age gracefully. As sugars dissipate over time, more complex umami flavors come to the front of the palate. Golden Russet in particular develops an intensely honeyed and leather quality after a few years in the bottle. Finding that right balance can ensure a delicious cider for years to come.

Another factor to consider with aging cider is the bubbles—and how they got there. The carbonation in force-carbonated ciders will fade over time as the bubbles become less integrated with the liquid. Classic-method ciders will continue to develop for years because they are conditioned (fermented) in the bottle. This is especially true if the cider has yet to be disgorged, because the lees continue to deter oxidation.

With time spent in the bottle, cider can often become more cohesive and complete than when it was first bottled. But on the flip side, cider is meant to be drunk. So do not sit on your supply when there is so much out there to try, especially when not all cider will reward the self-deprivation of cellaring. For every bottle that is transformed into a golden elixir, many others may be unsuitable even for adding to your next stew. Cans are especially suspect when it comes to aging. Can liners that separate the liquid from the aluminum continue to improve, but they also have the potential to break down over time and lead to safe but undesirable flavors.

Cider's Road Ahead

While cider is in an exciting moment in the United States, a few common challenges will continually surface throughout this book. We have learned from wine and beer that as American cider grows, its path forward will be long and arduous. There is a lack of diverse orchards from which to draw the complex apples that are suitable for quality cider. Whereas many beer and wine consumers can rattle off dozens of grapes, wines, hops, and beer styles, most cider consumers have little context for the cider flooding the shelves. All of this is magnified by a changing climate and a broken agricultural system that is driven by optimization at the expense of humanity and sustainability.

Prohibition has been the scapegoat for cider's "death" since, well, Prohibition. But the Eighteenth Amendment did not kill cider. Repeal of this amendment fourteen years later gave control and regulation of alcohol to the states, and cider's relationship within this system is complicated. On paper, the beverage is often said to fall somewhere between wine and beer. In some states, like Pennsylvania, cider was regulated as wine *and* beer until it became its own category in 2018. This, of course, says nothing of the immense cultural shifts that took place long before Prohibition, when the country was being founded.

What to Expect from This Guide

This book is divided into eight sections. Each highlights a region where apples have made—and continue to make—significant contributions to the area's social, economic, political, and cultural realities.

In each section we build on two narratives. The first pertains to the human history of the area, beginning predominantly with the arrival of Europeans and colonization. For that reason, the Southeast (home to the first European settlement in Jamestown) opens the book. We then move up to New England, down to New York and the mid-Atlantic states, and finally west, in tandem with the pattern of development in the United States. Rather than retell four hundred years of history in each section, we tell a successive history that begins with the English settlement of Jamestown in the Southeast, in 1607, and ends with massive, irrigated post–World War II orcharding in the Pacific Northwest.

The second narrative considers the region's specific apple history and infrastructure and celebrates the modern cidermakers, apple growers, and other folks contributing to cider's explosive growth. We highlight various cideries and orchards that we hope you'll visit and support as part of your growing understanding of this nationwide movement and product. Each section concludes with Core Takeaways, a summation of sorts including notable producers to visit. For brevity, some of these producers are not mentioned in the second narrative.

Before we explore the history and people, we begin each section with a (very) brief retelling of the region's geologic formation— laying the groundwork, if you will. Apples and orchards, like all agriculture, lie in the often fraught realm that is the relationship between humanity and nature. The landscape and terrain of the United States dictated its agricultural settlement, from the continent's Indigenous people to today's industries, from New York's wide Hudson River Valley to the swaths of irrigation in the Washington desert. Understanding cider and its relationship with the land and the communities it supports begins with what lies underfoot.

Continental lithospheres and supercontinents may seem far from the world of apples, but some 750 million years ago, the United States was nothing but a craton—a large, stable block of Earth's crust forming what eventually became North America.

Earth's outer layer, its crust, is made up of constantly shifting plates that slide past one another at times, and pull apart or collide at others. This movement shapes the land and its continents. It informs the soil and its minerals and the climate experienced by those who come to call the land home.

North America is roughly 200 million years old, resulting from a series of quite literally Earth-shattering rifts and collisions that left a supercontinent called Rodinia fragmented into smaller continents. Laurentia, the North American craton and geologic core of the continent, was one such fragment.

Throughout Laurentia's ancient history, roaming oceanic islands and microcontinents collided and sutured onto the growing craton. Born from these massive shifts and collisions is the unique and defining topography—the geologic makeup—of the United States. Humans developed over millions of years and formed civilizations that came to adapt, use, and cultivate that land. Down into the newly risen Earth go our sown seeds, and up comes the gift of eating.

Which is all to say: without patience and understanding, fertile soil, and profound human ingenuity, the explicit rise in today's cider market would not exist.

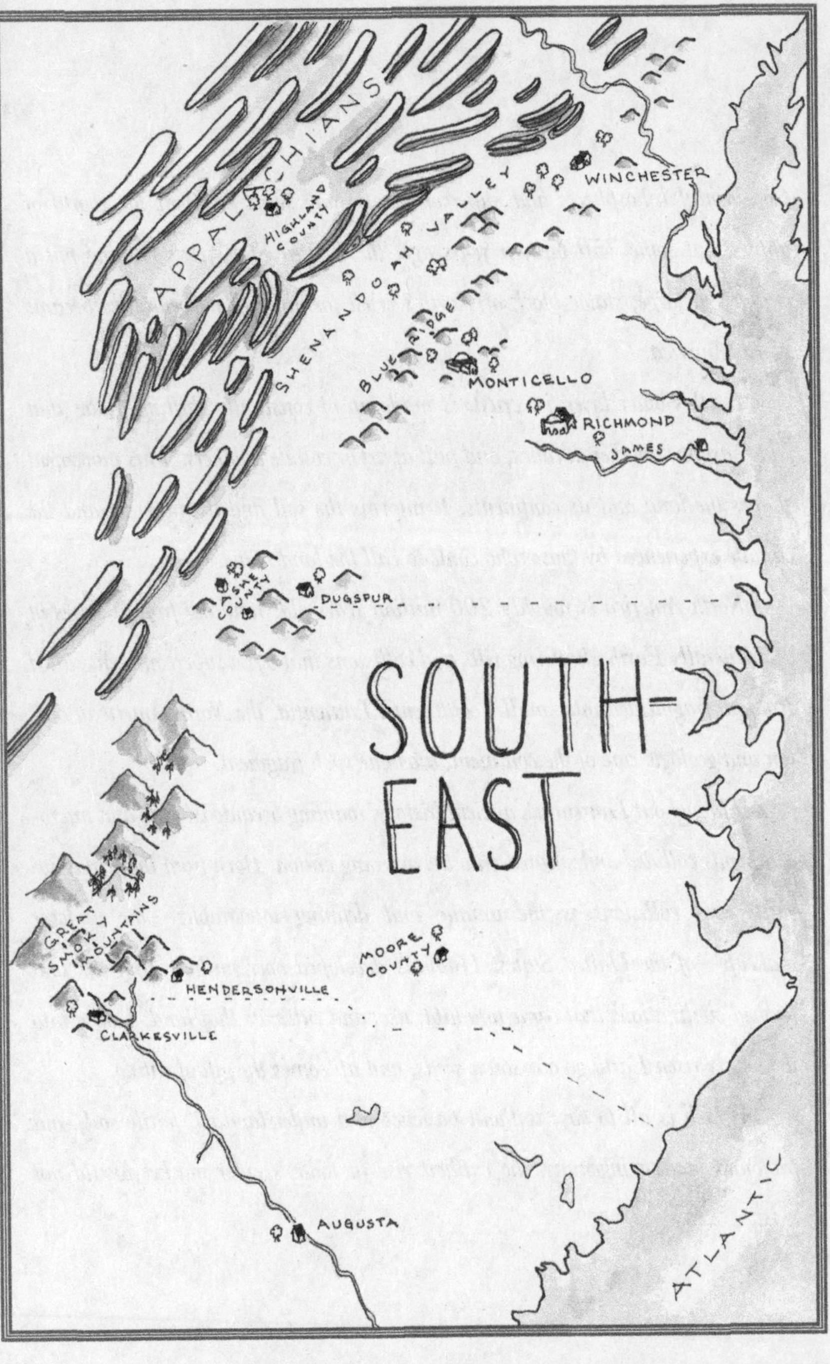

APPALACHIANS
HIGHLAND COUNTY
SHENANDOAH VALLEY
WINCHESTER
BLUE RIDGE
MONTICELLO
RICHMOND
JAMES
ASHE COUNTY
DUGSPUR
SOUTH-EAST
GREAT SMOKY MOUNTAINS
MOORE COUNTY
HENDERSONVILLE
CLARKESVILLE
AUGUSTA
ATLANTIC

THE SOUTHEAST

Some 500 million years ago, an island chain forcibly slammed into the East Coast. With steep and magnificent splendor, the Appalachian Mountains rose from the collision, and they stood in their formative years with the same grandeur and magnitude as the Himalayas. It is believed these mountains first formed from hard-packed mud on the ocean floor, at great depths void of light and warmth. Centuries later, long after the completion of the mountain-forming process, the Appalachian Mountains would come to stand not only as the backbone of the American South, but as the very spine of southern culture.

We start here, along the southern coast of the Atlantic Ocean in the shadow of the Appalachian Mountains. This is where, in 1607, the English established the first settlement in what would grow into the United States. From Jamestown, Virginia, along the James River, European customs, religions, agriculture, diets, and laws were first employed, and they spread through a vast new land of seemingly countless acres and endless opportunity.

The southern colonies were a more direct translation of European society and its class divisions than their counterparts in the North, where concentrated wealth developed along the coastal shipping industry. A landed elite were able to control the primary economic wheels, while in the North subsistence farms eked out an existence on the margins.

The United States' regional economic and cultural differences were shaped by the motives of the first European settlers. Where early New England colonies were defined by Puritan aspirations for religious liberties, southern settlers—who were funded by the ruling English aristocracy—were driven by the king's desire to acquire fertile land, expand the market for English goods, and discover what was then believed to be a navigable northwest passage from the Atlantic Ocean to the Pacific Ocean, along with the wealth and resources that would bring.

Systematic apple growing and cidermaking in the Southeast began with the arrival of Europeans. Starting in 1607 from the coastal English settlement of Jamestown, apples crept over the coastal plain toward the foothills, peaks, and valleys of the Appalachian Mountains.

Jamestown was North America's first permanent English colony. Apples were a proven part of the English landscape, culture, and diet, so settlers brought seeds with them. These seeds would find the southern heat and long summers favorable, but it took trees ten or more years to bear fruit, and Europeans struggled to survive while waiting.

After the third winter in Jamestown, known as the Starving Time, investors in the London-based Virginia Company realized that disease and starvation were preventing social and economic development. Faced with a failing colony, they began issuing sub-patents for land in Virginia. In what was known as the headright system, they offered fifty acres of land to anyone willing to pay their way—or someone else's—to make the transatlantic voyage. And so wealthy, educated colonists became the first landowners in the future United States.

The elite soon acquired more land than they had workers, settling the stage for the southern plantation system and a political and social structure that reverberated for generations. By 1630, Virginia was exporting more than 1.5 million pounds of tobacco per year, and the notoriously labor-intensive crop demanded large tracts of land, with many working hands, to maximize efficiency and productivity. Efforts were made to populate the colonies and produce a viable workforce, but none was able to supply enough labor or alleviate the growing rift between rich and poor. The answer, ultimately, came in the form of indentured servitude and slavery.

Indentured servants made up the bulk of Virginia's early workforce. Mostly men, they signed up for extended contracts and were promised land upon completion. Freed servants established subsistence farms on land they owned or rented from elite landowners, and their families lived with a degree of comfortable independence in times of dire uncertainty. Unwilling to parcel their land for free people, plantation owners began buying African slaves. Colonists first forced Indigenous people into labor, as the Spanish had done in Florida, the Caribbean, and South America in the sixteenth century. In the Southeast, colonists began shipping Indigenous people as demand for labor in Caribbean sugar fields rose. Into the turn of the eighteenth century, upwards of fifty thousand Indigenous people were shipped from Carolina ports. The first enslaved Africans arrived in 1619, bringing with them an agricultural expertise not found among the English colonists. While this expertise was mostly focused on rice, cattle, and row-crop cultivation, seventeenth-century slaves also tended to the early orchards of the Southeast.

Off of plantations, many subsistence farmers planted homestead seedling orchards because of the low initial investment and ease of maintenance. As trees matured, apples could be consumed fresh from the tree or cooked into sauce, butter, and jelly. Juice could be turned into cider and vinegar. Apples could be peeled and dried or stored through winter—the only fruit in the South with those bragging rights. As the region was colonized, apples became the premier edible crop.

Apple trees, because of their adaptability and versatility, added value to any and all property. Land leases often required subsistence farmers to plant apple trees, and small subsistence farms had as many as two hundred, mostly grown from seedlings. On sprawling estates of the cultural elite, apple trees were planted in the thousands, often from selected varieties.

Apple trees were adopted, nurtured, and cared for by people of different social, racial, and economic groups, and this led to an array of diverse methods, motivations, and capabilities in the orchard and cellar. Two distinct apple and cider identities developed: that of the cash crop plantations, defined by large enslaved workforces doing specialized tasks for a few crops along the eastern plains and hills, and that of the small subsistence farmers surviving in the mountains and other less desirable plots of land.

In 1642, William Berkeley, the first governor of Virginia, cultivated 1,500 fruit trees at his Green Spring estate. Two years later, he made the declaration that every planter must "for every 500 acres granted him . . . enclose and fence a quarter-acre of ground near his dwelling house for orchards and gardens." Thomas Jefferson, fellow founding father George Mason, and other early American aristocrats were often amateur practitioners of pomology. They grafted some of their favorite apples, like Hewe's Virginia Crab Apple (aka Hewe's Crab) and Newtown Pippin (aka Albemarle Pippin), and, together with their enslaved and hired help, studied, cultivated, and made cider from these apples.

Jefferson's primary cidermaker was Jupiter Evans, an enslaved man who was also Jefferson's personal butler from the time Jefferson was the age of twenty-one. Jefferson and the aristocratic cohorts were able to afford a consistent and deliberate cider experience, one that was worlds away from the rough seedling cider enjoyed by less prosperous farmers. Jefferson's reverence for cider and certain apple varieties, commonly celebrated by historians, is almost assuredly thanks to knowledge he gleaned from the masterful work and understanding Evans had of apples, orcharding, fermentation, and cider. But complete disregard for Black freedom and rights in the antebellum South and beyond has wiped significant pieces of African culture from history—and Black contributions to cider are no exception.

African cultures played a significant role in the development of the country, and the African community was often consulted for its knowledge of particular crops. Governor Berkeley, in the 1640s, learned about growing rice from African slaves. In this case and others pertaining to the likes of indigo and tobacco, the Black community built a foundation of knowledge for whites to execute certain crops, from which point on all Black contributions save labor were ignored.

Hewe's Virginia Crab Apple
(aka Hewe's Crab)

A true American cider apple, these small (1.5-inch diameter) green and black crab apples were first mentioned in 1741 but predate that entry by years. Cultivated by southern elites, Hewe's Crab made up Thomas Jefferson's entire north orchard at Monticello. C. Lee Calhoun, author of *Old Southern Apples*, said Hewe's Crab makes "dry cider unsurpassed in flavor and keeping ability." Its popularity spread throughout the South and coastal mid-Atlantic, where it remained a part of orchards long after hard cider had fallen from favor for pollination and jelly.

CIDER PROFILE

Intensely aromatic, savory, and pungent. Tropical notes of guava, passionfruit, and allspice. High in acid, tannin, and texture.

Subsistence farms sat inland, removed from coastal access and imported goods. Farmers there planted seeds—free, light, and portable—with minimal upkeep needed. Many of the seedling trees produced fruit that was sharp, bitter, and astringent, but cider was the perfect vehicle to hide the unpredictable nature of seedling fruit. It may have lacked the refinement of plantation cider, but it more than served its purpose as a facet of colonial culture.

Lee Calhoun, the late author of the seminal book *Old Southern Apples* (1995), which cites 1,500 unique varieties that predate 1928, explains, "There was a wide proliferation of seedling apple trees in the South that people were able to choose from to come up with some decent apples. Mainly, they were looking for apples they could use every day to feed their families. Cider was a sideline they would use for leftover, or wild seedling, apples."

The general recipe for farmstead cider was simple. Subsistence farmers, lacking the means and access to the dedicated cider apples of the elite, learned that their best cider came from a mix of half sweet and half sour apples. As farmers spread into the frontier and established backcountry orchards from seed, they tasted the fruit as it grew. Most of the sweet culinary apples fed the family. Some were traded, but many were saved and mixed with the sour crop to produce balanced ciders.

Unique to the Southeast is the fact that cidermaking took place on individual farms, either small farm holdings or large estates. This stands in contrast to the communal centralized presses that were the norm throughout New England. Likewise, because of the monoculture tobacco plantations and the population's social structure, much of the household cidermaking was done by women, which reflects earlier Old English customs. On small subsistence farms, families lacked the means and access to distill more potent, shelf-stable spirits, so cider was an especially common by-product, and, into the eighteenth century, it was women producing it.

For the wealthy class, demand for specific apples grew throughout the 1700s, and nurseries and commercial orchards were slowly established as nurserymen learned to graft. They began document-ing their work, and an inventory of unique southern apples grew into the hundreds. A market for these apples developed as the econ-omy strengthened, and the selling of apple and fruit trees com-menced Apple tree plantings reached into the tens of thousands as rural communities pushed further into the frontier.

Because the Appalachian Mountains, dense inland forests, and rough waters seemed impenetrable, colonists initially settled down the coast rather than move west. From 1730 to 1750, Germans and Scots-Irish from Pennsylvania crossed the Blue Ridge Mountains, moved down the Shenandoah Valley, and populated the western Carolinas. Saddled on horseback and drawn in carriages were apple varieties unique to the mid-Atlantic climes of Pennsylvania. These cultivars thrived in cold weather. They were winter hardy, as many of them were descended from cooler parts of northern Europe. As Virginia, the Carolinas, and Georgia became settled, these seeds, scions, and seedlings developed into yet another new set of southern apples.

Each farm was a breeding ground for the next great southern apple. The apples were found to vary from community to commu-nity, county to county, and state to state. Ciders that resulted from this regional expansion and growth were distinct and varied.

As southern settlers began pushing west, territorial tensions grew, resulting in the Seven Years' War, known in the United States as the French and Indian War in reference to the two enemies of British colonists. Upon British victory—and although most of the war's bat-tles were fought in New York and Pennsylvania—in an attempt to assuage the Indigenous population, Britain issued the Proclamation of 1763, which forbade colonists from moving farther west, into the land between the Mississippi River and the Appalachian Mountains. But after the Revolutionary War, colonists flooded into that area.

As the federal government strengthened, it continually enacted laws targeted at minority groups, and Indigenous Peoples—whose dispossession and removal by Euro-Americans was deemed neces-sary for national conquest—were viewed as one singular culture.

Referred to as "Indians," the vast diversity among Indigenous Peoples has been historically whitewashed.

In 1830, Andrew Jackson signed the Indian Removal Act, continuing the genocide and forced expulsion of Indigenous Peoples, who were pushed even farther to designated Indian Territory west of the Mississippi. Waves of settlers moved into the frontier and found orchards filled with unique apple varieties that Native populations had selected and cultivated from European fruit seeds. Presenting at the annual American Pomological Society in 1901, horticulturist and nursery owner Prosper J. Berckmans spoke to the origin of southern fruit: "Apple seed came mainly through the Creek, Choctaw, and Cherokee tribes inhabiting the middle and upper sections of North and South Carolina, Georgia, and Alabama, who secured these from tribes farther north or nearer the white settlements of Virginia. Many of our best southern apples and peaches can trace their origin to the trees originally grown from seed by these Indians." By the end of the 1830s, Europeans had settled the entire southern region east of the Mississippi.

JARVIS VAN BUREN AND THE LEADERS OF THE FIRST SOUTHERN APPLE REVOLUTION

In 1838, Jarvis Van Buren, future President Martin Van Buren's cousin, moved from his home in New York's Hudson Valley to the mountains of northeast Georgia. Jarvis scoured orchards that had been planted by Natives throughout Appalachia and began naming apples like Nantahalee, the Cherokee word for "maiden's bosom," and Junaluska, after Chief Junaluska, who refused to sell his land because it was the site of his favorite apple tree.

"King Cotton" reigned during this time. By 1860, cotton reached a value of $30 million in Georgia, the equivalent of almost $1 trillion in 2020. Subsistence farms and diversified harvests disappeared as cotton grew with the frontier. Pockets of the South became dependent on orchard fruit from the North, and the South fell under national scrutiny as a region incapable of self-sufficiency. Appeals were made for the South to diversify its farming.

Van Buren helped organize the Georgia Pomological Society in the 1850s, with goals to clarify the language surrounding apples in the South and to identify and name the apples he was finding. He made amazingly detailed drawings of apples and coupled them with thorough and, at times, scientific descriptions. Van Buren also argued that a regional vested interest in fruit and horticulture would encourage the development of diverse agriculture and help shift the economy away from one based on slavery.

Yates

The Yates apple was discovered in 1813 in Fayette County, in northern Georgia. Despite its small size and difficulty harvesting, it has become one of the Southeast's rising cider apples for its surprising abundance of juice. Ideal for the southern reaches of Appalachia, it also grows on the coastal plains, where apples like Hewe's Crab and Harrison struggle.

CIDER PROFILE

Textured, almost vinous, and reminiscent of white grape juice.

Van Buren's Gloaming Nursery, near his home in Clarkesville, Georgia, grew to boast the largest selection of southern seedling fruits in the United States. His efforts produced exceptional mountain fruit and helped establish a commercial growing market in the South. Dependence on northern fruit stopped, and the first apple revolution started.

Modern Cidermakers and Apple Growers

As in the rest of the country, small orchards in the Southeast were abandoned or swallowed in the jaws of commercial agriculture. By the end of World War II, large, homogenous orchards became the norm, and they grew fewer varieties, with consideration for appearance rather than flavor.

In the early twentieth century, as wet, humid, and freezing weather spawned diseases and pests that slowly killed trees, small-scale farmers could not afford the sprays and chemical-based combatants they needed. But well-funded commercial growers, who planted eating apples, could, so they were able to grow and maintain their massive eating-apple orchards. This fact, together with the temperance movement, Prohibition, the development of cities, and the consolidation of capital among the rich, swung the axe that chopped down small, diversified orchards. Generations later, these national concerns have fostered contemporary pioneers in the region who are inspired in ways not unlike Van Buren to reinvigorate what once was.

Apples grow in the Southeast from the tidewaters of Virginia to the Gulf of Mexico, and from northern Arkansas to northern Florida. But they thrive and are made into cider in three distinct areas: the Piedmont, a plateau region that runs from New Jersey to Alabama between the Atlantic coastal plain and the Appalachian Mountains; the Shenandoah Valley in northern Virginia; and the Appalachian Mountains.

The history and legacy of these places and people are evidenced today in the apple varieties, growing practices, and cider being produced there. Cider leads the charge to reclaim the identity, culture, and diversity of the southern orchard.

CHARACTERISTICS OF SOUTHEAST CIDER

Cider from across the region, like the topography itself, is distinctive in different ways. While each cidermaker is unique, applying their own techniques in the cellar, each vintage is also different, and every apple renders its own expression. Southern cider is marked by hot summers, which translates to ripe fruit high in sugar and cider that is not shy of alcohol. With ABVs exceeding 8 percent, cider throughout the Southeast exhibits sweet citrus and tropical profiles that run from Meyer lemon and guava to ginger and charred pineapple.

In the heights of Appalachia, apples are pushed toward higher acid content. Unlike the lower orchards, the mountains experience a dramatic fluctuation from daytime to nighttime temperatures, known as the diurnal shift. This allows the fruit to ripen with high levels of acidity, a prime characteristic of mountain apples. Certain valley soil pockets, like the northern Shenandoah, are washed with lime deposits that cater to certain apple varieties, like Newtown Pippin, that crave calcium and will likewise result in high acid. Apples maintain their acidity during cool nights after days under the heat of the southern sun. This acidity is gentler and riper on the palate than that of cider from states farther north, keeping these ciders vibrant, leaning toward brilliant.

Eastern Virginia and Coastal Carolina

In eastern Virginia, centered around Charlottesville and Richmond, plantations and estates built along the James River during colonial times still dot the landscape. It was on these sites that many of the classic apples of the Southeast were identified, cultivated, and celebrated. The fertile soils here are dominated by James River sediment and red clay from the imposing Blue Ridge Mountains to the west, which protect the region from inclement weather moving east from the plains and into Appalachia. There are nearly eight thousand acres of apple orchards in Virginia east of the Blue Ridge Mountains with increasing numbers of heirloom cider apples like Hewe's Crab and Arkansas Black.

In Jefferson's time, his most notorious farm failure may have been his inability to cultivate grape vines. Today, Virginia's wine industry contributes more than $1 billion annually to the state's economy. The thriving wine industry only helps cider producers like Albemarle CiderWorks and Castle Hill Cider. Their proximity to metropolitan areas and busy highways caters to the established wine culture of consumers visiting tasting rooms.

Monticello

Outside of Charlottesville, at 1,200 feet in elevation, Monticello—the former home of Thomas Jefferson—has been critical for southern apple preservation. The recreated eighteenth-century garden, grounds, and orchards see half a million visitors each year, giving Newtown Pippin and Hewe's Crab an unparalleled audience. Preservation efforts have been led by Peter Hatch, Director of Gardens and Grounds Emeritus for the Thomas Jefferson Foundation, and the late Tom Burford, a legendary seventh-generation apple grower, historian, and author. Throughout the harvest season, the historic site hosts apple tastings and workshops and highlights the work of Jupiter Evans, Jefferson's cidermaker.

In 1986, the Shelton family bought a farm that had been depleted from decades of tobacco and corn farming. Their intention was to raise beef cattle, but after tasting apples at Monticello with grower and educator Tom Burford, Charlotte Shelton started planting apple trees. Her hobby evolved into a small nursery business that now boasts 250 varieties. In 2008, Charlotte and her brother Chuck began Albemarle CiderWorks, which produces about four thousand cases of cider a year.

Chuck Shelton, cidermaker at Albemarle, draws inspiration from the history of apples and cider in the American South, including their prestigious cuvee Jupiter's Legacy and ciders from recipes penned by nineteenth-century pomologist William Coxe. Albemarle CiderWorks focuses on two- and three-hundred-year-old heirloom apples native to the Southeast United States, and their single-variety ciders are a great glimpse into what these apples can do in the twenty-first century.

Also in the Charlottesville area, Castle Hill Cider is the revitalized estate of Colonel Thomas Walker, a mid-eighteenth-century explorer, physician, and guardian of Thomas Jefferson. Stuart Madany, cidermaker since 2009, came to the property to restore and repair barns and stayed for the cider. Like the Sheltons, he seeks to better understand the local apples, and he says his best decision in the orchard was to graft over European bittersweet apples like Michelin and Medaille d'Or—which were not productive under the intense disease and fungal pressures in the humid heat of eastern Virginia—with local southern varieties.

Qvevri

One of the most unusual and forward-thinking features of Castle Hill is Madany's use of Georgian qvevri, earthenware vessels that are buried and used for fermentation. Because of his past in architecture, Madany is interested in how shape and material affect people's consciousness. Inspired by winemaker Josko Gravner, he imported the clay vessels for fermentation. His single-variety ciders fermented in qvevri are a blend of heirloom fruit and modern sensibility. They are intensely savory and rich in texture—driven by extended contact with the lees—and are a distinct voice in the national cider conversation.

In Richmond, Blue Bee Cider draws upon the energy and collaboration of the craft beer–centric city. The existing infrastructure is extremely useful to many of the cidermakers in the region because, like the winery tasting room relationship, it allows them to sell most of their cider on premise, rather than having to figure out channels for distribution. At Blue Bee, cidermaker Courtney Mailey pushes to make interesting cider amid the expanding beer market around Richmond's hundred-year-old Scott's Addition industrial neighborhood, recently turned chic.

Mailey's ciders blend tradition, experimentation, and collaboration. In addition to an exceptional Hewe's Crab varietal cider, she has partnered with the Virginia Historical Society to replicate colonial American ciders. Mailey, who apprenticed with Chuck Shelton, works closely with local brewers for beer and cider hybrids that are uniquely of a place, and she is developing communal affinity for her orange crab cider, made from a recently cultivated seedling apple. Her collaborative efforts speak to the growth of a changing city, but her influence is statewide: Silver Creek Orchard, a 150-year-old farm a hundred miles west in Nelson County, has planted a thousand orange crab trees.

Farther south, in the eastern Piedmont of North Carolina, David and Ann Marie Thornton have been experimenting with close to sixty varieties at their James Creek Orchards. The Piedmont is a challenging place to grow apples, as fruit there faces early springs, hot summers, and the occasional hurricane. Their efforts are rewarded with unique apples that are high in sugar with diminished acid, and their ciders as a result, on offer at James Creek Cider House, are dense and richly balanced, a distinct expression of the Piedmont's distinctive terroir. The Thorntons' experimental orchard has larger implications for the rest of the country. As climate change pushes existing growing regions into the unknown, the extreme growing conditions at James Creek may become the new normal for many established orchards.

Western Virginia (Shenandoah Valley)

The Shenandoah Valley has long been considered the breadbasket of the South. Deep, fertile shale and limestone soils tend to be

consistently moist, with good drainage and annual soil temperatures that remain well above freezing. The Blue Ridge Mountains
act as the valley's east wall, offering protection from coastal storms,
while the system of ridges and valleys in West Virginia shields
against the worst weather brought down from the Great Lakes.
These factors have historically enabled high crop yields and productive agriculture.

Black Twig
(aka Mammoth Black Twig and Paragon)

Black Twig is an incredible apple—big, bold, tart, and twangy—as well as an
incredible keeper. But its origins are muddy at best. Until 1900, Black Twig
was often used as a synonym for Winesap. Because Black Twig is such an
enchanting spectacle of an apple, reminiscent of Winesap but bigger and
darker, its origins were at once defended and attacked, as Arkansas and
Tennessee both claim the apple as their own. Contention peaked at the
1884 New Orleans Exposition, where Colonel Babcock, who led the fruit
exhibit, declared Mammoth Black Twig and Paragon the same apple. The
USDA later officially ruled the two apples were separate varieties, but the
difference is close to zero.

Black Twig was Lee Calhoun's favorite apple. He chose it as the name
for the road he built his Pittsboro, North Carolina, home on in the early
1970s. Calhoun recalled:

The first time I saw a Black Twig tree was about twenty miles north of
Pittsboro. I heard a guy had one so I went and knocked on his door. I
said, "I understand you have a Black Twig tree." He said it was down in a
pasture. I told him I'd like to graft it and asked if I could have some twigs
off the tree. It was a big old standard tree about twenty-five feet tall.
Way up on the top of the tree there were still four or five apples on it.

This was February! I thought, "How am I going to get the apples down?" I looked around and saw pieces of board, so I started sailing them up at the apples. Sure enough, I knocked a couple down. I grabbed one and took a bite. It was the best thing I'd ever had. Black Twig has it all. It's big, it's red, it's crisp, and it's got what I call that Winesap twang because it's half Winesap. It'll hang on a tree and be frozen and thawed ten times and still be edible. It's just a wonderful apple.

CIDER PROFILE

Full-bodied and lightly tannic, layered with ripe melon and baking spices.

While growers east of the Blue Ridge Mountains oriented themselves for farmers' markets and local retailers, Winchester—at the northern mouth of the valley—and the rest of the valley remain home to large apple processors, producing everything from juice to sauce to vinegar. Most of the valley grows multipurpose apples like York Imperial, Winesap, and Stayman Winesap that are also excellent for cider, and the calcium- and mineral-rich soils also produce exceptionally ripe, aromatic cider fruit. Apples like Newtown Pippin, Grimes Golden, and Hewe's Crab are being planted with greater regularity, and will soon bear the next generation of Virginia cider.

But the valley's 250-year history of agriculture and apple growing is under pressure, as other countries produce apples commercially, with a cheaper price tag. Not only has it become less lucrative to grow fruit on a large scale, but apple orchards around the town of Winchester are also becoming victims of Washington, DC's suburban sprawl. It's more profitable to sell real estate for houses than for apple orchards.

Helmed by a growing interest in cider, existing orchards are replacing commodity eating apples with cider and multipurpose apples throughout the Shenandoah Valley. Diane Kearns is a fifth-generation grower at Fruit Hill Orchard outside Winchester. Her farm has been growing fruit for local juice facilities since 1929—the height of Prohibition—when culinary apples were being planted in haste. "But the model needs to change," Kearns says. So she started a cidery, Winchester Ciderworks, in 2012.

In the same way that cider was a crucial part of subsistence farms in the colonial south, Kearns's impetus to make cider was to get more use—and revenue—from her farm products. Her mission now is to experiment with what cider varieties grow best at Fruit Hill and produce a microregional cider unlike any others on the market.

Arkansas Black

Most likely a descendant of Winesap, first grown in Benton County, Arkansas, in 1870, this high-acid apple was originally grown throughout the Southeast because of its storage abilities. Its skin turns from dark reddish-purple to near-black as the apple ripens, and it can last well into spring in proper cold storage, intensifying with age. When first picked late in the season, the apple can be starchy and unappealing, but after the snow melts the apple is one of the finest.

CIDER PROFILE

Slightly tannic and robust, with notes of strawberries and pineapple.

The Glaize brothers are on a similar quest. Their family has farmed apples in the valley since 1937. Fourth-generation brothers Philip and David recently "top-worked" varieties like Arkansas Black, Hewe's Crab, Black Twig, and Golden Russet in their orchard. Top-working—a form of grafting—changes the variety of mature trees, and the top-worked grafts produce a crop sooner than other methods. Of their six hundred total acres, twenty-five are cider and multipurpose fruit, with more on the way as top-worked fruit that proves successful is planted in their nursery. In 2015 the brothers created Glaize and Brother Juice Company, which supplies juice pressed at their farm exclusively to cidermakers. This fruit, and what's being planted by Kearns, helps drive and support the growth of cideries throughout the Commonwealth and beyond.

Appalachian Mountains

The mountains are an unpredictable but exciting place for apples in the Southeast. Stretching from Highland County, Virginia, to North Carolina, Georgia, and Alabama, the Appalachians never experienced the same level of agricultural intensity as the lower elevations surrounding them. Steep, challenging terrain meant homesteads remained small and limited up until the twentieth century.

The mountain climate here is more akin to southern New England than it is to the coastal plains and Piedmont foothills that lie to the east. Late frosts and mountainous terrain meant that in the past, orchards rarely grew beyond personal plantings. But the unique microclimate has also bred a prolific set of diversified apples.

Older residents recall times before the Blue Ridge Parkway was built, in the early 1930s, when their families would bring apples down from the mountains on horse carts to the small town markets in eastern Tennessee. Orchards planted before the Civil War can still be found full of heirloom varieties, like Limbertwig and Virginia Beauty, that never entered the modern market. These same hills are where enthusiasts like Jarvis Van Buren and, more recently, Lee Calhoun tracked and plotted the apple's past and paved the way for its future.

In 1996, Diane Flynt purchased acreage at an elevation of three thousand feet in Dugspur, Virginia, to plant a cider orchard. She was the first person to commit to growing southern varieties and European bittersweets on a commercial scale in the Appalachian conditions. Flynt believes that her apples have more flavor, texture, acidity, and grip than the apples in the lowlands. She harvests the

Lee Calhoun, Horne Creek Farm, and the Southern Heritage Apple Orchard

Horne Creek Farm, in the northeastern piedmont of North Carolina, is a working, living historical farm (and a North Carolina State Historic Site) that maintains the farming customs and traditions common at the turn of the twentieth century. To preserve the orchard that once thrived on the farm, Horne Creek's staff called on Lee Calhoun, who had begun scouring the South with his wife, Edith, in search of lost southern apples. Their discoveries ultimately led to the book *Old Southern Apples*. Ten years before that, in 1986, the couple started a nursery that grew to an excess of 400 apple varieties, most of which were unique to the South. For sixteen years, Lee and Edith grafted as many as 3,000 trees a year.

In 1997, the Southern Heritage Apple Orchard at Horne Creek became a reality. Lee grafted 800 trees, two of each variety from his nursery. Today, the nearly 1,000 trees in excess of 400 varieties make up one of the most culturally significant orchards in the country. And into the turn of the twenty-first century, thanks to a project called Apples for Africa, scions from Horne Creek's orchard are sent to Uganda, Zambia, and Rwanda. Because many southern apples are particularly heat-tolerant, they have found success growing in a central African climate and provide African farmers a comparatively easy crop to maintain.

Lee and Edith's contributions to southern apple culture remain immeasurable and unsurpassed.

apples after they naturally fall to the ground, ensuring only the ripest fruit is selected.

Flynt began producing Foggy Ridge Cider in 2004, to marry the intensity of bittersweets with Appalachian terroir, but she retired her cider in 2017 to focus on the orchard. She now sends fruit to a few cider producers in the region, including newcomer Molley Chomper Hard Cider in Ashe County.

Kate and Tim Arscott began Molley Chomper Hard Cider in 2015, using apples from Appalachia and the North Carolina Piedmont apple belt that stretches a hundred miles from Wilkesboro to Hendersonville. These foothills produce many of the same culinary apples found in the Southeast, including Winesap, Rome Beauty, and occasionally Arkansas Black. While commercial orchards never took root at high elevations, the warmer, drier Piedmont has been growing apples since the time of Jarvis Van Buren.

Retired agriculture extension agent Doug Hundley is also privy to the characteristics of mountain apples. He lives in Ashe County, which sits at 3,600 feet in elevation—nearly 3,000 feet higher than Charlotte in the Piedmont. Ashe County grows more Christmas trees than apple trees, but Hundley came across countless old apple trees while traveling throughout the mountains of northwestern North Carolina for work. In addition to native heirloom apples, he found northeastern favorites like Golden Russet and Roxbury Russet that thrived in the high elevation.

These trees were planted by turn-of-the-century subsistence farmers on standard rootstocks, nearly forty feet apart, and benefit considerably from the mountain breezes that help keep pests and disease away. Hundley noticed that these apples were about half the size of anything grown commercially and had more flavor, acid, tannin, and intensity.

Also in Ashe County, a stone's throw from the Virginia border, Ron and Suzanne Joyner are further proof that a diversity of apples is not just a relic of the past. At their Big Horse Creek Farm, they preserve many southern heirloom apples like Mattamuskeet and

Limbertwig

Limbertwig is not a variety but a large family of more than fifty varieties, including Myers Royal Limbertwig and Swiss Limbertwig, which are reputed to be great for cider. Limbertwigs are mountain apples, mostly originating around the Great Smoky Mountains where Kentucky, Virginia, Tennessee, and North Carolina converge. When the Great Smoky Mountain National Park was established in the 1920s and '30s, orchards of Limbertwigs were abandoned, only to be rediscovered and championed by the late Henry Morton, a Baptist minister from Gatlinburg, Tennessee. Their name comes from the trees' weeping growth habit. Thin, "limber" twigs sag late in the season when they're loaded with ripe fruit. Not all Limbertwigs grow in this fashion, however, and the only way to know a Limbertwig, enthusiasts say, is to taste one. Big Horse Creek Farm owner Ron Joyner offers his description from his first bite into a Limbertwig:

> "As I sat quietly beneath the [Myers Royal] tree savoring that first bite, I was immediately taken by the unique combination of flavor and aroma, which surprised and intrigued me. How do I describe what I was tasting? Here were flavors that I normally would not associate with fresh apples—a light, earthy, smoky, somewhat musky flavor that I sensed more as an aroma than an actual taste. Underlying these unusual flavors was a smooth, juicy sweetness, wonderfully counterbalanced with just the slightest hint of herbal spiciness that lingered on my tongue."

CIDER PROFILE

Musky, smoky, and full-bodied with slight signs of caramel and ripe melon.

Yates while growing cold-climate heirlooms like Calville Blanc d'Hiver and Wolf River. The Joyners get severe snow from the Great Lakes at their elevation, making their climate similar to that of western New York.

Kirk Billingsley, cidermaker at Big Fish Cider in Highland County, Virginia, forages throughout the county for wild apples grown from seed. Overlooking the Shenandoah Valley to the east, at an elevation of three thousand feet, Billingsley is just as likely to find apples that originated in the cooler Northeast, like Baldwin and Northern Spy, as he is traditional southern varieties like Smoke-house and Grimes Golden. He presses feral, wild apples into limited-release ciders, while southern fruit like Arkansas Black and Stayman Winesap make up his more consistent annual ciders.

Core Takeways

Contemporary cider in the Southeast is the marriage of different apple cultures that have co-evolved over the centuries. Landowners, subsistence farmers, and enslaved and Indigenous Peoples have each made contributions to a re-envisioned craft. The history of many of these cultures is filled with suffering and dispossession, which played a large role in shaping the region's orchards and farming. Whether through the manicured orchards of Hewe's Crab at Monticello, or Limbertwigs and Junaluksa on annexed lands, yester-day's echoes are still heard in today's cider.

EASTERN VIRGINIA AND COASTAL CAROLINA
- **Location and Geography:** West of Richmond and Charlottesville, the coastal plain slowly rises up into the foothills of the Appalachian Mountains.
- **Soil:** A soft composition of clay, sand, and silt with gravel due to erosion at higher elevations.
- **Climate:** Humid subtropical. Fire blight and other humidity-related ailments pose a serious threat. While some of the worst weather is diverted because of the mountains to the west, the area is still prime for autumn tropical storms. USDA Hardiness Zone 7a.*

---

* USDA Hardiness Zones look at a thirty-year average extreme temperature to suggest what plants will do best in a particular area. https://planthardiness.ars .usda.gov/

- **Orchard Location:** Orchards are found mostly at higher elevations from 500 to 1,000 feet in Albemarle and Nelson County, abutting the mountains.
- **Orchard Type:** Most of the orchards were intended for fresh packing, especially in Nelson County.
- **Significant Apple Varieties:** Black Twig, Golden Delicious, Stayman Winesap, Winesap, Ginger Gold, Hewe's Crab, Harrison, Ashmead's Kernel.
- **Cider Apple Plantings:** Many of the cideries located near Charlottesville and its existing wine tourism have their own estate cider orchards as well. Hewe's Crab has been championed at Monticello. Larger growers are beginning to plant more multipurpose and cider-specific apples.
- **Producers to Visit:** Albemarle CiderWorks (North Garden, VA), Castle Hill Cider (Keswick, VA), Blue Bee Cider (Richmond, VA).

WESTERN VIRGINIA (SHENANDOAH VALLEY)

- **Location and Geography:** Running 150 miles long and 25 miles wide through Virginia and West Virginia, this wide valley is situated between the Ridge-and-Valley Appalachians and the Blue Ridge Mountains.
- **Soil:** Limestone and sandstone over loam and gravel, hillsides are eroded granite and gneiss at higher elevations.
- **Climate:** Humid continental climate, defined by relative dryness and hot summers and cold winters. USDA Hardiness Zone 6b.
- **Orchard Location:** Orchards are located throughout the valley's hillsides, but most are clustered near Winchester, VA.
- **Orchard Type:** Winchester's prime location near north-south transportation lines make it home to a few apple and fruit processors—notably White House Foods, which has provided a local market for many of the apples grown in the valley.
- **Significant Apple Varieties:** Golden Delicious, Grimes Golden, York Imperial, GoldRush, Stayman Winesap, Winesap, Arkansas Black.
- **Cider Apple Plantings:** Cider apples are being embraced by both large and small growers looking to diversify. GoldRush has been widely adopted because of its dual uses and ease of growth. The area has seen sizable investment in not only apples but other cider-related projects like pressing infrastructure and nurseries.
- **Producers to Visit:** Winchester Ciderworks (Winchester, VA), Old Hill Cider (Timberville, VA).

APPALACHIAN MOUNTAINS

- **Location and Geography:** Extending from West Virginia to Alabama, these mountains once rivaled the Himalayas but have been eroded over the eons.
- **Soil:** Gravelly loam mixed with sand, silt, and granite.
- **Climate:** Subtropical highland climate with high diurnal shift, making for cold nights and winters and hot days. USDA Hardiness Zone 5a–7a.
- **Orchard Location:** The apple-growing region extends over several states at generally high elevation. Orchards are pocketed in several more concentrated areas, including North Carolina's Hendersonville, Brushy Mountain (south of Wilkesboro), and south of Asheville, as well as Yates County in northern Georgia.
- **Orchard Type:** Some intensive areas grow for the local fresh market and retail, but most orchards are small homestead plantings. This area remained agriculturally self-sufficient into the twentieth century.
- **Significant Apple Varieties:** Stayman Winesap, Winesap, Hewe's Crab, Harrison, Limbertwig, Black Twig, Arkansas Black, Yates, Winter Jon, Virginia Beauty.
- **Cider Apple Plantings:** Foggy Ridge Cider in Virginia was the first to plant cider apples. Plantings have remained small-scale, mostly for small estate cideries.
- **Producers to Visit:** Molley Chomper Hard Cider (Lansing, NC), Botanist and Barrel (Cedar Grove, NC), Noble Cider (Asheville, NC), Bold Rock (Nellysford, VA), Gypsy Circus Cider Company (Kingsport, TN).

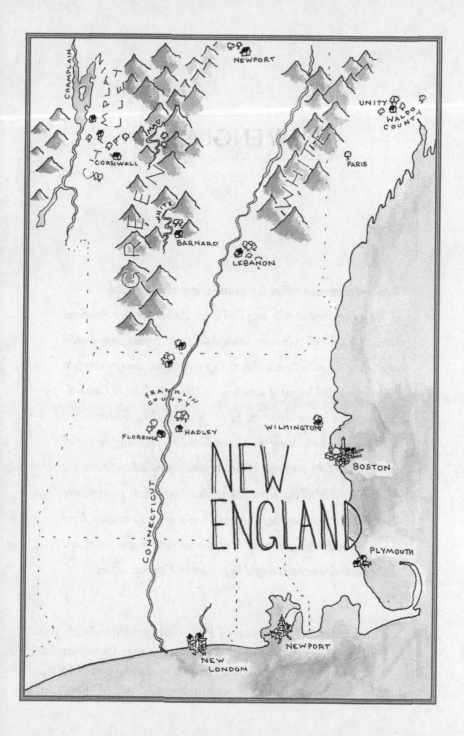

NEW ENGLAND

*Repeated continental collisions—crashing and retracting landmasses—
ripped a four-hundred-mile-long valley into the northeastern American
fabric. Millenia of volcanoes, earthquakes, and erosion formed sediment along the valley floor, which rose up and turned slow streams into
rushing rivers, the longest of which is the Quinnehtukqut, or Connecticut, named by Algonquins as the place "beside the long tidal river."*

*A two-mile-thick sheet of ice covered New England during the last ice
age, some 15,000 years ago. When it gradually melted and receded, it
left behind glacial till that formed the gentle rolling hills of pastoral New
England. But it is along the rich, loamy banks of the Connecticut River
where the earliest recorded evidence of human activity was found, and
where the earliest orchards would be planted by European settlers.*

New England's first colony of Plymouth, settled in 1620, was
intended as a self-sustaining place of refuge for separatists
of the Church of England. Known as the Puritans for their
desire to "purify" corruptions within the Church of England,

these separatists emigrated from Europe aboard the *Mayflower*, intent on joining the colony in Virginia. But rough seas and high winds landed the ship in Plymouth, Massachusetts, rendering the patent under which they sailed worthless, so the Puritans established their own form of colonial self-government, until their formal permission was granted from the king. Subsistence farms and agriculture were vital in both Plymouth and Jamestown, but Puritan values of religion, family, community, and education were the unique pillars on which Plymouth and ensuing New England colonies were built.

New England's geography—small and compact relative to the Southeast, and replete with capes, harbors, rivers, and lakes—primed the region for a thriving shipping industry as markets developed in Boston, Massachusetts; New London, Connecticut; Newport, Rhode Island, and beyond. In the years between the Revolutionary and Civil Wars, for New England, the birth of a nation came not just with a newfound star-spangled patriotism, but with a market revolution, diversified industries, and a new diet.

Plantations and commodity crops—drivers of the southern economy along with enslaved laborers—were constrained by New England's rugged, boulder-strewn landscape. Save for coastal plains and river valleys, New England terrain is dominated by the White and Green Mountains. Each range creates a rocky, uneven inland landscape that is prohibitive to scalable cultivation but suitable for growing apple trees.

Rather than agriculture, early commerce developed in trade and resources like timber and fur. With no land dedicated to commodity cash crops, families acted as the primary source of labor to provide necessary subsistence. But slavery was still present throughout colonial New England for more than 150 years. After the Pequot Wars, in 1638, Puritans captured and sent members of the Pequot tribe to the West Indies in exchange for African slaves. Three years later, the Massachusetts Body of Liberties made slavery legal, and it would remain so until 1780.

What developed in New England, because there was a lesser demand for—and therefore fewer—slaves, was a system of chattel slavery, whereby the children of enslaved Africans could be sold into bondage. The limited number of Black people in New England meant there was little hope for revolt from, justice for, or community to develop within the Black population. And although slave numbers were fewer than in the South, New England colonies were intricately tied to slavery via sugar plantations in the West Indies. Because of the monetary value of sugar, Caribbean islands were so deeply devoted to the crop that they relied on staples from elsewhere. In some instances—as with lumber and food—early New England colonies succeeded as a direct result of catering to the needs of the Caribbean elite.

Grain crops—which provided much of the region's food and labor—were sown on a significant portion of what cultivable land there was, so early New England developed as a region of beer drinkers. Colonial households made beer or took their barley and hops to public malt houses. Beer was brewed and barreled year-round while settlers established homesteads, farms, and orchards.

Tolman Sweet

A true sweet apple, Tolman Sweet dates back to seventeenth-century Massachusetts. Sweet in this case is a function of not only the apple's high sugar, but also its lack of acidity. Sweet apples are less common today, but they were once highly valued—both fresh at the table and fermented in the bottle—as a welcome contrast to generally astringent seedlings. The greenish-yellow fruit has a distinct suture line on its skin that runs from top to bottom, and the tree's sturdy root system was once widely used as rootstock.

CIDER PROFILE

Notes of caramel and berries. Usually blended due to its low acidity.

These small orchards were typically planted near the home, close to vegetable gardens where harvesting in inclement weather was bearable. Additional apple trees were planted in outlying fields, on land unfit for cultivation. No matter if the soil was poor, too thickly wooded to be cleared, or rife with rocky glacial deposits, the vigorous apple tree could blossom.

With trees flourishing, cider was made, stored, and consumed from October to May, after the summer's beer supply was tapped and barrels depleted. Into the mid-eighteenth century, stores of cider lasted New Englanders through winter, spring, and summer and even into fall, when the cycle could repeat. By 1750, with cider-making on the rise, beer consumption significantly declined.

As families grew and younger generations matured, their farms were parceled out among the family members, meaning they had less room for grains and shorter periods of fallow—and fields often suffered from soil exhaustion. Farmers found orchards easier to maintain than grain. One harvest could provide a year's worth of cider, and apple trees required a single planting and no seasonal sowing.

The harmonious confluence of climate and soil, coupled with the Puritan value of self-sufficient agriculture, gave New England an unrivaled crop of apples. As the region was settled, easy transport via abundant waterways fueled the growth of the apple industry.

With more apple trees and increased quantities of cider, land could be converted from barley and beer grains to a more diverse planting of crops. Gardens diversified after the Revolutionary War. Summer vegetable harvests and dairy products were lasting families into winter, and roots, cabbages, and potatoes—planted aplenty—could be stored through spring. Variety became a reality on the New England table. Broader pantries and stocks of food presented sub-sistence farmers a taste of surplus for the first time.

With subsistence farmers producing beyond their personal needs, farmland soon became profitable, and farmers could provide enough food for their own families and still sell more at local and urban markets. Farmers began buying plots of land to increase production and pass on to future generations.

In 1790, more than 90 percent of Americans lived on farms and engaged in agricultural occupations. But as the culture shifted from an agrarian economy to one based on industry, the percentage quickly dropped. By the Civil War, just over 50 percent of Americans lived on farms. New England's population more than tripled in this time, from 1 million to 3.5 million, and farmers moved from the countryside to villages and towns along the fertile soils of developing river valleys. The Census of 1810 reveals town populations along the Connecticut River Valley to be as much as five times those of more rural, inland counties. Farmers retained ownership of their abandoned outlying fields—upland lots and meadows that were granted to them before the Revolutionary War—leaving apple trees there to grow unchecked. Cider was the perfect fate for the neglected apples.

The Industrial Revolution was in full bloom early in the nineteenth century. Improvements were made to farm tools and equipment, increasing productivity and reducing labor costs. Agricultural societies ushered in a forceful movement that created a growing need for markets. New laws were passed, including two acts that prohibited American ships from trading with England and France. Farmers and merchants alike became champions of production and revenue management, and the gap was closed between rural self-sufficient economies and urban markets.

TAVERNS AND CIDER MILLS

Early colonial taverns were fixtures of New England culture, as significant as the church and country store. The Massachusetts General Court, which served as the governing body during colonial times, mandated that each town have a tavern, established to provide food and drink to churchgoers between morning and afternoon services. Taverns also catered to local militias and served as headquarters and hospitals during the Revolution. In post-Revolutionary New England, the tavern proliferated with the rise of markets, improved roads, and stagecoach traffic.

As transportation options grew, the rattle of stagecoaches, wagons, and carriages became fixed in the New England soundscape, and farmers hired marketmen and drovers to transport their produce to market. With more people traveling the roadways and the production and consumption of cider on the rise, New England's tavern culture was fortified.

Taverns appeared at crossroads, in mill towns, and along rural market routes on which drovers or farmers transported their goods. Trips were slow (it took three days to get from New York City to Boston) and required multiple stops. Taverns became a place to eat, drink, and sleep, with adjoining land to stable horses, graze cattle, and pen market-bound sheep and fowl.

Cider was the drink of choice at taverns. It flowed in abundant and liberal streams, and through wet lips came regional news with the day's gossip. Taverns were a spirited gathering place that contrasted the tame talks of the rural church. Fires burned bright in their great rooms while people discussed politics, attended town court sessions, or took part in elections. The tavern was New England's sanctuary of political, social, and economic transactions.

Stagecoaches relied on taverns the way railroads came to rely on train depots. Almanacs listed the distance between towns measuring from one tavern to another. Coach lines were routed and established from New England taverns in Boston and Narragansett, Rhode Island, and beyond to New York City and Canada. New modes of transportation also catered to the flow of goods and the growing population. Canals were flush with commerce. Steam power was applied to machines and industry. With more methods to transport goods, New England farm products spread west. From this wider distribution of fresh produce came a new focus on quality in the marketplace, and New England's premier apple crop began its ascent to national acclaim.

Cities and mill towns grew in tandem with local markets, typically sprouting along riversides where rushing water could supply power. Gristmills turned cereals into flour, sawmills made lumber from trees, carding mills prepared raw wool for spinning, slitting mills produced nails, fulling mills cleaned and thickened cloth, and cider mills turned apples into cider.

Cider mills, a common fixture in the early-nineteenth-century New England landscape, were typically built into hillsides, creating buildings with one story in the front and two in the back. Apples were unloaded in the front on the "top" floor, and cider was collected below. When the juice ran fresh from the press (before it fermented into cider), producers typically offered it for free to those who happened by. As American historian and author Alice Morse Earle wrote in 1898, "Yet is the sweet cider of country cider-mills as free and plentiful a gift to any passer-by as the water from the well or the air we breathe."

From Pomace to Fruit

Piles of pomace that resulted from pressing apples were the very source of the proliferation of apples throughout New England and beyond. Laden with apple seeds, pomace was spread about the farm, and the most viable seeds would grow into seedling apple trees. This resourceful practice contributed to some fifteen thousand apple varieties unique to the United States.

Farmers who couldn't afford to erect a building dedicated to a press, but still had a substantial orchard, often owned temporary milling equipment that consisted of a press and grinder, called a nut mill. They set up the equipment at the start of harvest season, broke it down at the end, and stored it in a barn for the remainder of the year.

If a farmer didn't have a press, one wasn't hard to come by. Unlike other mills, which employed an operator that collected a portion of the goods processed (known as a miller's toll), cider mills were available for rent and were a common necessity given the volume of small orchards throughout New England. Unique to the New England cider mill was that renters supplied their own processing equipment and labor. Farmers were responsible for bringing their own apples, barrels, straw (which was used as a filter and layered with ground apples in the press), and horse or oxen to transport the harvest and power the mill. After the threshing machine was invented for grain, farmers who could afford one used it in place of grinders to crush their apples.

Northern New England became nearly fully settled after the Revolution. Settlers aspired to engage in the growing market boom, beyond the self-sufficient economies of their own farms. Puritan values of home, family, and community provided the colonial roadmap for decision-making on the farm. The onset of industrialization reinterpreted these values from self-sufficiency and extended family into capitalism, markets, and profits.

Agricultural societies worked in conjunction with state and local governments to better American agriculture. Animal husbandry improved, and resources poured into the sheep industry, with the biggest splash made by the introduction of Spanish Merino sheep around 1810. Before the Merinos, prized for their high-quality thick, clean wool, domestic herds struggled through harsh winters, and sheep yielded small quantities of mutton and wool that required significant time to clean. But Merinos yielded more wool that sold at a better price. The breed kick-started the wool industry, and before long, the sheep population in New England reached six per capita. Wool became New England's first agricultural commodity.

While southern New England was cleared for cattle pastures and subsequent dairy products, the rugged northern New England landscape—optimal for grazing sheep—was deforested for pasture to accommodate sheep and the rising demand for domestic textiles.

By 1850, more than half of New England's landscape was deforested to extract raw materials and make room for agriculture. As white Americans overtook the land, apples followed in their wake, seeding themselves in the recently cleared land. Wool prices faltered as western farmers undercut New England farmers, hillside pastures were soon abandoned, and seedling apples naturalized themselves into the second-growth forests that now dominate the Northeast.

Contributions to the textile industry during these few decades transformed all other industries as well. Production had long been a singular craft, with one person completing a job from start to finish. But now, employers saw the value in dividing labor for the greater good. From prep and spinning to weaving and finishing, textiles become the first industrial product made under one roof by many different hands.

Orchard practices improved alongside the wool industry. Farmers learned the length and variations of growing seasons. They learned which apple varieties did well in their new climes, and knowledge was widely circulated regarding trees and apple varieties that were disease resistant, heavy bearers, early ripening, good keepers, and great for cider.

Grander livestock pastures meant a wider dispersal of seeds, thanks to animal deposits of digested fruit, and seedling trees moved and spread from homes to the edges of distant pastureland. While seed dispersal was common in colonial times, the ever-expanding deforested frontier resulted in seedling trees being dispersed into the deepest reaches of New England.

But heavy grazing damaged local ecosystems. Land clearing eroded the soils and eradicated the diversity found in centuries-old stands of forests. Competition and products from the West—easily shipped via new rail systems—cut into agricultural profits. New England farmers turned to producing goods that would not face competition from the west, and apple orchards and dairy farming became the ensuing commercial entities.

In the wake of the wool industry, children of farmers in the nineteenth century saw opportunity beyond that which could be gleaned from the rocky soil of their New England homes. They headed west with mercantile aspirations, and the significant migration brought Puritan ideals to all corners of the expanding country.

Sheep farmers who stayed behind replaced their herds with dairy cows. Cattle pastures moved to the riverside valleys and gentler lands of New England, where perishable dairy products could be shipped with greater ease. Abandoned pastures were left to nature's whim, and many of New England's seedling apple trees were swallowed by regrowing forests.

As seedling trees faded in the wood line, the roots of commercial orcharding were established. Whereas New England homestead farmers grew apples that worked for their families—cold hardy; suitable for fresh eating, cidermaking, drying, and storing; harvestable from late summer into winter—the commercial orchard and farmer considered these factors in unison with what the market demanded.

The 1830s welcomed a growing interest in grafting and grafted fruit, as farmers selected and planted apples with aesthetic values. Commercial orchards began along the Connecticut River Valley and Lake Champlain, and the hyper-regional apples of colonial times were soon being shipped worldwide. Markets in San Francisco and London became acquainted with New England apples like Baldwin, Porter, Rhode Island Greening, Roxbury Russet, and Hubbardston Nonesuch.

Apples from all over the world were likewise introduced to New England with success and acclaim. Canadian varieties like Fameuse (aka Snow) took root in Maine and the coldest parts of New England. In the 1830s, the Massachusetts Horticultural Society imported hardy Russian varieties, and Duchess of Oldenburg and Alexander apples thrived in regional markets, expanding apples even farther north, into the coldest reaches of New England.

Baldwin

This green and red-blushed apple began its journey as a chance seedling from Wilmington, Massachusetts, in the mid-eighteenth century. It was called Woodpecker, or Pecker, because of its frequent avian visitors. After the Revolutionary War, Baldwin was populated across New England and beyond by Colonel Loammi Baldwin, who came upon the apple during the construction of the short-lived Middlesex Canal. The apple industry in New England was built on Baldwin, which was prized for its thick-skinned durability, long storage capabilities, and tropical taste. The so-called Baldwin Belt stretched from southern Maine to the Berkshire Mountains along the border with New York. But three serious winters, the last in 1933–34, killed millions of Baldwin trees throughout the Northeast. McIntosh, a cold-hardy Canadian variety discovered in 1811, and its equally hardy and colorful progenies, like Macoun and Cortland, filled the void after the destruction of the Baldwin.

CIDER PROFILE

Stony and fruity, with bits of pear nectar and a slightly dry, herbal finish.

Consumers grew interested in specific apple varieties, and a horticultural contest ensued over which region could produce the best apples. New England consistently remained ahead of the curve.

Expanding markets gave farmers the confidence to learn the practices of pruning, grafting, and commercial planting through experience. Nurseries and commercial orchards began selling seedling trees and scion wood—pen-sized twigs for grafting—of fruit varieties that fetched high prices in the market, compounding the rapid development of market favorites. By the 1840s, apples were a consistent and reliable crop, and among the least expensive to establish and maintain, just as subsistence farmers had discovered. Hundreds of thousands of apple trees were planted throughout New England in the middle of the nineteenth century.

Fruit consumption was on the rise, be it fresh, fermented, cooked, or preserved. Historian Carroll Wright notes that up until 1807, apples were sold in Massachusetts only by the bushel (about 50 pounds). That year marks the first appearance of apples sold by the barrel (roughly 160 pounds). The peck (10 to 12 pounds) measurement first appeared in 1813 and, amid the proliferation of commercial orchards, the first distinction of apples sold at wholesale (in barrels) appeared in 1841. From that point on, barrel was the dominant measure by which apples were sold.

Rhode Island Greening

Reported in 1650 growing at Green's Inn in Newport, Rhode Island, the first tree—legend has it—died from the excessive scions taken from it. This large, firm, and waxy yellow-green apple was a popular counterpart to Baldwin, and It remains an important part of orchards in western New York and Michigan, where it is planted for juice, pies, and sauce.

CIDER PROFILE

Very green and lively, generally light in body and reminiscent of Sauvignon Blanc, carrying characteristics of lime zest, herbs, and wildflowers.

Industrialization and the evolution of the apple market, in some ways, planted the seeds of cider's demise. The market demanded fresh eating apples, and tannin and other cider qualities no longer appealed. Compounding the issue was heightened maritime trade, which brought increasing quantities of rum to New England. Laws were passed that show a government keen on collecting revenue from the flow of rum. Distillers, exporters, retailers, and tax officials profited from the spike in rum sales, and an increase in distilled spirits resulted in a diminishing consumption of cider.

Despite beer's hundred-year decline, beer culture developed anew as well, as nearly two million German immigrants arrived in America between 1820 and 1870. The U.S. population surged between 1800 and 1870, from 5.3 million to almost 40 million, a majority of whom were foreign born, and 25 percent of whom settled in cities.

Rural farmers, historically the makers and providers of cider, represented a diminishing demographic. They left their inland New England farms for opportunity in cities and towns or out west. The impetus for planting seedling orchards disappeared with the decline of subsistence farming and the rise of commercial orcharding. Marketable seedling varieties fit for fresh eating had been named, extracted from marginal inland farms, and sold in markets. These eating apples proliferated, and cider apples were overtaken by new forest growth. So while apples intended for fresh eating were shipped by the barrel in vast quantities, cider was made and consumed less and less, and professionalism in the orchard meant the decline of amateur cider.

Railroad expansion and communication networks continued to improve. Coach travel—and thus the tavern—suffered with the mobilization of the westward population. Railroads brought food to a nation once supplied by local farmers. Where colonial living was dependent upon agriculture and rural landscapes, the quickly industrializing America became increasingly urban. By the dawn of the Civil War, the rural New England interior—the birthplace of the region's cider culture—was significantly depopulated.

People still made cider—in cellars and barns—but it fell from public conversation. Life was no longer about establishing permanent homesteads, planting apple trees, and making cider. The economics and social preferences favored beer and factory work. The whisper of cider apples was drowned out by the screaming demand for eating apples, the chorus of commercial orchards, and the changing social landscape of America. Cider, and cider apple trees, became an antiquated facet of a once-rural country.

Modern Cidermakers and Apple Growers

Comprising six states—Maine, New Hampshire, Vermont, Massachusetts, Connecticut, and Rhode Island—New England and its cidermakers and orchards benefit from a handful of distinct natural features. Coastal orchards reap the benefit of a moderate climate, meaning slightly shorter winters and longer growing seasons. The Connecticut River Valley and Lake Champlain likewise help growers manage unwanted early and late frosts, while the valley flatlands get more daylight over the course of a year.

Cidermakers in New England are building upon the existing resources of the area, whether that be culled McIntosh or feral mountain seedlings. Cideries like Artifact Cider Project, Eden Specialty Ciders, and Rocky Ground Cider have found a unique path in bringing their message and cider to their communities and beyond.

Today, Vermont boasts the highest number of cidermakers in the country per capita, with around one commercial cidermaker for every thirty thousand residents. This is largely because Vermont remains a significantly rural and agricultural state. Both private and state investments flow into projects that support the existing apple and agriculture industries.

CHARACTERISTICS OF NEW ENGLAND CIDER

Ciders in New England rely on apples like McIntosh, Baldwin, and Cortland that are grown for fresh eating, but many are being supplemented with rare, characterful heirloom fruits. Apples grown for cider have been cultivated throughout the region for decades; because more of these are finding their way into New England ciders, an increasing number of them have a uniquely savory, tannic element.

Champlain Valley

Between the Adirondack High Peaks in New York and the imposing Green Mountains of Vermont, Lake Champlain has served as a border, highway, and cradle of agriculture for centuries. The lake sits within a 200-million-year-old tectonic rift valley carved up by sequential glaciers, and it marked the eastern boundary of the Iroquois Confederacy long before it divided Vermont from New York.

Compared to the granite hillsides found in higher elevations of Vermont, valley conditions primed the region for agriculture and drew settlers from New England and Canada. At more than 100 miles in length, Lake Champlain served as a major transportation route into the twentieth century, connecting Montreal and the Saint Lawrence River to the Hudson River and New York City. Apples, lumber, and leather were shipped from Burlington to the regional and global marketplace.

By the turn of the twentieth century, Vermont was a leader in fresh apple production. Newly introduced apples like McIntosh and Cortland were being grown and sold at previously unseen scales. Orchards grew, and though the Champlain Valley didn't produce as much as southern New England and New York State, the apples were renowned for their quality. What the region lacked in quantity was made up for by the premium price the apples fetched at market.

After World War II, the Champlain region invested in expensive climate- and chemical-control storage, allowing new thin-skinned apple varieties to get to consumers cleaner, fresher, and more intact. This facilitated their rise to premium status, despite competition from warm-weather regions that were able to saturate the market with apples that ripen sooner.

The introduction of new sorting, packing, and grading technology pushed the market toward uniformity over character. Orchards that managed to successfully commercialize were faced with another challenge: Alar. Alar (the trade name for daminozide) is a chemical spray that regulates growth. It was developed in the 1960s to keep apples hanging longer and push color to the skin, but it does so at the expense of flavor. After the prevalent chemical was purportedly linked to cancer in 1989, some forty million viewers tuned in to a *60 Minutes* exposé. Decades later, the threat that Alar posed remained unresolved, and growers switched to new chemicals in order to stay ahead.

McIntosh

Discovered by John McIntosh in 1811 among some seedlings on land he was clearing on his homestead in eastern Ontario, McIntosh did not go mainstream until after the destruction of the Baldwin in 1934. Its popularity was spurred on by the invention of pesticides, which kept the susceptible McIntosh presentable to the growing marketplace. Its unquestioned cold hardiness, petite size, and lush aromatic honey flavor made it a favorite of both growers and consumers throughout the Northeast.

CIDER PROFILE

Potentially intoxicating aromas of honeysuckle, quince jam, and saffron make McIntosh a frequent contributor to many New England ciders.

Vermont persisted through the scare, and the state has had a consistent, modern commercial cider presence since the early 1990s via Woodchuck Cider. Woodchuck, which is made by Vermont Cider Company, grew from a retirement project to one of the largest brands in the category. The company has had a rocky and uneven history. In 1998 it was acquired by H. P. Bulmer of Herefordshire, England, as part of an expansion that, after much fanfare, quickly fizzled. While most of the apples that go into Woodchuck today are globally sourced, the brand's presence has been instrumental in the growth of cider within the state.

Ben Calvi, Vermont Cider Company's operating manager, is a former Napa Valley winemaker, and he has been a source of great insight and technical knowledge for the growing cider community. His expertise, along with Vermont Cider Company's hardwired infrastructure, provides smaller producers access to resources like canning, filtering, and tank space that are not available in other parts of the country.

Large orchards that were forced to close after the commodity boom from international competition in the 1980s have been a starting point for many of Vermont's small growers. Amy Trubek and Brad Koehler, both trained chefs, moved to the Champlain Valley in 2002. The couple purchased a neglected orchard adjoining their home in Cornwall, with nearly eighty varieties that had been planted in the late 1960s, and turned it into Windfall Orchard.

Trubek and Koehler's hobby developed into a passionate career after they met Eleanor Léger of Eden Specialty Ciders. The trio made ice cider together in 2010, and by the following year Koehler was grafting many of the old trees at Windfall to European cider varieties like Yarlington Mill and Dabinett. The warmth from the lake during the growing season made all the difference for ripening these European apples, as well as American varieties like Arkansas Black that would normally never ripen at this latitude.

Windfall uses estate fruit and processes it at Eden's facility, and Koehler sells most of the cider at local farmers' markets. The European varieties Koehler planted will provide tannin for his cider as the trees mature, but the future for Windfall cider is to focus on domestic cider apples, be they named and known varieties or propagated seedlings that have proven to make excellent cider. Cider apples sell for a higher premium than eating varieties, a point that remains central in the world of apple growing.

Eden's facility is located in Newport, an economically depressed part of the northeast corner of Vermont (known as the Northeast Kingdom), just south of the Canadian border and sixty miles east of Lake Champlain, where Léger's great-great-grandfather blacksmithed before the Civil War. Léger's first taste of ice cider was in Montreal. Quebecois winemaker-turned-cidermaker Christian Barthomeuf developed ice cider after being inspired by the success that Ontario winemakers in Niagara were having with ice wine.

Léger recalls thinking that ice cider tasted of Vermont terroir and wondering why no one was making it in her home state. Vermont is one of the few places in the world where it is both cold enough to make ice cider and hospitable enough for apples to thrive. Léger suspected that ice cider from Vermont orchards could be sold for a premium, so she purchased an abandoned dairy farm in 2007 with intentions of recreating the specialty cider, the first time it would be introduced to the United States.

Ice cider is the apple equivalent of ice wine, made from either frozen juice (in a process known as cryoconcentration) or frozen fruit (via cryoextraction). When made well, it is concentrated, rich, honeyed, and full-bodied. Producing it is a time-consuming labor of love, and the alcohol by volume is slightly higher than traditional cider, so it is often bottled in smaller format and sipped rather than consumed by the glassful.

Cryoextraction draws out a concentrated nectar from the frozen apples as ice crystals develop and break the cellulose structure of the fruit. Characteristics of white grape, apricot, and often fig and walnut develop, depending on how long the fruit has matured. Cryoconcentration is a more widely practiced style of ice cidermaking, and the style for which Léger is the foremost advocate. With this method, ice cider is made from frozen juice rather than frozen apples—apples are pressed late in the season and the juice is left outside to freeze.

Léger believes that cryoconcentration does a better job of capturing and preserving the flavor and complexity of the heirloom fruit she uses. This is particularly important because she is not using commercial eating apples, but premium apples like Esopus Spitzenburg, Black Oxford, and Calville Blanc d'Hiver. The process also preserves the natural malic acid found in apples, which helps balance the concentrated sugar and prevent it from becoming too cloying.

Ice cider is one of the few alcoholic beverages in the nation that has a federally regulated process. It must be naturally frozen in the elements. Ciders frozen in freezers cannot be called ice ciders, largely because the thawing process is just as vital as the freezing. The gradual freezing and thawing separates the sweet cider liqueur from the water, something that is not feasible in a cold tank and is essential for concentrating sugars, acid, and flavor.

Vermont's Northeast Kingdom is a marginal place to grow apples, but Léger and her aptly named orchardist Ben Applegate manage to grow nearly four acres of apples holistically. They use natural pest deterrents like neem oil and Liquid Fish and cultivate active microbes that encourage orchard health. Admittedly, the yields are much less than you'd get from more conventional methods, "but the juice is amazing," Léger says, and quality is a hallmark of Eden Specialty Ciders.

Beyond the Northeast Kingdom, commercial eating apples like McIntosh, Empire, and Cortland still form the backbone of most cider made in the Champlain Valley, but new cider and heirloom varieties represent a growing portion of new plantings.

A majority of recent growth in the cider industry is propelled by cull apples—those deemed unfit for market. In the past, excess cull fruit was shipped to processors in western New York, mostly to be turned into applesauce or pressed locally into juice, but that has become increasingly less profitable. International competition came with the post–World War II shift to commercial orcharding, the development of regional processing companies, and bigger orchards using Alar. China was coming out of its Cultural Revolution, and reforms there encouraged the planting of expansive commercial apple orchards. That fruit entered the global market in the 1980s, and prices for commercial apples plummeted.

Today, large producers like Citizen Cider and Shacksbury Cider are exemplars of what cull fruit can do when fermented. As cider establishes its own identity—in the Champlain Valley and beyond—David Dolginow, cofounder of Shacksbury Cider with Colin Davis, has noticed that many consumers talk about their cider alongside Vermont's already-established identity of creating delicious agricultural products: Jasper Hill cheese, the Alchemist's Heady Topper beer, Ben & Jerry's ice cream, and Green Mountain Coffee Roasters have all paved the way for a national awareness of exceptional Vermont foods.

The rise of cidermakers seeking imperfect processing apples has helped reinstate regional value, and together with the introduction of new designer apples like Honeycrisp, apple growing has again become a sustainable operation in the Champlain Valley.

Vermont's Champlain Valley is fertile ground for genre-bending fermentations. Krista Scruggs of ZAFA Wines is a protégé of wine- and cidermaker Deirdre Heekin, of La Garagista Farm and Winery. Working in uncharted directions, Scruggs and Heekin both push the limits with their Vermont cider and wine. Heekin's solera-style cider builds complexity by blending multiple vintages aged in glass demijohns and barrels.

Scruggs, a native of interior California, is one of the few Black cidermakers in the country, a result of the systemic racism that oversaw a century of decline in the number of Black farmers. In 1920, there were nearly a million Black farmers in the country. A century later, there are fewer than fifty thousand—about 5 percent of U.S. farmers—and they collectively own less than 1 percent of the country's farmland.

Scruggs came to Vermont after working for one of the largest wine companies in the country, turning her attention to better farming and natural fermentation. Her first cider and wine vintage, in 2017, was sold out before it was labeled, having garnered advance press and acclaim. Early vintages of her ciders were foraged from trees in the mountain valleys, the fertile lakeshore, and Grand Isle, once the site of some of the state's most coveted orchards. Later cider iterations incorporate cultivated cider varieties with hardy hybrids grown in Vermont's unique terroir. Scruggs's coferments seamlessly blend grapes and apples with a hands-off approach that creates a singular narrative with many personalities. CO Cellars, the tasting room that she shares with Shacksbury Cider, is devoted to the unconventional, showcasing cider, wine, beer, and cocktails without the baggage of categories.

Connecticut River Valley

The Connecticut River flows from a beaver pond near the Canadian border in the remote north of New Hampshire, over four hundred miles south to the Long Island Sound. Formerly buried by an Ice Age lake that slowly drained over thousands of years, today it is defined by nutrient-rich soils, expansive floodplains, a narrow valley, and waterfalls that continue to cut into bedrock.

Dutch and English colonists built settlements and towns, like Hartford, Connecticut, and Springfield, Massachusetts, along the fertile valley near older Indigenous settlements. The valley quickly became one of the most agriculturally productive regions in early New England, sustaining field crops like wheat and corn in addition to row crops like squash and beans, as well as ever-present apple orchards.

While the Connecticut River Valley has a single geologic history, it can be split into two distinct apple-growing regions. From the northern Massachusetts border north, the upper reaches of the valley share much in common with the business models and orchard practices of northern New England—areas like Maine and the Champlain Valley. Below Massachusetts's northern border, the region is linked to New York's Hudson Valley. This region has warmer weather and apples that ripen faster, plus the advantages of being closer to the consumers in cities.

In the last decades of the twentieth century, the fate of many small growers in New England was bleak. Commercial orchards had become so efficient at producing apples that fruit flooded the

PICK-YOUR-OWN

Unable to stay afloat selling fruit wholesale in the 1960s and 1970s, many fruit growers began retail operations to market their goods directly to consumers. Since then, U-Pick or Pick-Your-Own orchards have become a common sight not just in the Connecticut River Valley, but throughout the entire country, especially on the East Coast and in the Midwest. Large operations draw thousands of visitors on harvest weekends, making U-Picks one of the few times Americans engage with agriculture firsthand, inviting a connection between experience and fruit.

market, triggering a race to the bottom as farmers rushed to unload their fragile crops at rock-bottom prices. Costs for packaging, transportation, and storage kept rising, and retailers and brokers set prices that often did not meet the cost of production.

In the 1980s, New England apple growing was in a similar pattern of decline to the one that had claimed the wool industry over a hundred years before. Improvements in technology and competition from cheaper sources negated any sense of quality and position within the existing market. Many larger growers were crushed by the load of their own debts, which they had accumulated in pursuit of efficiency.

Zeke Goodband of Champlain Orchards, and former orchardist at Scott Farm Orchard in southeastern Vermont, wanted to break away from this cycle. While living in Maine in the 1970s, he took inspiration from old apple varieties growing on neglected homestead orchards. Instead of competing with other McIntosh growers for the biggest, reddest apples, Goodband realized he could beat them with diversity. He began selling apples like Blue Pearmain and Roxbury Russet at prices he was able to control.

While many New England farms turned to commercial production, some of the older farms—especially in Maine and Vermont—remained diversified, with apple trees, modest dairy operations, and small herds of sheep. These were the "germ repositories," as Goodband calls them, "the library of Alexandria for old apple varieties," and the reason the heirloom orchard model continues to thrive in New England.

Eleanor Léger sources many of her heirloom and cider apples from Scott Farm, including the famed Kingston Black bittersharp, a scab-resistant early fall apple that has become highly prized among modern cidermakers. Kingston Black is an old apple of British origin, but it grows exceptionally well in New England's climate and lends complex tannin and structure to ciders. It is one of the few cider apples that has traditionally been made into a single-variety cider in the United States and the United Kingdom.

Poverty Lane Orchards, farther upriver in Lebanon, New Hampshire, is Léger's other main source for apples. Like many orchards throughout New England, Poverty Lane—owned by husband-and-wife team Steve Wood and Louisa Spencer—was built on Baldwin before McIntosh took over. Wood has been growing apples on the farm since he was eleven, and he says the best and most flavorful McIntosh in the Connecticut River Valley are smaller than 2.5 inches in diameter. In the 1970s, Poverty Lane had a substantial business exporting 2-inch flavor-bomb McIntosh apples to the UK for considerably more money than the apple receives today. When the market eschewed flavor for uniformity and size, the desire for small, irregular apples dried up.

As the market changed, orchards invested in equipment, warehousing, and storage to facilitate ever-bigger, redder McIntosh. Companies developed new sprays and mechanical grading lines that could handle the delicate, thin-skinned apples. Packers also began spraying an artificial wax coating on apples, which gave them a lustrous shine but removed the fruit's bloom, leaving no indication what condition the fruit was in. A majority of the smaller orchards that couldn't afford to mechanize went out of business.

Wood and Spencer saw cider apples as a potential way to reestablish value on their land. In 1989, they planted a thousand cider apple trees, making Poverty Lane the first modern commercial cider orchard in the United States. It took them over a decade of trial and error with European and American varieties to come up with what grows well and tastes great in their orchard. Since then, Poverty Lane has remained one of the largest cider orchards in North America.

Countless orchardists and prospective tree growers have collected scion wood from Poverty Lane Orchards. Apples they have grown successfully in Lebanon have spread across the country, laying the foundational norms for tannic fruit nationwide. Stewards of these trees often try to consult with Wood, but he is the first to admit that unless you are in northern New England, there is little insight he can offer about growing the apples he has made famous.

Farnum Hill Ciders, the label under which Wood and Spencer make and bottle cider, was born in the 1990s. Spencer says their goal has always been to create reliable ciders that maintain a certain level of expectation. Their sparkling extra dry and semidry, in addition to their still extra dry cider, have been standard bearers for tannic ciders, and for many years were among the only tannic American ciders to be nationally distributed.

Only a portion of the fruit under Poverty Lane's care goes into the Farnum Hill label. A large amount is sent to other cidermakers across the country seeking to bolster their own ciders with tannin, depth, and complexity. Growing demand has made Poverty Lane's high-quality juice some of the most expensive in the apple business.

Wood gives credit for the apples' quality to the glacial till soils, in which a high level of organic matter has been maintained. The orchard also simultaneously has good drainage but sufficient water retention, meaning he has never had to irrigate or fertilize his trees. In Lebanon's microclimate, springtime frosts can take away an entire crop if the buds have already developed. But in the fall, frosts can push certain varieties to new levels. Cold causes a rush of photosynthates from the leaves to the fruit—"scaring the fruit," as Wood says—which forces the tree to focus all its energy on the fruit, thereby building higher and higher sugars.

Adding to the quality, Wood and Spencer argue, is their approach to harvesting. Rather than picked early from the trees, most of Poverty Lane's fruit is harvested off the ground, after the tree says it is fully ripe and drops it. This ensures that their fruit reaches its maximum development and perfect ripeness.

Despite its owners' long list of firsts, Farnum Hill Cider was not the first commercial cidery in the United States. That distinction goes to West County Cider, located downriver in Franklin County, Massachusetts. Founders Terry and Judith Maloney's cider journey began in the San Francisco Bay Area late in the 1960s, when they made wine from grapes grown by friends and old Italian growers.

In search of cheap land to build something for themselves, and inspired by their winemaking experiences in the Bay Area, the Maloneys headed east and landed in Colrain. They cleared a homestead in 1972 and began to learn the region's history with apples. They began planting an orchard while Terry continued working as an ER doctor. Terry's approach to cidermaking blended ingenuity and local history with the rationality, precision, and cleanliness that came with his medical training. He sought to understand how the innovations in scientific winemaking that had developed since he left California could be applied to cider.

Field Maloney, Terry's son and the current proprietor of West County, remembers clearing forest when he was in fifth grade to plant orchards inspired by what his parents had read in nineteenth-century historical resources. They planted a smattering of different apple trees in their first orchard: three Chisel Jersey, four Sheep's Nose, and three Golden Russet. Field swears by the complexity that can be found only in fruit from old trees, since they grow and change over their lifespan—much longer than one human generation can see. Redfield, one of West County's signature apples and ciders, continues to be a source of learning as the years go by.

Redfield

A 1938 cross between Wolf River and Niedzwetzkyana, Redfield is a big, tart, high-acid, red-fleshed variety. One of the apple's initial purposes was to be added to applesauce, to make a more spritely and red-toned product. But because apples take years to develop, the applesauce industry advanced more quickly than the fruit with the advent of red food coloring. Redfield was rediscovered by Terry Maloney, who found it growing in a research orchard and saw the fruit's potential in cider. Thanks In large part to the contribution and success West County has had with the apple, Redfield is now one of the most widely recognized red-fleshed varieties in the United States.

CIDER PROFILE

Very tart, cranberries, crushed roses, dried cherries, and candy-coated raspberries.

West County has always been an advocate for the maligned McIntosh as a cider apple. While not every McIntosh develops the complexity that will make great cider, those that are grown with extensive care in the nutrient-rich soils of the Connecticut River Valley capture all the aroma, fruit, and florals that first made the variety popular. Field Maloney's favorite source for McIntosh is Singing Dog Orchard. Trees there grow on an all-but-abandoned property, and the neglect has come to produce low yields and intense fruit with intoxicating aromas and flavors.

Franklin County CiderDays

The Maloney family has been instrumental in creating and growing one of the greatest cider festivals in the world. Since 1993, Franklin County CiderDays has brought cidermakers, drinkers, and enthusiasts, along with leaf peepers and apple pickers, to the rolling hills and crunchy leaves of western Massachusetts. The weekend-long festival seamlessly integrates professionals with amateurs, the casual drinker with the dedicated enthusiast. Throughout the county, old churches, community centers, and storefronts are transformed into venues for discussion, education, and celebration of cider, apples, and orchards.

CiderDays is especially valuable for new cidermakers, who can swing by one of the orchards to fill up carboys and other containers with top-quality fresh-pressed juice from heirloom apples for their own cider projects. And Saturday night's tasting salon is always an unparalleled assembly of cider and cidermakers from around the world.

West County's contribution to cider in New England—and beyond—cannot be overstated. Cidermakers across the country cite their first experience drinking something from West County as inspiring and revelatory, the final push that led them down the cider road.

Artifact Cider Project got its start in Springfield, Massachusetts, moved to the Boston area, and has since headed back west to Florence, in Franklin County, closer to the source of many of its apples. Artifact founders and childhood friends Soham Bhatt and Jake Mazar source apples from up and down the Connecticut River Valley. Bhatt has created an ambitious selection of ciders (twenty-five varieties in 2018) that he says caters to the label's growing and diverse customer base. His first vintage was made under the supervision and tutelage of the Maloneys. Like the Maloney family, Bhatt is a believer in the power of McIntosh. The apple forms the backbone for Artifact's canned cider, Wild Thing, which makes up a significant portion of their overall production.

Bhatt makes cider that shows the diversity of what cider can be. In addition to McIntosh cider, Artifact focuses on limited bottlings that highlight heirloom apples like Roxbury Russet and Foxwhelp sourced from Scott Farm Orchard and the family-run Pine Hill Orchards in Colrain, MA. In working consistently with Connecticut River Valley fruit, he has gained an appreciation for the region's growing conditions, microflora, native yeasts that develop on the fruit, and the characteristic richness he says you can't find elsewhere in New England or beyond. This awareness plays into his wild fermentations, which are done without the addition of commercial yeasts, Bhatt's preferred way to ferment.

Roxbury Russet

Often touted as America's oldest named apple, this greenish-gray apple was first noticed from the rest of the country's seedlings in the early seventeenth century. The apple followed New Englanders on their westward expansion into Connecticut and then on to Ohio in the early nineteenth century. Coarse, sweet, and savory, it is one of the great cider and eating apples of North America.

CIDER PROFILE

Textured but not lush. Subtle spices accent candied lemons, minerals, and a distinct hazelnut finish.

Just south of Franklin County, in Hadley, Massachusetts, is Carr's Ciderhouse. Husband and wife Jonathan Carr and Nicole Blum got started in 2007, when they began planting their 2,500 trees along the Connecticut River. They work with forager and orchard expert Matt Kaminsky, who has collected a large assortment of wild and feral varieties from the Connecticut valley. These apples—cast off, random descendants of earlier apple generations—often prove to have superior cidermaking potential, and they are being cultivated in an orchard setting for the first time since the seedlings originated more than a hundred years ago. They have proven to be the most resilient in Carr's nursery—which uses a no-spray system—often exceeding the imported varieties that can succumb to disease and suffer in the valley's erratic rain patterns.

Kaminsky is not alone in the feral apple endeavor. After most of the Northeast was deforested with the arrival of European settlers, the forests began to return and apples naturalized themselves into the landscape. These seedling trees, referred to as pippins, favored the marginal areas between the forest and the pasture edge, and their fruit is often more astringent, acidic, and tannic than their cultivated cousins. Henry David Thoreau rhapsodized about their elusive appeal in his 1862 essay for *The Atlantic* "Wild Apples," in which he eulogized seedling orchards, once the norm in New England but now replaced by rows of nursery trees. Today, numerous cidermakers throughout the Northeast are working with these apples—chasing the long-lost tart, acidic, tannic, and resilient apples that have made compelling, distinctly terroir-driven cider for centuries.

In Central Vermont's Mad River Valley, known more for its ski resorts than apples, Teddy Weber of Tin Hat Cider helps manage a small orchard that was planted in the 1990s with the intent to make cider. The trees were planted in marginal soils low in nitrogen, but Weber says this makes for long, slow fermentations, which gives his cider time to develop depth and complexity.

Because of the orchard's relatively small size (250 trees spread out on seven acres), Weber looks to the bounty of wild seedling trees among the conifers in nearby mountains. As the national quest for the next great cider apple continues, Weber believes these trees warrant important observation, having survived natural selection in less-than-ideal conditions. Above all, these trees, Weber feels, are the future for regional American terroir.

South of Tin Hat, in the hollows flowing into the White River, brothers Jon and Chris Piana of Fable Farm Fermentory originally produced cider from feral apples to subsidize their community-supported agriculture (CSA) vegetable farm. The landscape of Barnard, the closest town, boasts abundant cellar holes, the remnants of former homesteads. Near these stone-lined holes are typically organized rows of trees, the former kitchen gardens of Vermont's first European settlers.

The Piana brothers incorporate the apples planted generations earlier with seedlings to produce savory, rich, unique ciders in their cellar. Bitter wild apples lend structure and phenolic complexity, which contributes to mouthfeel and structure, while cultivated apples bring fruitiness and perfume to the ciders. Grape skins and local botanicals, like sumac, lend other layers to these taut, acidic ciders that are defined by minerality and creativity.

Maine and Coastal New England

Maine was the New England state hardest hit in the triad of freezing disasters, culminating in the winter of 1933–34, which proved to be a devastating setback for commercial growers. Baldwin had been Maine's premier commercial apple, and the winter freeze wiped out nearly 90 percent of the state's remaining trees. Local apples, in addition to the cold-hardy Russian varieties, tolerated the freeze, as they had for decades, and persisted on homesteads throughout the state.

As in the rest of New England at the close of the nineteenth century, many of Maine's small farms were replaced by larger market-oriented orchards. Numerous navigable rivers and channels allowed for easy transportation of apples to markets in Boston and Europe. But still, on a smaller scale, many apples remained local, spreading from farm to farm in ways unique to Maine, because of an early reliance on small seafaring boats for transportation.

Homesteader, historian, self-accredited pomologist, and apple detective John Bunker has spent decades decoding and deciphering the people and apples of Maine's unique past. Maine's unofficial apple ambassador through the Maine Organic Farmers and Gardeners Association (MOFGA) and Fedco Trees (which specializes in distributing local apples), Bunker is a master of identifying and tracking old apples from pre-industrial Maine as they spread from a single tree to become regional and local favorites. In the past, hundreds of distinctly Maine apples could be found on farms alongside other New England favorites like Baldwin, Duchess of Oldenburg, and Rhode Island Greening. Some apples, like Collins from Cherryfield, Maine, never traveled farther than their local community, or even the farm where they originated, as with the Canadian Strawberry, which remained the secret of a single farmer.

Bunker has tracked down hundreds of varieties, and more than three hundred of them now survive on the Maine Heritage Orchard in Unity. He also seeks out unloved apples from all places, like a

Black Oxford

Black Oxford originated in the western Maine town of Paris in 1790, before becoming a favorite of the Fedco Trees catalog. Nearly black, with slight white blooms on its skin, the apple could be confused for a plum with a passing glance, says John Bunker. Sweet, lush, and creamy, Black Oxford epitomizes the potential of antique apples, and several multicentury-old trees can still be found on homesteads throughout Maine.

CIDER PROFILE

Warm peaches with walnuts and cream, and an important aromatic for Eden's Heirloom Ice Cider.

seedling apple grown down the road from his farm that he calls Bitter Pew, which has more tannin than typical European cider apples. Bunker's apples are not just relics of the past. Many have come from the university system for breeding and research. Bunker lobbied the University of Minnesota for years to have access to an apple that was later named Frostbite (a grandparent to Honeycrisp), whose unique blackstrap molasses and vegetal qualities kept it out of wide propagation for decades. Bunker feels that cider may be a realistic venue to preserve some of these unique apples and give them an avenue for sustainability.

Bunker and his wife, Cammy Watts, are at the center of a growing cider community in Maine. The heirloom orchard on their home at Super Chilly Farm, though not commercial, has been a source of endless knowledge for hobbyists and pomologists alike. Every year farms across the state send apprentices through MOFGA to Super Chilly, training the next generation of farmers.

John Bunker and MOFGA provide resources to a wide community of passionate people interested in apples, fruits, and plants. Khristopher Hogg of Perennial Cider Bar and Farm Kitchen is one such person. He moved to Waldo County from Marrowstone Island in Washington State in 2016, and by 2019 he was set on opening a restaurant to highlight that community. Few places other than Maine have such well-attended scion swaps or classes. Programs like the Common Ground Country Fair and Maine Apple Camp, held at an old summer camp in August, serve to educate countless people on the beauty and diversity of Maine's agricultural ecology.

Many of Maine's cideries, including Rocky Ground Cider, Whaleback Cider, and Portersfield Cider, come out of the tradition and culture of MOFGA and the Maine Heritage Orchard. They combine the culture of foraging with dedicated orchard work, looking to the flora and fruits around them in addition to imported cider apples and exploring cider through the lens of the place the apples come from.

Core Takeaways

New England's agricultural landscape and orchards have changed dramatically since the early twentieth century, as the orchards that once sent apples around the world have shrunk and specialized. As progress marches on, the remnants left behind are being retooled and reimagined to serve a new purpose, and New England cider has become an excellent expression of the region's terroir. By encompassing the geography, historical resources, underutilized infrastructure, and diverse population of the region, cider is emerging as part of a new New England identity.

CHAMPLAIN VALLEY

• **Location and Geography:** This wide valley is centered on a large freshwater lake, the remnant of a former sea sandwiched on the border between the Green Mountains of Vermont and the Adirondack Mountains of New York.
• **Soil:** Fossil-rich shale, clay, and silty loam were deposited when the land was submerged.
• **Climate:** Humid continental climate, moderated by Lake Champlain, protecting fruit and buds from the worst of winter and spring's weather whims. USDA Hardiness Zone 5a.
• **Orchard Location:** Orchards are located on both sides of Lake Champlain, with several also remaining on the islands in the lake.
• **Orchard Type:** McIntosh and its derivatives, grown for the fresh market, have been king for nearly a hundred years. Smaller orchards focus on direct-to-consumer sales.
• **Significant Apple Varieties:** McIntosh, Empire, Honeycrisp, Cortland, Somerset Redstreak, Dabinett, Franklin.
• **Cider Apple Plantings:** Larger orchards on the Vermont side are beginning to invest in American and European cider apples.
• **Producers to Visit:** ZAFA Wines/Shacksbury Cider/CO Cellars (Burlington, VT), Citizen Cider (Burlington, VT).

CONNECTICUT RIVER VALLEY

• **Location and Geography:** Running four hundred miles from the Canadian border to the Long Island Sound, this wide river valley is dotted with farms and mill towns. It starts between Vermont and New Hampshire and runs into Massachusetts and Connecticut.

• **Soil:** A wide variety of soil types are found along the course of the river as a result of former glacial movement and splayed floodplains. Nutrient-rich farmland exists along former glacial lake beds.

• **Climate:** Humid continental, with rain throughout the year and lots of snow but excellent air drainage from the river valley and hills. USDA Hardiness Zone 5a–6a.

• **Orchard Location:** Most orchards lie in the hills above the river, taking advantage of the air drainage from the pressure differential.

• **Orchard Type:** The heart of the former Baldwin Belt, some wholesale orchards still exist, but many have moved to direct retail, specializing in heirloom and unique varieties.

• **Significant Apple Varieties:** Baldwin, McIntosh, Cortland, Calville Blanc d'Hiver, Roxbury Russet, Tolman Sweet, Northern Spy, Rhode Island Greening, Golden Russet, Fameuse (aka Snow), Kingston Black, Yarlington Mill, Ashmead's Kernel, Black Gilliflower, Blue Pearmain, Hubbardston Nonesuch.

• **Cider Apple Plantings:** Poverty Lane Orchards first planted cider-specific trees in 1989, and others have followed in their mold. Direct retail orchards have been home to many heirloom varieties for decades.

• **Producers to Visit:** Artifact Cider Project (Florence, MA), West County Cider (Colrain, MA).

MAINE AND COASTAL NEW ENGLAND

• **Location and Geography:** Small coastal rivers wind through rocky gentle hills, dotted with former homestead orchards. Most of the area remains forested.

• **Soil:** Rocky gravel influenced by centuries of glaciers.

• **Climate:** Humid continental climate moderated by the Atlantic. USDA Hardiness Zone 4b–5b.

• **Orchard Location:** In Maine, commercial orchards are mostly in the southwestern part of the state, with many others around the cities of Augusta and Bangor. Duchess of Oldenburg and other hardy apples have seeded in northern Aroostook County, which became largely unpopulated with the decline in lumber demands after the nineteenth century.

• **Orchard Type:** Larger orchards in southern Maine are more focused on fresh packing for grocery stores. Small orchards throughout the rest of the state are more focused on on-premise sales. Feral trees can be found throughout the landscape.

- **Significant Apple Varieties:** McIntosh, Duchess of Oldenburg, Baldwin, Northern Spy, Black Oxford, Alexander, Wolf River, Honeycrisp, Tolman Sweet.
- **Cider Apple Plantings:** Larger orchards are beginning to follow the mold of pioneer Farnum Hill Ciders, while smaller estate cideries are also planting new trees. Fedco Trees and other nurseries have sustained homestead orchards for decades, and the Maine Heritage Orchard has a number of cider-specific apples in its collection. Feral apples throughout the state provide excellent raw materials for the state's cidermakers.
- **Producer to Visit:** Portersfield Cider (Pownal, ME).

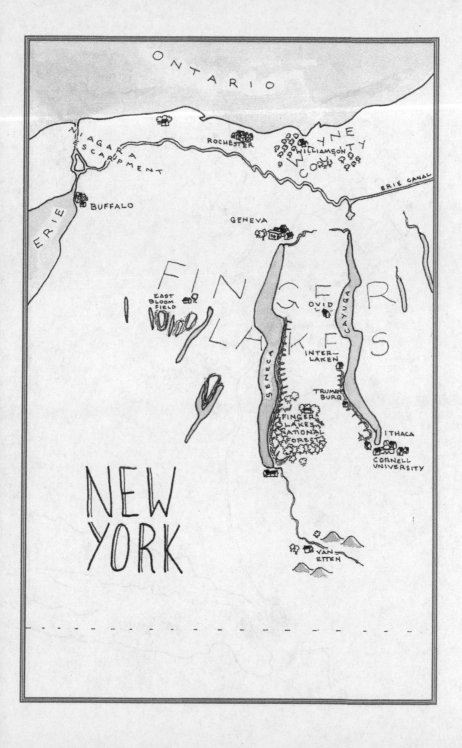

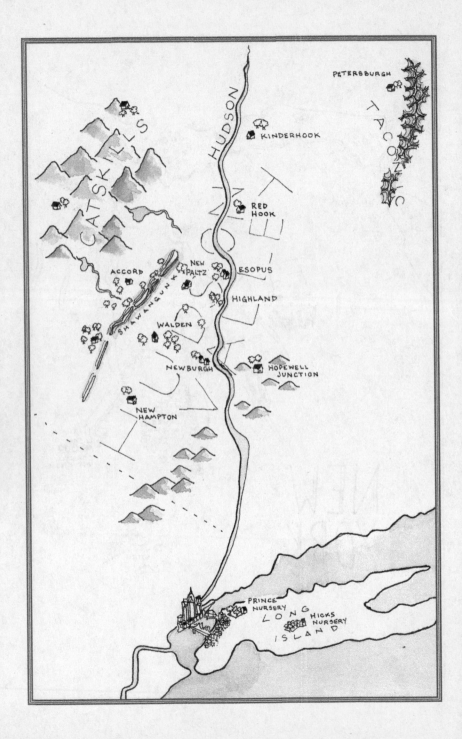

NEW YORK

Rising sea levels millions of years ago covered New York State in a shallow oceanic pool that eventually drained and left a bounty of sediment in its wake. This sediment formed an additional layer of continental crust called the Grenville Province, which extends throughout the northeast United States and eastern Canada. From that layer came the Hudson Highlands, the Adirondacks, and the Thousand Islands. Around five hundred million years ago, further tectonic activity created the Taconic Mountains, whose stunning magnitude eroded to a humble standing of black marine shale in the upper Hudson Valley. Farther south, twenty-five million years ago, white quartz pebbles and fluvial sediments came to form much of the Shawangunk Ridge. Constant uplift and erosion of New England's ancient Acadian Mountains left behind hardened sediment that formed a plateau cut through by water, known today as the Catskill Mountains.

Collision between the protocontinents of Laurentia and Amazonia spawned mountains and valleys throughout New York. Their north—

south orientation gave water little course but to flow south into the Atlantic, and when glaciers formed moraines and then melted during the last ice age fifteen thousand years ago—putting the finishing touches on the Finger Lakes and Long Island—the Hudson Valley filled with water and, eventually, the ancestral river became the main artery for Dutch settlement and economic development in New York.

New York State was the largest producer of apples in the country at the turn of the twentieth century. The preceding century's apple boom and subsequent commercial industry was particularly beneficial thanks to the state's many canals and waterways, which then advanced to railroads and highways. These improvements had a significant impact on the settlement, growth, culture, and orchards of New York, and the state became a nexus of new-age thought and industry.

Before it became New York, the region was home to the first Dutch colony in North America. Settled as New Netherlands in 1624, it was built around the proto-city of New Amsterdam at the mouth of the Hudson River. Fifteen years earlier, Henry Hudson, sailing under the Dutch East India Company, navigated the North American coast in search of a possible Northwest Passage. He never found one, but his voyage up the Hudson became the framework for early Dutch settlement.

While the colony lived under a Dutch flag, nearly half of the residents came from other parts of Europe. French-speaking Walloons from modern Belgium, Germans, Scandinavians, and both free and enslaved Africans made up the diverse society of early New York. In the 1650s, after the loss of a Dutch colony in South America to the Portuguese, many Portuguese- and Spanish-speaking Christians and Jews moved to New Amsterdam.

The fledgling colony was the flashpoint for clashes among the

Haudenosaunee (more widely known as Iroquois), Algonquin, French, English, and Dutch as they vied for control of the state's great wilderness and viable waterways. While the colony was eventually ceded to the English, during the annexation, Governor Peter Stuyvesant negotiated favorable terms to preserve the religious freedoms that built the diverse society, which drew ambitious outcasts and radicals from New England and Europe.

While main trading ports were established at New Amsterdam (New York) and Fort Orange (Albany), colonists from northern Europe began to carve out farms all along the Hudson River. Settlers established small apple orchards near their homes, as they did in other colonies, and relied on the fruit for seasonal subsistence and the juice for cider.

Fruit trees found great success along the river's temperate banks. In 1650, Adriaen van der Donck, acting as lawyer and ethnographer for the Rensselaerswyck colony near Fort Orange, made detailed notes of the landscape and climate of his adopted home. He noted the ease of cultivation, the diversity of fruits and vegetables, and the superior taste of seedling apples grown in the Hudson Valley.

Huguenots—French Protestants fleeing persecution and war in Europe—settled several Hudson Valley communities in addition to Staten Island and what would become Bushwick, Brooklyn. They brought with them a variety of fruits and an enthusiasm for horticulture, and they found that the soil along the north shore of Long Island grew exceptional fruit trees. Woodlands there were cleared early on for homes and fuel. After sawmills were introduced, clearing increased to support barrel making and shipbuilding, and the newly cleared land fostered the development of orchards and nurseries. Towns like Great Neck, Herricks, Oyster Bay, and Manhasset had extensive orchards whose owners sold thousands of barrels of apples early in the eighteenth century.

In 1730, Robert Prince established Prince Nursery in a Huguenot community along the Flushing Bay in modern-day Queens. It was the first large commercial nursery in the country, and it remained a preeminent nursery in the industry for nearly 150 years. The nursery began on an eight-acre plot just east of Flushing Creek, where the Queens Botanical Garden is today. It grew to sixty acres, with fifty employees, as generations of sons expanded the operation to meet growing demands for nursery trees.

Prince Nursery constructed its own docks to easily ship grafted apple varieties, as well as native and European plants, flowers, and trees, up and down the American coast and overseas to Europe. Many of the early grafted apple orchards in the Northeast and down into Virginia were planted with trees grafted at Prince Nursery. A 1771 advertisement for Prince Nursery lists twenty-four apple varieties, eight of which are European imports, while the other sixteen grew from seed and originated in the North American colonies.

From New York Harbor, the Prince family set many of the norms for fruit growing across the country. The nursery drew acclaim and visits from the first three presidents, and it was so respected internationally that during the Revolutionary War, British Commander-in-Chief William Howe sent a military detachment to the nursery to ensure its security. Many growers followed the path paved by the Prince family, including Samuel Parsons, whose Kissena Nurseries supplied famed landscape architects Frederick Law Olmsted and Calvert Vaux, and also Isaac Hicks, who started Hicks Nursery in 1853 in Westbury, where it still operates today.

Commercial nurseries and extensive orchards were not the only contributors to building New York's apple industry. The Haudenosaunee readily adopted European fruits brought to their Central New York territory by early settlers. Their confederacy and its political alliances dated back to the twelfth century, with influence extended throughout western New York into the Great Lakes and down the Ohio River Valley. Jesuit missionaries and other European travelers through Haudenosaunee territory observed apples, peaches, and plums growing alongside native crops.

Haudenosaunee orchards, planted along the warm slopes of the Finger Lakes, were destroyed in 1779 when General George

Washington called for the complete destruction of those Haudenosaunee settlements that supported the British. His troops devastated thousands of homes and orchards, displaced communities, and forced many refugee Haudenosaunee, regardless of their involvement in the war, out of New York and into British-controlled Canada.

While the Haudenosaunee found refuge in Canada, the new—heavily indebted—American government parceled out land west of the Appalachian Mountains to veterans and their families in lieu of payment after the war. Veterans from New England began pouring into western New York to build farms and societies for themselves on land formerly cultivated by the Haudenosaunee.

As New York developed, a societal rift grew between the city and upstate—between rich and poor. The elite, domineering class vied for control of the workforce, many of whom were immigrants. Business owners relied on skilled laborers, who in turn were able to demand higher wages, but the marginalized factory worker received little social power, justice, or consideration.

As settlements multiplied in western New York, the Hudson River remained a central feature of trade and transportation. Steamboats, introduced early in the nineteenth century, diminished travel time between Albany and New York City by 75 percent. In 1838, Robert Livingston Pell planted one of the first large-scale, export-focused orchards along the Hudson River in Esopus, New York. By the 1850s, Pell Orchards had more than twenty thousand producing apple trees covering more than two hundred acres.

The town of Esopus had more than a century of fruit-growing history. Noteworthy varieties like Esopus Spitzenburg and Jonathan grew there from seedling orchards planted by early settlers. In a declaration by the New York Assembly in 1852, Pell's orchard was recognized as the largest in the world. Pell's contributions fortified a statewide shift that began with Prince Nursery. For the first time, growers leaned toward commercial fruit growing with a focus on quality and the intent to sell.

Presidential Election of 1840

In 1840, presidential candidate William Henry Harrison's campaign capitalized on the nation's convoluted relationship with cider. Harrison, a Whig, triumphed against the incumbent Democrat Martin Van Buren. After the convention that set Harrison toward the White House, a Democratic reporter was quoted as saying, "Give him a barrel of hard cider and settle a pension of two thousand a year on him, and my word for it, he will sit . . . by the side of a 'sea coal' fire, and study moral philosophy." The Harrison campaign seized on this quote and painted the former Indiana governor and general as champion of the everyman. Faux log cabins were rolled out at cider-fueled rallies, whipping voters into a frenzy of nostalgia for simpler times and a humbler way of living.

The irony was that Harrison was born into a wealthy aristocratic family from the tidewater of Virginia. Van Buren, the son of a Dutch-speaking shopkeeper in the Hudson Valley, was the rightful owner of the humble origin story. Harrison bought his commission into the military, and his time on the frontier was often spent with the finest coastal and European imports. Nonetheless, he was portrayed swigging jugs of cider, which was the perfect vessel for his populism. With the election of 1840, cider became a co-opted symbol of earlier times, a tangible relic for a country in the grip of dramatic social and economic change.

While steamboats revolutionized transit and facilitated early apple growing along the Hudson River, canals transformed the rest of the state. Inspired by successful canal projects in France and England, New York State set off on a canal building campaign to connect the state's navigable waterways. In 1823, Lake Champlain was connected with the Hudson via the Champlain Canal. Two years later, the Erie Canal opened, connecting Lake Erie to Albany and the thriving commerce along the Hudson River.

Exceeding 350 miles, the canal became the only significant water passage through the Appalachian Mountain range from Alabama to Vermont. Other canals followed, connecting the Finger Lakes and the Delaware, Susquehanna, and Chemung Rivers, fostering a trading network and facilitating the growth of commercial orchards throughout the state.

The Erie Canal enabled farmers to move from Hudson Valley counties to the more unencumbered flatlands of western New York. Intent on growing grain for coastal markets, farmers established small "kitchen orchards" and harvested grain while those trees developed. But as farms in the Midwest began growing greater quantities of grain more cheaply, apples found favor in western New York counties, specifically Wayne and Orleans. Ambitious orchards and nurseries began developing in areas close to the canal, perhaps most notably in Rochester, where Ellwanger and Barry Nursery was founded in 1840 and exceeded five hundred acres of fruit trees and ornamental shrubs by 1860.

As New York's grain industry saw a boom and bust akin to New England's sheep industry in the second half of the nineteenth century, many New York growers replanted their grain fields with commercial orchards, relying on Pell and Prince and modern literature to show them the way. State pomology and horticultural societies were founded to further understand, promote, and encourage fruit cultivation, and New York became a breeding ground of apple research and development.

During the mid-nineteenth century, grafted varieties slowly replaced seedling orchards throughout most of the United States. In New York, this began in the Hudson Valley, where access to New

Dried Apples

By the turn of the twentieth century, evaporated (dried) apples had become a multimillion-dollar industry. With the growing bounty of fruit, a result of increased commercial orcharding, drying apples was a way to preserve the excess. The fruit became shelf stable while still retaining flavor, and it was lightweight and portable, which catered to the increasingly mobile nation. In 1899, the United States produced 144 million pounds of dried apples. Wayne County produced 75 percent of New York's entire dried crop, to ship around the country and world. Massive buildings called dryhouses cleaned, sliced, and kiln-dried apples, creating shelf-stable fruit long before the advent of climate control.

York City and international markets provided economic incentive. But the practice thrived throughout the state beginning around 1860.

In 1845, Hudson Valley native and horticulturist Andrew Jackson Downing described 133 apple varieties in his seminal book *The Fruits and Fruit Trees of America*. Downing and others, like Bernard McMahon (*The American Gardener's Calendar* in 1806) and Spencer Ambrose Beach (*The Apples of New York* in 1905), provided the early language, education, and recommendations for farmers looking to understand new and grafted varieties. With their efforts, apples like Northern Spy and Gravenstein were among the earliest grafted fruit varieties planted in commercial orchards.

Fruit breeding became common as both a professional practice and an amateur hobby. Farmers across the country sought new and better varieties to cultivate, as the next successful apple could bring wealth and fame. They cast seeds about their marginal land and let trees come up as they would, hoping for a new marketable variety. Fruit that was unfit for market catered to home cidermaking, and the seedling trees could be sold as sturdy rootstocks for others to graft on to. Census records from the time reveal that the people doing this were not nurserymen but farmers, looking to make a little extra money.

In 1875, the New York census counted more than eighteen million apple trees. *The Apples of New York* describes over a thousand varieties, as does the first revision of Downing's *Fruit Trees* in 1869. From 1850 to 1900, while the country's population tripled, the value of orchard products leapt from $7.7 to $83.7 million. These numbers showcase the growth of commercial orchards as farmers learned which apples did best on the farm and in the market.

Railroads would eventually replace canals, but initial freight costs during the early days of rail transportation, in the 1830s and '40s, were prohibitive. The Erie Canal initially survived the boom of railroads, increasing its tonnage year after year into the 1870s. Still, railroad improvements stifled the use of canals after the Civil War. Trains were quicker and could operate year-round, whereas the canals of the Northeast were subject to freezing winters and being out of commission for months each year. Lock systems built into canals also added time to trips. It took five days to get from Albany to Lake Erie outside Buffalo, and additional time to navigate the 150 miles down the Hudson River and into the port of New York City. By train, the trip took less than a day.

In the second half of the nineteenth century, with reliable railroads, it was common for entire orchards to be established with grafted nursery trees and specific apple varieties. But success was slow as farmers learned the challenges of commercial orchards. Monoculture plantings welcomed new insects, diseases, and pressures that threatened to eradicate orchards.

Rural pockets diminished as transportation networks and urban development increased. Modest, traditional farm methods no longer sufficed, and farmers were left with a diminishing set of options.

Those without means to farm commercially were forced into cities, where factory work was plentiful. Farmers could move west and re-create what failed in the east, or they could adapt to the more pro-gressive, specialized farm systems and contribute to the thriving market economy.

Modern Cidermakers and Apple Growers

In line with early colonial expectations, New York has positioned itself as an economic center of the globe. More recently, springing up from a long history of successful commercial apple orchards, the state has also been at the center of the growth surrounding cider production.

For centuries, New York's heirloom varieties like Newtown Pip-pin and Esopus Spitzenburg have been prized in local and distant markets, and their success encouraged growers to continue planting these heirloom trees for generations in the face of commercial agri-culture. It is on this foundation that modern New York cidermakers are able to forge success.

In 1976, New York State's Farm Winery Act created the oppor-tunity for winemakers to sell wine directly to consumers. Since 1976, laws have been extended to include spirits (2007), beer (2012), and cider (2014). Each license has its own qualifications, but for cideries or wineries making cider, the law stipulates that 100 percent of the apples must be grown in New York State. Since the farm cidery license was passed, the number of cidermakers in New York has risen from fewer than ten in 2010 to the most in the country—nearing one hundred—in 2020.

The state's many distinctive growing areas help drive local and regional cider appreciation, while the urban metropolis consumes its fair share. While New York was an early adopter of tannic apples at commercial scale, most of the ciders in the state continue to be made from apples planted with other intentions.

CHARACTERISTICS OF NEW YORK CIDER

New York ciders are defined by the diversity of apples at the disposal of its many cidermakers. Large, older blocks of Northern Spy, Baldwin, and Golden Russet provide the backbone for many of the state's finest ciders. Empire, Liberty, Cortland, and Idared are all excellent and subtle varieties being grown in abundance that bring fruit and freshness to both apple-centric and flavored ciders. Because of the state's climate and soil, cider from New York tends to share characteristics of high acid and embracing structure.

Hudson Valley

The Hudson Valley is the birthplace of commercial apple growing in the United States. At the turn of the twentieth century, the valley was the most productive apple-producing region in the country. Eating apples formed the backbone of production, starting in the mid-nineteenth century with Newtown Pippin and Jonathan, and leading to contemporary shiny, waxed Gala and Fuji. Today, the Hudson Valley accounts for 40 percent of New York's total apple production.

Mohicans called the Hudson River Mahicantuck, meaning "great waters in constant motion," or "the river that flows two ways." Because of its unusual tidal habits, the river ebbs and flows with ocean water pushing up the channel and meeting downstream runoff from the Adirondack, Catskill, and Taconic Mountains.

From the Hudson's headwaters in the Adirondacks to New York Harbor, the valley's varying climate zones are affected by the mountains and hills that frame it, along with the moderating warmth of the Atlantic. Glacial movements up and down the valley deposited long tracts of rich, sandy loam soils that provide an abundance of organic nutrients. These bands of well-drained soils encourage trees to establish deep root systems, fortifying health and longevity, and the valley channels airflow that helps deter insects, disease, and fungal pressures.

The longer growing season in the Hudson Valley, generally a

few weeks ahead of cooler New England, means that the Hudson Valley determines the prices for the rest of the Northeast market. But late-spring frosts can sometimes happen after early warm days bring out a tree's buds, wreaking havoc on Hudson Valley trees.

Orchards in the valley have long benefited from easy access to New York City. Growers are able to harvest ripe fruit and get it to market weeks before their cooler northern counterparts. For this reason, orchards have been geared toward supplying fresh eating fruit to market in New York City for generations. Apples like Golden Delicious, Fuji, and Gala are among the most common, but they are sold alongside older varieties like Northern Spy and Golden Russet.

West Counties and Wassails

The West Counties of England are Herefordshire, Devonshire, Somerset, Worcestershire, and Gloucestershire. Collectively, the counties are home to some of the longest continuing cider traditions in the world, chief among them the wassail. The celebration has its roots in pre-Christian celebrations and gives thanks to the trees and wards off blights and evil spirits to ensure bounty in the upcoming season.

The word *wassail* comes from the Anglo-Saxon phrase "in good health," which can be hard to remember, as the festivities take place in the orchard at night during the middle of January. Warmth is generally provided in the form of torches and brandy. Wassail revivals have taken root across England and have been adopted by the cider community in the United States, drawing people to orchards and farms at a dormant time to build community.

The commercial eating apple industry has dominated the Hudson Valley since the days of Pell's Esopus orchards, leaving little room for cider until Elizabeth Ryan founded Hudson Valley Farmhouse Cider. She came to the Hudson Valley in the early 1980s after graduating from Cornell with a degree in pomology to grow apples and grapes, but after traveling to the West Counties of England, she was won over by the cider culture there and began making cider commercially shortly thereafter. A constant historian, entrepreneur, and social bee, as anyone who has shared her table can attest, Ryan creates ciders that have become a staple at farmers' markets up and down the valley.

The town of Kinderhook, home of President Martin Van Buren, loser of the cider-tinged presidential election campaign of 1840, is now home to Samascott Orchards. Many of their apples end up in Albany, at Nine Pin Cider Works, which was the first cidery to take advantage of New York State's 2014 farm cidery laws.

More recently, in 2016, the well-known cider brand Angry Orchard took over sixty acres of trees in Walden, giving a local face to the country's largest cidery. Launched in 2012, Angry Orchard's nationally distributed products are made in Cincinnati from mostly Pacific Northwest cull and European tannic apple concentrates. But Walden is home to innovative styles and collaborations with leading cidermakers like Soham Bhatt, Eleanor Léger, and the UK's renowned cidermaker Tom Oliver. In 2016, the orchard's old Red Delicious trees were replaced with Dabinett, Yarlington Mill, and other cider apples. In the center of the orchard is the innovative cider house, where Angry Orchard pushes the limits of cider expectations.

Angry Orchard cidermaker Ryan Burk has been leading the charge at Walden. Since the brand is owned by Boston Beer Company—the brewer of Samuel Adams—Burk has a well of resources to join international cider cultures and some of the country's best apples. Weekends at Walden are a busy, inspiring affair.

People from all over the region tip back glasses of Newtown Pippin and bittersweet cider alongside the rest of the Angry Orchard collection.

Part of Angry Orchard's on-site draw is that the ciders being made there are different from what's found in grocery stores across the country. Their nationally distributed ciders are complemented by ciders made from apples grown across the country, but the ciders at Walden are made from the likes of New Hampshire's Poverty Lane Orchards, Red Jacket Orchards in the Finger Lakes, and E. Z. Orchards in Oregon.

One of Angry Orchard's most interesting Hudson Valley ciders is Extension, crafted from the remnants of the last great cider investment in the Hudson Valley. It is made from an unknown collection of bittersweet and bittersharp apples planted at the Cornell extension office in Highland, just south of Esopus. These unknown apples were planted by H. P. Bulmer, the United Kingdom's largest cidermaker. When Bulmer purchased Vermont Cider Company, they contracted a western New York nursery to custom graft several thousand bittersweet and bittersharp trees to aid in their conquest of the American market. But custom grafting takes several years, and by spring of 2002, when the trees were ready to be planted, Bulmer was pulling out of the country, leaving the nursery with thousands of cider apple trees. The hillside behind Cornell's extension office, along with several commercial orchards in the valley, ended up fostering some of the orphaned trees.

While this was not the first time cider apples were planted in New York, this widespread planting created a foundational resource for cidermakers across the state. Today New York producers are able to draw upon these apples to give backbone, structure, and tannin to their ciders.

Bulmer's leftover trees were a small step toward jump-starting cider in the Hudson Valley, but Glynwood, an agricultural nonprofit based in the valley, took the largest leap. Glynwood began its cider initiative in 2011, at a time when the valley was home to just a few cidermakers, one of whom was selling unmarked mason jars to local college students with dubious legality. One of the program's backers, originally from Normandy, France, thought to bring together the two rural international cider communities to talk about their issues, futures, and resources.

The meeting of Hudson Valley apple growers and brandy- and cidermakers with their French counterparts was an inspiring give-and-take, whereby U.S. growers and producers learned centuries-old techniques and traditions of Normandy cidermaking and apple growing, while the French contingent gained knowledge of the innovation of the Hudson Valley. The program helped seed many Hudson Valley cidermakers and led to the foundation of Cider Week New York. Glynwood's efforts grew in scope, and the non-profit became a founding sponsor of the New York Cider Association, dedicated to the growth of cider throughout the state.

Just north of Glynwood, Fishkill Farms abuts the northern slope of Fishkill Mountain, part of the Hudson Highlands that separate the central Hudson region from the lower, more maritime Hudson Valley. The farm became a U-Pick in the 1980s after a devastating hailstorm damaged a nearly harvest-ready crop meant for distributors. With unsellable apples still on the trees, the farm threw open its doors to the community, who hurried to pick their favorite apples themselves. What looked like the end of the farm quickly became its best year to date. Today, Fishkill, in Dutchess County, hosts thousands of visitors a day throughout the fall season, all searching for apples, pies, cider doughnuts, and cider.

The Morgenthau family has owned Fishkill Farms since 1913, when Henry Morgenthau Jr. purchased the land and converted it from Christmas trees to apple and other fruit trees. Morgenthau became close friends with his Hudson Valley neighbor, then-governor of New York Franklin Delano Roosevelt, who took him to Washington, DC, as the head of the Farm Credit Association and then appointed him Secretary of the Treasury. Many of the programs that Morgenthau enacted helped farmers throughout the country keep their land in cultivation during the Great Depression.

Henry's grandson, Josh Morgenthau, returned to the farm in 2008 to paint, but he found farming more rewarding and traded brush for spade. Josh has progressively moved the farm to more organic and sustainable practices while transitioning the orchard from mainstream eating apples to heirloom and cider apples. In 2016, the farm released its first vintage of Treasury Cider, aptly named in honor of grandfather Henry's government gig.

A similar story is playing out forty miles north on Dutchess County's oldest fruit-growing farm. Rose Hill Farm started in 1812 on land purchased by Peter Fraleigh in the 1790s, and it remained in the family until the turn of the twenty-first century when it was sold to the Scenic Hudson Land Trust. In 2015, entrepreneurs Holly and Bruce Brittain purchased the farm with Chris Belardi, an ER doctor with an affinity for historic restoration. Using sustainability as their guiding force, the trio upholds the farm's bicentennial vision of quality fruit and has since ramped up Rose Hill's U-Pick model. They hired Mike Biltonen as an orchard consultant; he in turn put the new owners in touch with bike-mechanic-turned-cidermaker Matthew Sanford. Rose Hill Farm launched their cidery in 2018.

Turns out Sanford is the perfect fit for Rose Hill's diverse collection of apple varieties and fruit trees, as his ethos is centered on the fact that anything with sugar is fermentable. The farm recently added a thousand trees, mostly bittersweet, to their expanding four-acre cider block. While those trees mature, Sanford sources and masterfully balances the complexities of European cider fruit with the farm's decades-old varieties like Golden Delicious, Mutsu, and Empire. His natural, hands-off approach in the cellar mimics the vision shared by the farm's owners, and his enthusiasm for fermentation extends beyond apples and into the realm of other fruit wines, made with the likes of plums, cherries, and blueberries. Neighboring breweries like Plan Bee Farm Brewery and Suarez Family Brewery use the farm's fruit in collaborative beers cherished up and down the Hudson Valley. At Rose Hill, coferments and macerations have become commonplace, and the resulting products are some of the most exciting expressions of old-meets-new and of cider and fruit wine.

Soons Orchards, across the river in the heart of Orange County, partnered with Karl and Carolyn duHoffmann and Andrew Emig in 2013 to operate Orchard Hill Cider Mill, whose ciders grant the farm freedom from annual cycles of feast and famine that hold many family farms hostage. In prolific apple years, like 2015, Orchard Hill takes full advantage of the bumper crop, including the cull fruit, to make cider and pommeau from cosmetically damaged fruit that could not be sold fresh.

Pommeau

A traditional beverage of Normandy, France, pommeau is a fortified cider beverage akin to port wine. Fresh, unfermented juice is blended usually in a ratio of 5:1 with apple brandy (distilled apple juice). In Normandy, there are requirements for aging the brandy and pommeau both before and after fortification, but there are no such restrictions in the United States. Typically, after the juice is fortified with brandy to around 20 percent ABV, the pommeau is aged in barrels until it is deemed ready for release, generally one year but often longer. As pommeau ages, it takes on a more oxidative, nutty, and caramel character. Any apple variety can be used to make pommeau, and each lends its own fresh, acidic, or tannic profile to the glass.

The town of Esopus lies farther upriver, in the shadows of the Catskill Mountains. As riverfront development creeps into farmland orchards, Esopus has seen a diminished scale of production since the days of Pell, but the town remains an exciting apple growing area. Kimberly Kae and Matt DiFrancesco of Metal House Cider are working to rebuild some of the town's remaining orchards, including nine hundred trees on the estate of a former presidential candidate that were neglected for decades and then damaged by overly ambitious pruning crews. None of Pell's original trees have survived, but some of the trees on the property are approaching one hundred years old. The trees are titans of an earlier era, widely spaced with a mixture of typical early-twentieth-century apples, including McIntosh, Jonamac, and what Kae believes to be a Blue Pearmain—an apple of exceptional quality that was widely grown throughout New York in the nineteenth century.

Kae's goal is to keep the orchards intact as long as possible. An old orchard of Idared and Empire sparsely planted along the river consistently fruits year after year. With a reverence for big, hardy trees, Kae intends to leave the old trees and fill in new trees at the same scale and standard size as what is already there. Kae, like many cidermakers, is willing to play the slow game. Patience, quality, and passion are all evidenced by Metal House's steadfast commitment to Champagne-style cidermaking. Beyond the occasional assist from their son, and only after upwards of two years aging on the lees, the couple disgorges by hand every bottle of cider they release. Their approach, coupled with the aromatic foundation of certain varieties, results in some of the most complex yet approachable cider being made anywhere in the country.

Over the northern tail of the Shawangunk Ridge, in Accord, New York, is Westwind Orchard. Husband and wife Fabio Chizzola and Laura Ferrara first came to the area for its renowned rock climbing. Born in Italy, they moved to New York City and, in 2002, bought their farm more for the majesty of the intact eighteenth-century farmhouse than anything else. Their plan was to lease the land to a farmer and keep their fashion jobs in the city, but that reality shifted as they got more and more involved in revitalizing the property's old neglected orchard. Westwind expanded from U-Pick to jams, syrups, and other products before making cider an integral part of their operation. Westwind Orchard comes alive in the summer and fall, with wood-fired pizzas made from garden-grown ingredients that are paired with estate-grown Kingston Black cider.

Chizzola and Ferrara are part of a longer tradition of agricultural immigration to the Hudson Valley. First-generation Italian immigrants established orchards in the early twentieth century to supply the burgeoning Italian vegetable and fruit markets in New York City. Today it is a different immigrant story. In 1986, the government established the H-2A visa, which allows U.S. employers to bring foreign nationals to the United States for temporary farmwork. Since then, a significant portion of the day-to-day orchard labor in New York has been supported by Jamaican and Mexican workers. These workers return to the same farm year after year, often for decades, leaving at the end of the harvest.

For cidermakers producing on a smaller scale, labor is less of a concern. Inspired by his time making wine in Germany's world-class Rheingau, Leif Sundström started making cider in the States while he was working in restaurants. Up to that point, Sundström had worked throughout the wine industry, first in Oregon restaurants and vineyards and then in New York. Cider came as he grew more interested in following his own explorations; when most of his 2013 cider vintage was stolen from the stoop of his apartment, he decided to increase production.

Sundström Cider ambitiously balances precision with experimentation. Sundström has no orchard of his own, so he sources apples from some of New York State's premier orchards. He may pay a premium for quality fruit, but he is able to do so without the overhead of owning his own production facility.

For Sundström, each year is an experiment as techniques are continually adopted, thrown out, and redeveloped. While peers warn that extended macerations may be a costly mistake, because the pectin found in apples can interfere with viscosity and clarity in cider, Sundström found that varieties like Golden Russet were improved by their lengthened contact with the pulp. Instead of being a volatile disaster, the longer maceration layered aroma, texture, and nuances in the final cider. Today, macerations are becoming more common for these coveted varieties, as cidermakers have better access to suitable fruit.

In addition to Samascott Orchards, Sundström has sourced from Montgomery Place Orchards in Dutchess County. Montgomery Place is owned by Bard College but operated by Talea and Doug Taylor, some of the most knowledgeable and enthusiastic growers in the state. Part of what makes Montgomery Place unique is the quality and diversity of apples. Doug's ardent interest in cider led to plantings back in the 1980s of Golden Russet, Newtown Pippin, and Cox's Orange Pippin. Other apples followed, many of which date back to the late nineteenth and early twentieth centuries, and today the orchard grows nearly seventy varieties. While most of Montgomery Place fruit ends up sold at their seasonal farm stand for fresh eating, amateur cidermakers are always pleased to find an array of discounted seconds, from Black Twig and Maiden's Blush to Blue Pearmain and Rhode Island Greening, during harvest.

Another key to unlocking the complexities and subtleties of cider, for Sundström, is found in lees, which are deposits of dead and inactive yeast cells that have fallen out of solution after fermentation. Most of the development of aroma, flavor, and texture in cider takes place after fermentation, when cider has a chance to rest in contact on its lees. The vast majority of cider is taken off its lees, either siphoned or pumped, within a few weeks of fermenting, maintaining fresh flavors but at the expense of certain compelling secondary complexities. Sundström often leaves cider on the lees for up to a year, where it is able to take on character, texture, and true personality.

Extended lees contact can prevent oxidation and the formation of acetic acid, but it can also lead to off flavors if not properly managed. Bâtonnage, the process of stirring the lees back into solution, is often practiced in winemaking, and it leads to a softer, rounder, and more unctuous product. For cider, Sundström has found that it opens up aromatics, builds texture, and increases stability without compromising the nerve or tension, thereby extending the aging potential of his cider. Sundström bottles his cider with lees to help improve the stability and evolution. Sparkling ciders with extended lees contact, like the best Champagnes, can last for years without fading.

Kyle Sherrer of Graft Cider in Newburgh also takes a very different approach to cidermaking than most of the rest of the valley. He got his toes wet with his dad, Curt, making decidedly peculiar cider in Maryland at the since-closed Millstone Cellars. Wild, explosive, and always funky, Millstone ciders were unlike anything else. Sherrer continues to carry the torch by drawing from a large palette of fruit, spices, hops, and botanicals to paint against his uniquely sour ciders. Many Graft ciders draw direct comparison to the beer world, a place Sherrer cites as a gateway to cider. The company's stylized can design and unique flavors reach new cider consumers every day, adding diversity to the styles and expectations of what cider can be.

Catskill and Taconic Mountains

Flanking either side of the Hudson Valley, the Catskill and Taconic Mountains are northern extensions of the Appalachians. They were never home to large orchards, as high levels of slate and shale were frustrating, if not outright prohibitive, for prospective farmers. But over time, the area has become home to millions of uncultivated apple trees. During the first hundred years of European settlement, many of the mountainsides were clear-cut for lumber to send to markets downriver. As old forests were cut back—removing competition—apple trees began popping up throughout long-abandoned pastures and at field edges. They developed naturally to withstand crippling May and early-June frosts that can eliminate entire cultivated commercial crops.

Historically, the relative isolation of the Catskills, compared to the rest of New York State, meant a higher cost of transportation to bring goods to market. In order to offset those costs, whatever products farmers brought to market had to be of exceptional quality. Butter and dairy brought the region the most prestige, but apples from these elevations were highly sought after. Schoharie County author Chauncey Rickard, in "Story of the Apple" from 1925, boasts that the best Esopus Spitzenburg is in his own backyard, where the rich alluvium of the Schoharie Valley and its generous sprinkling of lime and humus grow fruit like no place else. The quality of the apples was so high that, even without railroads, farmers' diaries of the time note they were seeking to export their relatively small crop of apples to Europe.

Esopus Spitzenburg

One of New York's oldest apples, Esopus Spitzenburg, or just Spitzenburg for short, was discovered along the Hudson River in Esopus in the early 1700s. Spitzenburg roughly translates to "top hill" or "top peak," which is most likely where the apple was "discovered" by a Palatine German. The apple's fame reached down the Atlantic and into Virginia, where it is often cited as one of Thomas Jefferson's favorite apples, as evidenced by records of his frequent requests for scion wood. But he most likely grew it poorly, because he frequently requested more scion wood.

CIDER PROFILE

Exuberant stone fruit and bold, fleshy acid. What it lacks in tannin it makes up for with mouthfeel and complexity.

In the southern Catskills, where slate intersects with the sandstone-rich Shawangunk Ridge, husband and wife Andy

Brennan and Polly Giragosian ferment wild, uncultivated apples and were among the first to introduce them to the public. Their endeavors in cidermaking began after the housing crash in 2008, when they cut back on spending where they could create instead. Surrounded by old abandoned apple trees in their home in Wurtsboro, Brennan and Giragosian began harvesting wild apples to make and bottle cider. In 2011, they established Aaron Burr Cider.

Brennan is a steadfast believer in the concept of regional—even microregional—cider. He works with a seemingly boundless vision, striving to show both the subtle and bold variations that exist from apple to apple and from place to place. His book, *Uncultivated* (2019), is an extension of his cider philosophy, which may be defined as a quest to understand the relationships between people, apples, and nature. In the bottle, this philosophy translates to balance and individuality, and Brennan's passion is tangible in every sip.

In the western Catskills, Wayside Cider is the brainchild of Irene Hussey and Alex Wilson. After beating Wilson in a local amateur cider competition, Hussey teamed up with the UK native to turn the feral apples around them into a business. Their taproom, opened in 2017, is a renovated wagon shop that once hosted some of the area's fiercest horseshoe tournaments. Wayside draws thousands of visitors a year to enjoy the mountains over some of their fine cider and food. Hussey, a stoic stonemason, and Wilson, a former film editor, blend their precious tannic feral fruits with softer apples from lower lying parts of the state, but they maintain the structure and weight of the native Catskill apples.

Few sensations are as intense as taking a bite from a wild Catskill pear. These rock-hard fruits are all but inedible, possibly descended from seeds carried by Swiss-German immigrants, with a passion for brandy, who flocked to the banks of the Delaware River. Hussey uses these special pears and their neighboring apples to make powerful ciders that can stand up to even the heartiest meals.

Perched above Rickard's beloved Schoharie Valley, in the

hamlet of West Fulton, is the comparatively small Scrumpy Ewe Cider. At the helm is musician-turned-stonemason-turned-part-time-cidermaker Ryan McGiver, one of a new generation of growers in the Catskills investing in cider. Because of the project's size, McGiver is less concerned with scale and more interested in learning what will grow in his small orchard. McGiver's dialed-in vision and understanding of what apples blend well together result in ciders that showcase place, structure, and complexity in a rare and unique way. His passion for the nuances of still cider are evidenced by the fact that a majority of Scrumpy Ewe selections are not sparkling.

The Catskills region can never compete on price or consistency with the flatter, larger, warmer orchards of the Hudson Valley, but cider may be able to command the premium needed to make these hillside orchards of cider apples sustainable. Many new orchards, some of considerable size, have been recently carved out of the hillsides, but they remain too young to reveal what effect they may have on the larger cider community.

While the Catskills rise up over the Hudson to the west, the Taconic Mountains extend south from Vermont to the east. The mountains are some of the oldest in the state, and lower elevations are pocketed with dairy towns and early-twentieth-century industrial mill towns. Seth and Yasemin Jones came to the Taconic town of Petersburg, looking for refuge from their jobs and life in Manhattan. Abandoned apple trees got Seth digging into historical texts as an escape from his design job. After his visit to Franklin County CiderDays, new trees were going in the ground and honeybee hives were established nearby to pollinate.

Jones launched East Hollow Cider in 2017, using mostly fruit from the old, abandoned orchards he came upon in Petersburg. Excellent cider varieties like Ashmead's Kernel and Redfield can be found in Other People's Pommes, a second label of East Hollow Cider that utilizes fruit not grown on the couple's mountain orchard. As of March 2020, 50 percent of all weekly proceeds are being donated to charities and foundations. The move is an extension of the greater vision the couple has for East Hollow Cider, which is not to make money, but to make real and deep contributions to the community and world. According to Seth, "The money is part of our activism to try and fight for real change."

Finger Lakes

Central New York's Finger Lakes were once a series of northward-flowing rivers that intersected with a southward-encroaching glacier. Before the lakes formed, the rivers were pushed below nearly two miles of ice, digging hundreds of feet into the bedrock. Seneca Lake (618 feet deep) and Cayuga Lake (435 feet deep) are the deepest, and the focal points of cidermaking in the region.

The depth and size of the lakes make them act as climate moderators. Freezing over only in the worst of winters, the lakes extend the fall season while delaying the onset of spring. In summer, cool lake water keeps temperatures from spiking, and it helps fend off cold snaps in winter. The lakeside slopes extend back from the shore several miles, creating warm hillsides with excellent air drainage that encourage the development of ripe, healthy fruit.

Finger Lakes soil lends itself to unique flavor profiles in the ciders produced there. Glacial activity created a soil with fairly low pH that is high in calcium and magnesium. In apples and cider, this translates to flavor profiles that are mineral-driven and flinty, reminiscent of graphite and gunpowder.

While the lakes themselves dominate the landscape, the thriving wine industry and Cornell University fortify the efforts of Finger Lakes cidermakers today. The cider community often looks to the established Finger Lakes wine industry for knowledge, information, philosophies, and even wine equipment—often sharing tanks, pumps, and filters. These institutions represent some of the world's greatest sources of knowledge and research when it comes to better understanding fruit, and they have helped create a synergy between cidermakers and apple growers that further benefits the region's cider.

For one, thanks to the region's wine-savvy consumers, Finger Lakes cidermakers have noticed an innate interest in single-variety ciders—a direct result of the international success of the region's Riesling. In some instances, this has encouraged cidermakers to consider fruit independently, isolating varieties that can stand out on their own. From a marketing perspective, cidermakers can steer the conversation to single varieties, instead of using terms like "craft" and "orchard-based."

Finger Lakes cidermakers have unparalleled access to cider varieties because of the USDA apple germplasm, in Geneva, New York, one of the world's largest collections of national and international apple varieties. Since its creation in the early 1980s, researchers have traversed the globe in search of genetic diversity throughout the dozens of species that make up the genus *Malus*. They have brought back unique apples from expeditions all over the world, creating a library of genetic information in Geneva that is unmatched. It helps sustain research in new apple varieties, rootstocks, and other agricultural improvements, which just might bring about the next great cider apple. While anyone in the United States can request free scions from the repository, Finger Lakes growers and cidermakers can request with an understanding and confidence of what varieties will do well in their climate.

In the past, little research was geared toward translating the existing collection of apples in Geneva into cider apples. But the collection is getting a reexamination from Dr. Gregory Peck, an assistant professor in Cornell's department of horticulture. Peck, charged with the same spirit of mid-nineteenth-century nurserymen, has been researching and grafting apples for the potential of finding the next great American cider apple. Elsewhere on campus, new breeding trials by Dr. Susan Brown are also an attempt to develop the next generation of cider apples, combining the tannin

Geneva Tremlett's

This unknown bittersharp masqueraded for years as Tremlett's Bitter, a powerful bittersweet apple from Devon in southern England. During its introduction to the United States, mistakes, erroneous labels, and lost information compounded the confusion, until DNA testing proved that what people in the United States were calling Tremlett's Bitter was not the same apple found in the United Kingdom. While the apple is most likely a named European cider apple, its true name is currently unknown. It is an excellent apple, both in the orchard and in the glass.

CIDER PROFILE

Full bodied and rich with a direct through-line of high acid. Notes of clove, cinnamon, makrut lime, and curry leaf.

and acid of European bittersweets with the blight resistance, ease, and scalability that commercial orchards require.

In 1990, when Dr. Ian Merwin—Peck's predecessor and professor emeritus of horticulture—began working at Cornell, he experimented with fermentation, but not of apples. Before he moved to the Finger Lakes in 1985, Merwin was working in the Bay Area, where he ventured north to Italian vineyards to pick grapes and make wine. When he came back east, high-quality red-wine grapes were rare in the Finger Lakes, but apples could be picked freely. So, out of thrifty necessity, Merwin began making cider, and it ultimately led to the launch of Black Diamond Cider in 2014.

Back in the day, Merwin and his friends would take their apples to States Cider Mill in Odessa, joining a line of pickup trucks full of apples. They had all bought used whiskey barrels for twenty-five dollars each from across the street. The cider mill in those days attracted an eclectic bunch, from students like Merwin to a wild collection of longtime locals looking to fill their barrels with cider the way they had for generations.

Regional cider mills once dotted the New York landscape, built roughly every ten miles so farmers could get there and back in a day's carriage ride. But at the end of the twentieth century, foodborne pathogens became a global concern, and the FDA took action. It developed the Hazard Analysis Critical Control Point system, which required many farm products to undergo extensive food safety procedures. For cider, this included pasteurization, whereby juice was heated to a point below boiling to kill pathogens and extend shelf life.

Pasteurization is not necessary in cidermaking, because dangerous bacteria like *E. coli* cannot survive in alcohol. Crude pas-

---

Escherichia coli (E. coli)

In New York and many other states, it is illegal to sell unpasteurized fresh cider. The leading reason is the rise of *E. coli* 0157:H7, a new acid-tolerant strain of an otherwise benign bacterium that evolved on dairy farms sometime in the late 1980s because farmers, on a national scale, had changed what they were feeding their herds.

The new diet lowered the pH of cows' multiple stomachs, gradually making them more tolerant to the pathogen that formerly could not have survived in their stomachs or in acidic fruit juice from the likes of apples. The bacterium evolved into a toxic strain, and that is when people started getting sick—even dying.

With the rising frequency of *E. coli* scares, people stopped drinking fresh, unpasteurized cider. In some instances, people stopped eating apples altogether. Large commercial growers lobbied for the pasteurization of fresh cider, to eliminate public fear and ensure their crops could be sold.

teurization contributes to a homogenous profile, and it changed the flavor people had become familiar with over generations. Pasteurizers cost thousands of dollars, and the new regulations were an economic hurdle that backcountry operators could not jump. Countless cider operations closed, while others prohibited people from bringing their own fruit. Gradually, small community cider mills were abandoned.

Long before Merwin launched Black Diamond Cider, he and his wife, Jackie, bought Black Diamond Farm in Trumansburg in 1992. Over the years they experimented with 150 different apple varieties, settling on two dozen that made great cider and could be sold at the farmers' market in Ithaca. Merwin's intention to this day is to stay small, to not exceed five thousand gallons of cider or more than fifteen acres of trees. It allows him full control of the process, from orchard to bottle.

In 2002, when H. P. Bulmer suddenly retreated from North America, Merwin stepped in to foster the abandoned trees. Many found a place at his home orchard, while others went to Cornell's research orchards in the Finger Lakes and the Hudson Valley. Merwin convinced several forward-thinking orchards like Hicks, along the Vermont border and now home to Slyboro Ciderhouse, and LynOaken Farms, along the Niagara Escarpment in western New York and home to Steampunk Cider, to take a chance on tannic apples.

Bulmer's blunder was not the first time tannic apples were propagated in New York. In 1994, Dr. Jim Cummins—a former Cornell professor and consultant developing hardy rootstocks for Geneva— and his son Steve were the only people to bid on a defunct nursery that had been aligned with Cornell. In 1999, Dr. Cummins, who does not drink, had the idea to begin aggressively investing in cider apples. For years, Cummins Nursery was one the few suppliers of rare and tannic apples, and cider growers from the Carolinas to Puget Sound got their collection started with stock from Cummins.

Many of Cummins's surplus pears and apples, like Ashmead's Kernel and Hendre Huffcap, ended up in a small U-Pick orchard owned by Steve's brother south of Ithaca. He had recently partnered with a young apple enthusiast named Autumn Stoscheck, who began Eve's Cidery in 2001 out of tips she earned waiting tables in Ithaca.

When Stoscheck read an article about Steve Wood bringing European cider apples to Poverty Lane Orchards in New Hampshire, she visited and returned with inspiration and new apples for her orchard. Wood had been growing some of the varieties she was experimenting with in her orchard for years. Over time, her business evolved to organic orcharding. Her husband, Ezra Sherman, moved from practicing law to join the cidery full time, and, in 2015, they moved to making cider strictly using their own estate-grown fruit.

Located south of the Finger Lakes in Van Etten, along the Chemung River, Eve's does not benefit from the moderating effects of the lakes. They have colder winters and hotter summers, with a longer and more intense growing season, as bud break can often come a week before their lakeside neighbors. Estate fruit comes with its own unique set of challenges, especially when it is grown organically. Apple crop yields are never consistent, and in off years, trees may not provide enough fruit for cider.

Organic orcharding is a challenge in itself in the Northeast, where hot, wet summers invite numerous diseases, fungi, and pests that threaten orchard health. Weather aside, since pesticides and herbicides are not used, mice can become a huge threat during the winter. They seek cover under compressed grasses buried under the snow, feeding on and killing trees by destroying tree roots. Stoscheck and Sherman have lost hundreds of trees to mice over the years. The upside is that trees grown using an organic approach struggle more, which makes them produce higher-quality apples with more concentrated characteristics. The cider, as a result, tends to have more weight, body, and texture.

Eve's ciders have walked a long path, as Stoscheck and Sherman have learned, adapted, and changed with the trees. As certain fundamentals are established and championed, cidermakers can pursue new goals and work toward a cider that represents the apple, the grower, and the place as acutely as possible—say, to the effect of Pinot Noir in Burgundy, or Zinfandel in California.

Golden Russet

Golden Russet has long been revered for its admirable flavor, making it a perennial favorite of cidermakers across the country. Its true identity is a bit muddled, as English Russet, American Golden Russet, Golden Russet of Western New York, and Hunt's Russet are all often referred to as Golden Russet. All of these apples are high in sugar and have fully russeted skin, like a potato. In *Plain and Pleasant Talk About Fruits, Flowers, and Farming* (1859), Henry Ward Beecher recollects a response from asking a farmer how to plant a thousand-tree orchard: " 'Set out nine hundred-ninety-nine Golden Russets,' came the reply. 'The others you can choose for yourself.' "

CIDER PROFILE

Full bodied, rich, and pear-like with excellent structure and longevity. Certain strains lean toward dried apricot, while others are more lemon curd and crushed flowers.

When Eric Shatt and Deva Maas purchased a house and property on Seneca Lake, they intended to plant a vineyard. But when Shatt picked and tasted apples from a wild seedling orchard up the road, those plans went into the proverbial lake. He was so blown away by the intensity and complexity of the fruit that he, like Ian Merwin, switched his grape goals to apple aspirations, and Redbyrd Orchard Cider was born.

Shatt and Maas push the potential of cidermaking in both the cellar and the orchard. In the cellar, Redbyrd does trials with lees stirring—which develops complexity by agitating the yeast—and with extended aging for traditional sparkling cider, which has helped inform cidermakers across the country. Shatt is experimenting in the orchard with different animals, like ducks, geese, and sheep, in attempts to promote orchard health through minor grazing. His orchard is also filled with experiments in new varieties of foraged and propagated wild trees. One of these, Gnarled Chapman, is a bittersweet possible Northern Spy offspring that Shatt says makes amazing cider and is now available from Fedco Trees.

But the discovery process is a slow one. The wild seedling fruit has to first be grafted and transplanted to a nursery setting, which has an entirely different ecosystem than a hedgerow or forest. It takes more than five years for those trees to bear fruit, and after being cultivated, the apple may not have the same captivating traits that it did in its wild setting, on its own rootstock. If it does retain its wild complexity, trees then have to be evaluated for their bearing habits, whether they are precocious growers or biennial, meaning they produce fruit only every other year. Bloom and harvest dates have to be assessed and fit into the orchard's existing schedule. For Shatt and others, each of these are key to deciding whether a seedling has potential in a cultivated setting.

Because the Finger Lakes is home to such a high concentration of great cidermakers, it can be a challenge to stand apart. Shatt and Maas chose to differentiate by taking the leap into getting their farm certified biodynamic. While Redbyrd's orchards have been practicing biodynamics for a number of years, 2018 was their first certified biodynamic crop. At Redbyrd, the ultimate goal is to use the best possible fruit to tell a story that encompasses the apples, the Finger Lakes, and the makers. "It's important when you make a beverage on a small scale," Shatt says, "to really be able to connect with people, to make sure they get the right information. It's easy to lose the value of the importance and complexities of everything that goes into it if it's sitting on a shelf with a bunch of other products." Shatt and Maas are forming new ways to invite the public to their farm, beginning by offering tastings by appointment, and looking to expand to orchard tours accompanied by tastings, which is a very good thing, because Redbyrd produces some of the best cider in the country. While it took decades to build a market for Finger Lakes wine, cidermakers are now using the existing bridges to find an audience for their own austere styles.

Biodynamics

Biodynamics is a method of farming that seeks to explore the systems, connection, and (human) inputs that exist within agriculture. Many producers and consumers feel that the organic label has become ambiguous and lax, as the spirit of the movement becomes co-opted by large industry. Organic simply looks at what is going into the soil, while biodynamics considers the entire farm system. For orcharding, the biodynamic mindset is to aid the plant or tree and encourage it to perform to its utmost ability in its given environment, rather than bombard it with protectant aides.

Nowhere are the comparisons between wine and cider more transparent than at Finger Lakes Cider House in Interlaken. There, cider easily integrates into an agricultural landscape that has become inundated with people tasting their way from wineries to distilleries to breweries during summer and fall months.

Finger Lakes Cider House is located on Good Life Farm, a bio-restorative farm that, since 2008, has brought life, fertility, and diversity back to land decimated by industrial agriculture. Where there was once only corn and soybeans, asparagus now dances between apple and peach trees as a host of animals and native plants have been brought back to the land. Their Kite and String Cider uses apples from across the region, drawing on other orchards to supplement the fruit from their young trees.

While there are abundant, diverse orchards throughout the region, other interesting apples can be found in the Finger Lakes

National Forest. Lying on the ridge between Seneca and Cayuga Lakes, the forest is framed by plots of land that were deeded to Revolutionary War veterans from Haudenosaunee farms. Intensive farming throughout the nineteenth century depleted the thin soils as prices for commodity grains continued to drop. By the 1930s, the situation became untenable for many farmers, and as part of President Franklin Roosevelt's New Deal, the federal Resettlement Administration bought out over a hundred farms. Finger Lakes National Forest today is a patchwork of former homesteads. Surviving stone fences and foundations offer a glimpse into early American agriculture and orchards. Left to nature's whim, the trees have reproduced to create multiple generations of new trees.

Steve Selin got turned on to cider from friends he plays old-time music with. He started South Hill Cider in 2015 and obtained a permit to harvest from the Finger Lakes National Forest. He found that the feral apples he could pull out of the forest were unlike anything available in local orchards, and they proved to make unrivaled cider. Though South Hill has grown in scope, Selin still hauls apples out of the forest for his Packbasket cider. He established his own orchard and partnered with other orchards to continue to grow, and while his own orchard is a mix of European bittersweets with American heirlooms, Selin is shifting his focus to native apples like Shatt's Gnarled Chapman to round it out.

The intensity and power of seedling fruit is often a reflection of its environment. For example, Selin once cleared the choking honeysuckle and blackberries off one of his favorite feral trees in the national forest in order to make it easier to harvest the following year. But that year, and all subsequent years, the fruit did not have the same tension of life that he loved so much before clearing the wild brush.

Selin is one of many cidermakers in the Finger Lakes inspired by the late paleontologist, music collector, documentarian, and Finger Lakes legend Peter Hoover. In the 1980s, Hoover planted a small orchard behind his house to make cider and spirits. He had caught the fermentation bug while attending graduate school in Pittsburgh, and later became prolific in the art of distillation in the Finger Lakes. Handling the fermentation and bottling himself, Hoover would bring his traditional-method sparkling cider to a local winery to be disgorged. Late in his life, he had mobility issues, but even seated, at close to seven feet tall, the man was still a giant. Selin took over the regular management of Hoover's orchard and bottled the fruit from it as South Hill's Stone Fence Farm Cider. Hoover's mature plantings of cider fruit were intended to create a well-balanced and complete cider, an ethos that can be found in every bottle of Selin's offering.

Hoover's decreased mobility did not stop his passion for distillation. He rigged a small still that he could operate from his wheelchair, and his legendary Finger Lakes Light was made from apple, pear, and a small amount of quince that was fermented in the fall. Cherries would then be added to the fermentation frozen or in the summer, during harvest. Finger Lakes Light served as the backdrop to some of the finest pommeau ever produced. Hoover passed away at the age of eighty, late in 2019.

Hoover's curiosity and passion for fruit are echoed by John Reynolds of Blackduck Cidery. He and his wife, Shannon O'Connor, grow a vast array of weird, unknown fruit at their Daring Drake Farm along Cayuga Lake. While many commercial growers skew toward more conventional offerings, Reynolds serves his local farmers' market customers with an ever-changing selection of gooseberries, currants, and sour seaberries. Their orchard is filled not only with heirloom apples and pears, but Russian quince, pawpaws (a native Appalachian mango-like fruit), and medlars (similar to rose hip). Apples, pears, quince, and berries alike all end up in their cider, and while most of the Finger Lakes' cidermakers subscribe to a similar high-acid, bright, fresh, and clean style of cider, Blackduck's ciders are the exception that proves the rule. Reynolds's hands-off approach to fermentation yields ciders that are somewhere between sour beer and natural wine, but neither Reynolds nor O'Connor is particularly interested in labels.

Reynolds and O'Connor, along with their daughters, scour the National Forest for old apples and pears, finding many powerful varieties once favored by displaced homesteaders. Seedling pears, at times more so than seedling apples, are not for the faint of heart, as one bite can leave an unwelcome taste in your mouth for hours. These seedlings, in addition to some English perry pears and American pears like Seckel, give their perry (fermented pear juice) unmatched weight and power, making for one of the best bottles in the country.

Western New York

The Great Lakes contain 21 percent of the world's fresh water and stretch over a thousand miles from the mouth of Lake Ontario in Alexandria Bay, New York, to the western shore of Lake Superior in Duluth, Minnesota. Lake Ontario's shores are a bountiful place to grow fruit, and the region produces 55 percent of New York's apple crop. The lake itself is the smallest of the five, but it is the second deepest. Similar to the Finger Lakes, Lake Ontario acts as a massive heat sink and delays the changing seasons.

In Wayne County, east of Rochester, orchards hug the shoreline of Lake Ontario and benefit directly from its moderating abilities, making it the third-largest apple-producing county in the country. Orchards surrounding the town of Williamson produce a huge volume of apples for processors like Seneca Foods, Mayer Brothers, and Mott's, turning out applesauce and juice and every other apple product possible.

Mott's has been a leading processor in New York's apple industry since 1842, when Quaker Samuel Mott started making cider and vinegar at his mill in Bouckville, about a hundred miles east of its current location. Mott's introduced new products early in the twentieth century, marketing what it called Mott's Champagne Cider—made from Golden Russet apples—to restaurants from New York to California, where thousands of cases were sent by clipper ship. Applesauce was introduced in 1930 and helped the brand thrive through Prohibition and the Great Depression.

In 1955, when Mott's opened a production plant in Wayne County, it cornered the commercial orchard market and made processed fruit king of the county. Over the years, orchards adjacent to Mott's grew to upwards of a thousand acres per family, whereas nearby Orleans County orchards—focused more on fresh market apples—remained under five hundred acres.

Consolidation in the 1970s and '80s left Mott's in the hands of out-of-state conglomerates, far removed from the realities of commercial growing in New York. In the ensuing decades, the company scaled from buying dozens of varieties to a mere handful. Apples that had long been New York staples, like Northern Spy, Baldwin, and Golden Russet, were removed from the list. With no one to buy the fruit, growers ripped out many of the old trees and replaced them with more profitable apples.

But in the wake of cider's rise, even though Mott's stopped buying Northern Spy and Baldwin, those apples have been able to command a premium among cidermakers, reaching three times the price that Mott's once paid. Cider creates new opportunities for processing-fruit growers like Jake Lagoner of Lagoner Farms and Embark Craft Ciderworks. His family has been growing processing apples for five generations. Throughout the years, the farm went from dozens of varieties down to ten. Lagoner did not like this monoculture direction and encouraged the farm to look at other options for their apples. Having grown up with Ryan Burk of Angry Orchard and sharing his passion for fermentation, in 2013, Lagoner attended CiderCon, an annual trade conference for the cider industry. As a grower, he wanted to better understand what people were looking for in fruit and cider, and he went home and fermented forty different varieties in five-gallon carboys. Two years later, New York passed the Farm Cidery law, and Lagoner dove in.

Lagoner's stubborn grandfather did not adopt the high-density plantings that were in vogue in the mid-twentieth century despite demand from the likes of Mott's, instead planting larger trees that are still bearing fruit decades later. The old blocks of apples like Northern Spy, Golden Russet, and Newtown Pippin are prime multipurpose apples that make exceptional cider. For Jake Lagoner, these old fresh-eating fruit trees are less finicky than the fifteen acres of European cider apples and American crab apples he recently planted with the express purpose of making cider. Now with over a hundred varieties, the farm presses 150,000 gallons of juice a year, half of which they bottle, and half of which is sent to cidermakers from the Hudson Valley to Texas.

Northern Spy

Originally from East Bloomfield in western New York, Northern Spy is a seedling that sprouted in the early nineteenth century from pomace brought from Connecticut. The first tree died before it bore fruit, but a cutting from its roots was propagated and the apple was widely disseminated by the mid-nineteenth century. Northern Spy trees can often take several years to come into bearing, but the apple's large size made it a favorite for homestead and commercial orchards across the Great Lakes and into the higher elevations of the Southeast. It makes excellent cider and is also popular as a baking apple.

CIDER PROFILE

Suggests dried flowers, plums, and strawberries. Incredible sense of minerality and an excellent blending apple.

West of Rochester, lake effects are compounded by the Niagara Escarpment, a long hilly outcropping of preglacial limestone that forms the basis of Niagara Falls. The escarpment captures and intensifies the lake's moderating air as it passes over the orchards and collides with the cliff, sending the air back down over the orchards and toward the lake. This cycle creates a microclimate that allows even southern heirloom apples like Limbertwig to ripen long into the fall.

In the shadow of the Niagara Escarpment, the Oakes family of LynOaken Farms has been taking advantage of this microclimate for over a hundred years. What began as a poultry and tomato farm in 1918 has grown into one of the state's most exciting orchards for cider fruit. The farm shifted to fruit just before World War II, and in the late 1990s, Darrel Oakes spurned convention and planted vinifera grapes in the gravely, lakeshore land. He soon established Leonard Oakes Estate Winery. Then, thanks to a longstanding friendship with Ian Merwin, Oakes came to learn about the Cornell research and cider project, and apples became a natural next direction. In the early 2000s, Oakes planted over a hundred apple varieties, including many of the surplus European Bulmer trees, using scion wood from Merwin.

Jonathan Oakes, Darrel's son, returned to the farm after college with an oenology degree. Operating with a self-described "progressive mindset that has been passed down from generation to generation," Jonathan made his first cider—a dense, richly tannic sparkler bottled with expensive corks—from the European cider apples in 2008. He called it Old English, and, at $14 per bottle, no one bought it. Aware that the market was not ready to embrace that style of cider, Jonathan and his brother Christopher launched the more accessible Steampunk Cider in 2010, using a blend of the farm's tannic European apples with the more approachable, sweeter Fuji apples. While it was not their original intention to make cider with residual sugar, Jonathan calls it a step in the right direction, a start down the path he hopes will lead people to drier, more austere cider.

New York City

Orcharding and cidermaking efforts throughout the state are supported by the thirsty city at the mouth of the Hudson River. Ciders from around the country and world flow through its harbor and glasses, sipped and swirled at farmers' markets and fine restaurants alike. Notable restaurants like Gramercy Tavern brought cider to the table when it was still an oddity, and New York City has been quick to incorporate cideries into its cityscape.

Newtown Pippin

A chance seedling that grew along Newtown Creek in modern Queens early in the eighteenth century, the Newtown Pippin was heavily promoted by Prince Nursery, and its reputation was solidified by Pell Orchards, which shipped the apple around the world. Noted for its durability and flavor, few other American apples reached the international fame of Newtown Pippin, as orchards from New York to New Zealand grew it for the globalizing nineteenth century.

Whether the Yellow and Green Newtown Pippin are separate varieties is a point of much contention among growers around the country. The popular Albemarle Pippin of Virginia was also thought to be different, but they are all most likely the same variety. More than any other apple, Newtown Pippin's quality is determined by its soil. In the Southeast, Newtown Pippin takes on a distinct sweet lime or Meyer lemon note. In New York, it carries more baking spice and subtleties, and in sunny California it is brawny and sarsaparilla-inflected.

CIDER PROFILE

Notes of yellow stone fruits, green plums, spring herbs, and citrus blossom. Often shows baked bread aromas from extended lees contact. Elevated alcohol, usually over 8 percent ABV.

In 2014, from a tiny warehouse in Maspeth, Queens, Alex Fisk and Jahil Maplestone started Descendant Cider Company, the city's first cidery. Their pomegranate-infused cider was a magnet for attention during the surge of new breweries and beer bars. Originally a homebrewer, Maplestone was at first interested only in the fermentation process. But as he got deeper into understanding how trees behave in orchards, he set about establishing his own orchard in the foothills of the Catskills, planting the roots for more exciting cider to come.

On the other side of the fabled Newtown Creek, siblings Peter and Susan Yi have transformed a massive warehouse into a cider shrine. Peter, who previously owned PJ Wine in Manhattan's Inwood neighborhood, dealt with the finest wines in the world before he was struck by inspiration on a trip to northern Spain. The cider house, or sagardotegi, is central to Basque cider culture. During spring, visitors are served an assortment of traditional foods—like cod omelet (tortilla de bacalao) and porterhouse steak (txuleton)—while drinking cider directly from large barrels. Patrons hold glasses out some ten feet away from the barrels and catch the mysterious, savory, distinct, and fruity cider. The meal and cider catching is called txotx, and the Yis wanted to bring it back home. In 2017, they opened the doors to their Basque-inspired Brooklyn Cider House. Visiting the cider house makes it easy to drink up the Yis' gospel of cider's food-pairing possibilities, as they recreate the txotx experience, from the steaks to the massive chestnut barrels they imported from Spain. As in Spain, patrons can catch the Yis' unique and always fresh cider straight from the barrel.

Unfortunately, Brooklyn Cider House was forced to close early in the summer of 2020 due to the Covid-19 pandemic. Since the cider house doubled as an event space and wedding venue, the social distancing and limited capacity resulting from the pandemic made it impossible to sustain their high operating costs. Peter Yi continues to make cider, and it is available online and in retail stores throughout New York and other places as far south as Washington, DC.

Before they opened their doors in Bushwick, the Yis—like Jahil Maplestone—started looking at orchards to help fuel their cider ambitions. In 2015, they purchased Twin Star Orchards outside of New Paltz. The historic U-Pick orchard was in need of reinvestment and vision, and now McIntosh apples grow alongside cider apples as the orchard's fifty acres are converted to biodynamics.

Cider is likewise found east of the city, in suburban Long Island. Before the island became synonymous with city sprawl, it was an active agricultural region. Up until the early twentieth century, Paulding Cider Mill in Jericho supplied many of the finest restaurants in the city with Newtown Pippin cider. While some tree fruit is still grown on the eastern tip of Long Island, most of the island's orchards are now only remnants seen through fences. From these ruins came a unique project that allowed Long Island native Erik Longabardi to see his home in a new light. In 2018, Longabardi introduced the first commercial vintage of Floral Terranes, ciders and wines that he makes in the garage of his eighteenth-century home. By day, Longabardi is a special education arts teacher in Queens; in the evenings and during the weekends and summers, he combs the island for forgotten trees with fellow Long Island native Benford Lepley.

Most of their apples come from trees attached to former Gold Coast estates along the north shore of the island. These Gatsby-esque estates were built by the rich and powerful of the late nineteenth and early twentieth centuries, but they quickly became untenable after World War II and were transformed for new purposes. Many of their orchards remained through benign neglect.

Core Takeaways

Transportation networks established New York as a global center for industry, resources, and capital. New distribution networks in the nineteenth century provided outlets for the state's developing commercial orchards, leaving a lasting impression on the state's culture.

Today, new networks are creating identities for each of the state's distinct cidermaking regions. The unique and diverse orchard patterns, intentions, and varieties within the state have created multiple paths to cider for farmers, fermenters, and enthusiasts. The result is a wide range of cider made throughout the state from vastly different fruit growing wild on mountainsides, manicured homesteads, and endless, meticulous rows of commercial orchards. Together, New York ciders are a commanding voice in the American cider dialogue.

HUDSON VALLEY

- **Location and Geography:** North of New York City, the Hudson River runs 134 miles from Troy, NY, to the tip of Manhattan. Rolling hills extend out from the river along small waterways and streams.
- **Soil:** Loamy, sandy silt with more clay closer to the river.
- **Climate:** Humid continental with cold winters and hot summers and year-round rainfall. USDA Hardiness Zone 5a–6b.
- **Orchard Location:** Orchards often sit at elevations overlooking the river, as in Ulster County above the towns of Marlboro and Highlands, while in Columbia and Dutchess Counties, they are generally several miles back from the river.
- **Orchard Type:** Orchards still grow fruit for fresh packing, but U-Pick and retail orchards have been an important part of the ecosystem for decades. Cider was first introduced widely through these direct-to-consumer avenues.
- **Significant Apple Varieties:** Fuji, Gala, Golden Russet, Northern Spy, McIntosh, Esopus Spitzenburg, Red Delicious, Macoun, Dabinett, Yarlington Mill, Brown Snout, Major.
- **Cider Apple Plantings:** Cornell University's experimentations in the early 2000s, along with developing interest in cider at the same time, have led many producers large and small to begin planting cider apples more aggressively.
- **Producers to Visit:** Rose Hill Farm (Red Hook, NY), Orchard Hill Cider Mill at Soons Orchard (New Hampton, NY), Angry Orchard (Walden, NY), Fishkill Farms (Fishkill, NY).

CATSKILLS

- **Location and Geography:** West of the Hudson Valley, southwest of Albany, the area is defined by rolling hills and mountains carved by glaciers.

• **Soil:** Rocky slate and shale with deeper soils in the Delaware River valley.
• **Climate:** Humid continental, significantly colder throughout the year than its neighboring areas. USDA Hardiness Zone 5a–5b.
• **Orchard Location:** Never a large apple production area, but wild apples can be found along roads and fence lines.
• **Orchard Type:** Orchards going in the ground today almost all have their eyes set on cider.
• **Significant Apple Varieties:** Esopus Spitzenburg, Liberty, McIntosh, Fameuse (aka Snow).
• **Cider Apple Plantings:** Several ambitious cider projects have started to experiment with the possibilities of the hills. Many cider producers began by building off the area's tourism.
• **Producers to Visit:** Wayside Cider (Andes, NY), Scrumpy Ewe Cider (East Fulton, NY), Seminary Hill (Callicoon, NY).

FINGER LAKES
• **Location and Geography:** A series of eleven very deep lakes in western New York, running north to south, were formed by rivers that were subducted by encroaching glaciers. The two largest lakes are Seneca (618 feet deep, 38 miles long) and Cayuga (435 feet deep, 40 miles long).
• **Soil:** Shale, slate, glacial till, and loams.
• **Climate:** Humid and temperate, moderated by the largest lakes. Excellent air drain onto the lakes prevents frost damage. USDA Hardiness Zone 5b–6a.
• **Orchard Location:** Orchards have been an essential part of this largely agricultural community. Most orchards are set back off from the lakes on the gentle slopes that slowly meet the lakeshores.
• **Orchard Type:** While most orchards sell to on-premise consumers, packing orchards and cider orchards can also be found throughout the region.
• **Significant Apple Varieties:** Northern Spy, Golden Russet, King of Tompkins County, Golden Delicious, Gnarled Chapman, Geneva Tremlett's, Porter's Perfection, Dabinett, Idared.
• **Cider Apple Plantings:** A number of well-established cider orchards in the area, especially between Cayuga and Seneca Lakes and around Ithaca, are easily marketed because of the existing beverage tourism from the Finger Lakes' world-class wineries. Larger orchards have begun planting cider apples to sell, as well.

• **Producers to Visit:** South Hill Cider (Ithaca, NY), Finger Lakes Cider House (Interlaken, NY), Eve's Cidery (Van Etten, NY), Blackduck Cidery (Ovid, NY), Grisamore Cider Works (Locke, NY).

WESTERN NEW YORK

• **Location and Geography:** The easternmost and third deepest Great Lake, at 801 feet, Lake Ontario is divided among Ontario, Canada, and New York. The Niagara Escarpment runs a few miles back from the lakeshore, while soft hills, drumlins, and old lake bottom all lead to the water.

• **Soil:** Gravel, sand, and limestone make up the soil along the escarpment, while lake-bottom gravel and clay appear closer to the lake.

• **Climate:** The lake is a large heat sink, moderating the climate, delaying spring bloom, and moderating summers and winters. The area has long, extended falls. USDA Hardiness Zone 6b.

• **Orchard Location:** Orchards are found mostly in eastern Wayne and western Orleans Counties, within close proximity of the lake.

• **Orchard Type:** Wayne County is the home of large processors like Mott's, while Orleans has always been more oriented toward the fresh market.

• **Significant Apple Varieties:** Northern Spy, Rhode Island Greening, Idared, Golden Russet, Baldwin, Fuji, Jonagold, Major, Dabinett, Brown's, Honeycrisp.

• **Cider Apple Plantings:** Many large plantings of cider apples have begun producing great fruit for the state's cidermakers. There is a lot of enthusiasm from growers looking to innovate on existing practices.

• **Producers to Visit:** Steampunk Cider at LynOaken Farms (Medina, NY), Embark Craft Ciderworks (Williamson, NY), Seed and Stone Cidery (Rochester, NY).

Temperance and the Protestant Pursuit of Control

Although New England was founded in pursuit of religious freedoms, the United States was not a church-going nation after the American Revolution. Few Americans believed God was involved in their daily lives: In 1776 only 17 percent of Americans attended church regularly, down from 80 percent seventy years earlier.

Those religious institutions that lasted became irrelevant as state constitutions were drafted under the new federal government. Separation of church and state was established with the First Amendment, and churches were no longer financed by states. Concern for how to promote the Puritans' Protestant faith while adhering to new religious liberties was at the forefront of democratic architecture. Adding to the discord, the Industrial Revolution and early-nineteenth-century transportation improvements rearranged the way traditional society was structured.

As mobility, a market economy, and a growing working class framed the new republic, religion became a social force dedicated to fostering a moral people. The American Temperance Society formed in 1826 with the goal of social reform, and alcohol became an easy scapegoat for societal troubles. Advocates viewed alcohol as a seed that grew into social disorder and called for a complete abstinence pledge.

When temperance reform was in its infancy, members were permitted to make, use, and dispense cider, beer, and wine in the privacy of their homes. Early temperance sponsors advocated for these lower-alcohol drinks as a less dangerous alternative to distilled spirits. But the years leading to the Civil War saw an increase in the demonization of all alcohol.

With the new factory system acting as a form of control, employers demanded consistently reliable workers. Drunkenness was judged as an obstacle in the path of economic gains, and temperance was a leap toward a more productive workforce. Employees were encouraged—if not forced—to join churches and engage in moral practices like temperance.

As the frontier expanded west, churches faced new challenges, and charismatic missionaries of all sects capitalized on the westward growth. They went into the frontier, organized multiday camp meetings, and preached a progressive gospel to pioneers eager to socialize, trade, and rejoice during unforgiving circumstances as they moved toward unknown futures.

Church attendance swelled. Methodist, Baptist, and other denominations saw astounding growth as the withdrawal of state funds leveled the field for formerly underfunded, stifled upstart devotions. This religious fervor grew into the Second Great Awakening—a revival with Puritan roots that took on new life in the frontier. But the lack of churches and ministers upholding pre-Revolutionary ideals meant that lay ministers and politically minded demagogues—not religious scholars—were interpreting the Bible. National support for temperance, and a focus on a more just and moral society, fortified their mixed messages.

Temperance became a form of cultural dominance as the foreign-born population rose exponentially throughout the country. More than 5.5 million immigrants made up nearly 15 percent of the population by 1870. Many were Irish Catholics escaping famine and German idealists fleeing failed revolution. The surge in new populations gave rise to hate, conspiracy, and discrimination in the form of a nativist movement and the Know-Nothing party, which put forth the fear that the young nation would fall under the pope's rule unless Catholics and immigrants were denied jobs and election to political office.

Cider, once shipped from rural areas into cities, began to evaporate as rural Americans, fueled by nativist sentiments, began drinking less. Newly arrived Europeans moving to growing cities built their civil society around drinking outside their cramped living conditions. German immigrants brought many of the comforts of home with them to the United States, including the finest beers and wines, and modern brewing technology. Along with alcohol, immigrants brought Catholicism. It became easier to characterize people crammed into slums as part of a papal conspiracy if they were seen as drunks. This meant that places of religious fervor, like western New York and Ohio, quickly became dry, as taverns were replaced by churches and temperance halls.

The religiously steadfast communities of Puritan

New England cast a collective wary eye on the new pioneering and immigrant populations. Much of the political writing from the time is coded with anti-immigrant rhetoric that calls for deportation, mandatory Bible reading in schools, and exceedingly long naturalization periods for immigrants. Through temperance, the movement-wide suppression of alcohol became a unifying form of control over the new populations, as Protestant groups argued for moral superiority. Temperance societies called for assimilation, and the movement forced conformity onto immigrants seeking life in new communities.

With alcohol cast as the devil, white Protestant Europeans, the demographic that gave rise to New England's cider culture, turned on fermented apple juice. They equated cider with the devil, the product of rot, good for little more than hog feed. The once-common beverage was a gateway to the depravity of alcoholism and moral corruption.

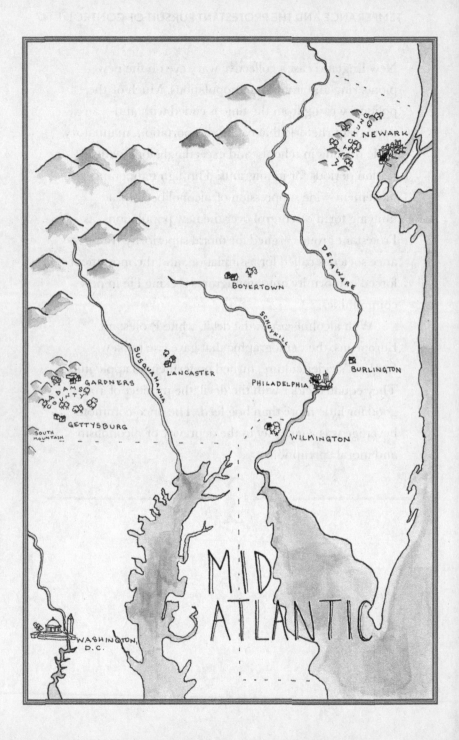

MID
ATLANTIC

NEWARK

DELAWARE

BOYERTOWN

SCHUYLKILL

SUSQUAHANNA

LANCASTER

BURLINGTON

PHILADELPHIA

GARDNERS

ADAMS COUNTY

GETTYSBURG

SOUTH MOUNTAIN

WILMINGTON

WASHINGTON, D.C.

MID-ATLANTIC

When the Atlantic Ocean formed 130 million years ago, resulting volcanic activity pushed black basaltic magma through Earth's crust, forming the ridges of Gettysburg and the Palisades of New Jersey. As these giants eroded, the Delaware, Susquehanna, and Potomac Rivers carved the plains into fertile river valleys and the Great Chesapeake Bay. Heat and pressure lined the mountains with coal that, millennia later, fueled the growth of cities downstream.

The Swedish, in their own colonization efforts, were the first Europeans to settle around the Delaware River. Those settlements and, later, the English Quaker colony of Pennsylvania bridged the gap between the plantation economy of the Southeast and the mercantile economy of the northern colonies. The colony of New Sweden, centered in modern-day Wilmington, Delaware, was established in 1638 to bypass other European countries for sources of tobacco and fur. Settling along both sides of the Delaware River in modern Pennsylvania and into Delaware and New Jersey, farmers from Finland, Sweden, and Estonia cleared forests and planted seedling apples.

Rambo

For his book *Old Southern Apples*, Lee Calhoun collected information on Rambo from Peggy C. Troxell, a direct descendant of its founder. She says, "In 1640, the twenty-seven-year-old Swede, Peter Gunnarson Rambo, arrived in the Swedish colony of New Sweden on the Delaware River. In his pocket were seeds of a Swedish apple from which the Rambo apple originated."

In 2008, scions of the Rambo apple were sent as a gift by Swedish Americans to Sweden, where they were grafted and planted at significant cultural locations. The apple also served as the name inspiration for David Morrell's protagonist in the 1972 novel *First Blood* and Sylvester Stallone's 1982 movie of the same name.

CIDER PROFILE

Fresh fruits and vibrant with medium acidity and no tannin.

Where Puritan values bloomed in the elite, Protestant parts of England, Quakerism has its origins in the more rural, Roman Catholic part of northern England. As both groups settled the colonies, they marched into unknown futures in opposite directions—against one another. When the Quaker ship Woodhouse arrived in New Netherland, Governor Peter Stuyvesant—a member of the Christian Dutch Reformed Church—established anti-Quaker laws, subjecting Quakers to abuse and imprisonment.

George Fox, the founder of Quakerism, is reported to have seen a vision of places where the Lord intended his followers to be gathered. Within five years, twenty thousand people, referred to as Friends, had joined his movement. Fox and other early missionaries, escaping persecution in England and then the North American coast, established settlements late in the seventeenth century in the middle colonies—what would become Delaware, New Jersey, and Pennsylvania.

William Penn, a Quaker and the founder of Pennsylvania, was

a traveler with Fox and integral to the rise in Quakerism throughout the state. In 1682, much of the territory was handed over to Penn in payment for debts owed to his father by King Charles II. Penn's centrally planned city of Philadelphia quickly attracted residents from Europe and the early colonies of North America. The colony's religious tolerance toward other Christian denominations attracted dissident groups of Puritans, Catholics, Anabaptists, Mennonites, Amish, and Quakers. These groups set up their own farming communities in the counties surrounding Philadelphia and along the banks of the Delaware River.

Before the rise of temperance in the nineteenth century, Quakers made, consumed, and traded for cider. Account books held by John Bowne, a New York Quaker and cidermaker on Long Island, show that his friend William Penn was a sometime recipient of Bowne's cider. Late in the nineteenth century, though, minutes and accounts from yearly Quaker meetings show the religion's advocacy for the temperate use of alcohol, which altered their views on cider. In *Rules of Discipline of the Yearly Meeting of Friends: For Pennsylvania, New Jersey, Delaware, and the Eastern Parts of Maryland,* Friends posed queries unto themselves such as "Are they good examples in uprightness, temperance, and moderation?" Other discipline books share the same concerns, stating that "moderation and temperance are inseparable to the Christian religion."

Philadelphia was cemented as a horticultural center of North America in part thanks to Quaker John Bartram and his son William. The Bartrams traversed the coasts and interior of North America seeking, studying, and documenting plant life on the continent. John was the continent's first practitioner of Linnaean taxonomy—using binomial nomenclature to classify living things—and his botanical garden was the first in the continent.

The Bartram property, along the Schuylkill River in South Philadelphia, was spared from industrial development as the city grew, and Bartram's Garden stands to this day. In addition to the trees and plants collected by the Bartrams, the garden has preserved a cider mill that John carved into the bedrock. The mill used two large stones to grind apples into a fine pomace before it was sent to the press. While the top grindstone is now gone, the trench and bottom portion of the mill sit overlooking the river and acres of industry below.

The Bartrams did not have a monopoly on botany in the Philadelphia area. Pomologist and politician William Coxe lived on the other side of the Delaware River, in Burlington, New Jersey. Coxe's *A View of Cultivation of Fruit Trees, and the Management of Orchards and Cider* (1817) was one of the first deep dives into the unique diversity of American fruit. In it, he defines the premier apple-growing region as the land extending from the Mohawk River in New York to the James River in Virginia, at the center of which happened to be his orchard.

Cultivation of Fruit Trees is the culmination of years of experimentation—Coxe's lifelong pursuit to better understand how great fruit is grown in North America. His primary concern, and what he waxes most poetic about, is cider. Detailed lessons and trials on pressing, fermenting, and processing reveal different attributes of various apples to an unmatched degree. Coxe highlights his preferred

Winesap

Dating back to the seventeenth century along the Delaware River in western New Jersey, Winesap possibly sprang from a Swedish seedling. Widely grown throughout the mid-Atlantic and Southeast, across the plains, and into the mountains, Winesap is highly adaptable to a range of growing conditions. Highly productive trees would give fruit even when other varieties failed, and its resistance to many blights made the apple a leader until the rise of cold storage.

CIDER PROFILE

Reaches for citrus and apricots, tarragon and orange oils, with a rich, oily texture. William Coxe describes Winesap as the choicest cider fruit.

varieties for his own cidermaking: Harrison, Winesap, and Hewe's Crab. He was also an early advocate for aging cider, claiming that, when properly aged, cider can challenge the best European wines.

While Coxe rhapsodizes about his orchards and cider along the Delaware, Newark—on the other side of New Jersey—was the real center of commercial cidermaking in the mid-Atlantic. Cider was the earliest manufactured product in Newark and played a significant role in the industrial development there. In 1682, Colonial Governor Philip Carteret commented on how the quantities of cider made in Newark exceeded anything being made in Long Island, Rhode Island, or New England. By 1700, cider orchards were used as boundaries in deeds and wills, and thousands of barrels of cider were being produced each year. In 1810, Essex County produced 198,000 barrels of cider.

Cider surged in Newark thanks to orchards leading up to the Watchung Mountains, which overlook the Newark Basin. They featured grafted trees of Harrison, Campfield, Graniwinkle, and Poveshon, varieties that originally grew as seedlings in Long Island, Connecticut, and points farther north, and were named for the families who first cultivated them in Newark. Poveshon, an early

Harrison

First cultivated by recently arrived New Englanders in the eighteenth century, Harrison was lauded as the best cider apple in the world. It was thought extinct until 1976 when Paul Gidez, a fruit collector from Vermont, retrieved scion wood from a slow-to-be-destroyed orchard in Livingston, New Jersey. In 1989, Tom Burford obtained the scion wood and encouraged people to plant it throughout the Southeast, where it has been widely grown and consumed.

CIDER PROFILE

Earthy aroma and rich tannins accented with sweet mandarins and golden raisins.

ripening apple, has probably been lost, but Campfield, Graniwinkle, and Harrison are still being cultivated.

In an age when most of the cider across the country was made from seedling fruit, these notable New Jersey apples offered a consistent and reliable alternative and earned the state a reputation as a renowned apple- and cider-producing region. In *The Cider Makers' Manual* (1874), Jonathan Buell notes that Newark cider easily fetched twice the price of other cider in southern and Caribbean ports, and advertisements for Newark cider are found throughout nineteenth-century newspapers in the South and California.

Newark cider is also mentioned by numerous foreign and domestic travelers, and it seems to have remained a feature of common knowledge long after temperance took hold across the country. In a July 1879 issue of *Atlantic Monthly*, an American talking about his travels through rural England remarks on how dull and flavorless the cider is compared to Newark cider. This reputation, for a time, is what helped save the orchards of Newark from the wheels of industrial progress and temperance. But eventually, Newark orchards were uprooted as the city's apple and cider legacy was cleared for industry.

Modern Cidermakers and Apple Growers

Apple growing and cider production in the mid-Atlantic are largely confined to Pennsylvania, New Jersey, and the District of Columbia. But this unique history stretches into Delaware, northern Virginia, and parts of New York, and each area has a unique impact on agriculture, orchards, and the region's developing cider market.

Cider in the mid-Atlantic is in transition, as the region looks to both the North and South for inspiration. Cidermakers here rely on apples grown on both sides of the Mason-Dixon Line, even though many of these apples have their roots in the earliest settlements of the mid-Atlantic. The region's intersectional nature has allowed contemporary cider to follow the roots of cidermakers from centuries ago, but also to build a new beverage that crosses borders with its own independent sense of identity.

As mid-Atlantic cider begins to take shape, its outspoken cider-makers are catching national attention by staying true to what makes the region great: its orchards and growers. With the region's rich apple-growing history, it has constantly been searching for new ways to capitalize on its apple crop. Solutions are beginning to arise in nearby markets that are proving ready to back local beverages.

CHARACTERISTICS OF MID-ATLANTIC CIDER

Cider in the mid-Atlantic is largely made up of apples grown for the processing industry, such as York, Golden Delicious, Winter Banana, and Winesap. European cider apples have shown to be more successful here than in the low-elevation Southeast, but they make up only a small amount of the cider being made. Ciders sit between the high-acid style of the Northeast and the richer, more lush counterparts in the South. Luckily, older varieties like Winesap and York have the capacity to make great cider. Estate-grown cherries, peaches, and hops make frequent appearances in the ciders as farmers try to adapt existing resources. Sour ciders, pioneered by Maryland's defunct Millstone Cellars, have been a popular style for both the mass market and artisan ciders alike.

Adams County, Pennsylvania

Long before the famous battle that elevated the town into the international spotlight, Gettysburg and the surrounding Adams, Franklin, and Cumberland Counties attracted farmers with their gentle hills and fertile soils. The area lies within the northern extension of the Shenandoah and Cumberland Valleys, filled with similar limestone deposits with outcroppings of quartz and shale that influence the minerality and flavor of the region's apples. Development of early Quaker farms and orchards was followed by immigrants from modern Germany, Switzerland, and

Scandinavia. The arrival of railroads made the valley, and Harrisburg to its north, a crucial highway during the Civil War and into the twentieth century, and with it many of the regional orchards began growing for factories.

Informed by the success of these early orchards, Noah Sheely, in 1878, planted the first commercial orchard in Adams County. Sheely's twenty-three-acre orchard—and apples from Adams County—gained national acclaim shortly after 1893, when he sold 1,500 barrels of apples at the Chicago World's Fair. Chicago merchants then traveled to Adams County with an interest in buying apples, prompting farmers to begin commercial growing.

Today Adams County is the center of apple growing in Pennsylvania, with two-thirds of the state's orchards and about 70 percent of its annual crop. Orchards rest on the undulating hills west of Gettysburg, known affectionately as the Adams County Fruit Belt. The Fruit Belt lies against South Mountain, ironically the northern maxim of the Blue Ridge Mountains. It envelops the county from the west and shelters it against severe weather from the Great Lakes. The foothills offer excellent air drainage for the orchards and stave off the worst threats from spring frosts, which roll off the hillside orchards and down into the valley below. When surrounding counties are devastated by killing freezes, Adams County produces a nearly full crop. While all of Pennsylvania is adequate for growing apples, unpredictable weather can make growing fruit outside Adams County precarious.

Predictability is paramount when growing fruit at the scale that is done in Adams County. Nearly every hillside is lined with trees, and the density of cultivated land is staggering. Large Pennsylvania-based processors Knouse Foods and Musselman's buy thousands of tons of apples each year from local growers for a wide range of products.

In 1907, Christian High Musselman acquired Biglerville Canning Company and cut all produce save apples from the company's processing line. By specializing in apples, Musselman controlled the quality, creating a premium outlet for Adams County growers. He opened a second processing plant in Gardners to access fruit from the north part of the county and, at the onset of World War I, saw immense growth with the need for canned food to ship to Europe.

Around this same time, orchards in Adams County and the Northeast became infected with an insect dubbed San Jose scale. Having landed in California on flowering peaches from China in the 1870s, the scale spread throughout orchards across the United States by the turn of the century, decimating trees in small-scale, hobby-sized orchards. In an era of increased chemical sprays, San Jose scale proved to be the first insecticide-resistant pest in the United States. In the first decade of the twentieth century, one-third of all Pennsylvania apple trees succumbed to the scale.

While the insect facilitated the death of many small orchards unable to defend against it, commercial orchards concentrated in south-central Pennsylvania were able to outwit the pest by sheer volume. Similar stories played out across the nation: regional small-scale growers could no longer cater to the needs of their immediate communities, so less diverse commercial orchards filled the void.

During Prohibition, in 1928, with little interest in cider, Musselman built an apple butter plant in Biglerville to use the waste from fruit ill suited for canning at the neighboring plant. The business lasted through the Depression, and Musselman built the first cold-storage facility in the area. By his death in 1944, the C. H. Musselman Company operated so near to a monopoly within Pennsylvania that it was able to influence grower practices and dictate the price paid for farmed goods. Farms became specialized, centering on fruit production, which facilitated the growth of orchards in Adams County. The Musselman Company remained an unrivaled force until Mott's opened in Aspers in Adams County shortly after World War II.

Postwar inflation raised the cost of production for growers, but Musselman continued paying them low prices for their fruit. The Adams County Fruit Growers Association took action. They formed a cooperative, brought in growers from throughout the entire mid-Atlantic region, and bought a processing plant from M. E. Knouse in Peach Glen. Since Peach Glen was near Musselman's Gardners plant, it gave the cooperative a local outlet for their fruit, where they would receive higher prices than what Musselman was paying.

What became Knouse Foods Cooperative in 1949 gave growers freedom to sell their crop to processors of their choosing—unlike Musselman's. It was a big draw that incentivized more farmers to invest in apples.

Golden Delicious

A seedling discovered by A. H. Mullins in Clay County in central West Virginia around 1890, Golden Delicious catapulted itself onto the national stage when the tree sold to Stark Bro's for $5,000 in 1914. By 1916, Stark had begun to sell it around the country. They built such a great demand for the apple that the nursery put up a steel cage around the original tree to prevent the theft of scion wood. It quickly became one of the most popular varieties in the country and is still a widely planted counterpart of York Imperial throughout the Shenandoah Valley and beyond.

CIDER PROFILE

Can evoke honeydew and acacia flowers with high sugars. Because of its soft structure and minimal tannin, it is an excellent base for other varieties to play upon.

Adams County's mid-century boom was fueled by the Knouse cooperative and founded on excellent processing apples like Stayman Winesap and York Imperial, favored for their firmness and durability. In the case of York, the apple was complemented by Golden Delicious, its sugar-rich pollination partner. (Apple blossoms need to be pollinated in order to become fruit, but apple trees are not self-pollinating, so different varieties with corresponding bloom times are often planted together.) Marriage of the two apples formed the backbone of most juice blends coming out of Pennsylvania processing plants. In looking to differentiate from Musselman's, Knouse patented a chunky applesauce that became a leading product.

But, as in the rest of the country, the model of growing apples for the factory has gone into decline thanks to international competition. Mott's canceled many of its contracts with Adams County growers, and farmers were sent scrambling for alternatives. Many found refuge in Honeycrisp and other modern apples to satisfy today's consumers' yearning for crunch, and old processing trees are continuously being uprooted in favor of apples destined for grocery stores and the fresh market.

Since 2000, the National Park Service has undertaken a campaign to restore the landscape of Gettysburg to its pre–Civil War state. They are removing species that were not around in the second half of the nineteenth century, and have planted nearly three thousand apple trees on more than a hundred acres at thirty-five historic orchards. Good Intent Cider has collaborated with the Gettysburg Foundation to produce cider with some of these apples. Adam Redding, owner of Good Intent, coordinates groups of volunteers to harvest apples scattered throughout Rose Farm Orchard, the site of some of the bloodiest fighting during July 1863.

Adam's County lies at a type of crossroads: How many of the area's three million yearly visitors will continue to visit the battle site as time marches on? With cider, Gettysburg has an opportunity to innovate into new spaces and create experiences for people built on the richness of the community, rather than on its tragedy. While Gettysburg tourists rarely head into the orchards, the area's proximity to large cities provides Adams County farmers like Ben Wenk of Three Springs Fruit Farm and Ploughman Cider many opportunities, especially through farmers' markets. Wenk is a fifth-generation farmer, and his family now manages 450 acres, on which they grow tomatoes, cherries, and peaches in addition to apples. In the 1950s, encouraged by the presence of processing plants, Wenk's grandfather moved the farm to a more substantial apple crop. His father, David, expanded the farm after he returned from college, and Ben followed in his dad's footsteps in 2006. After working for Penn State and hearing the buzz of employees talking about which farmers' markets they visited over the weekend, Ben was on a mission to take Three Springs into the markets, which he did the following year.

Ben was discovering craft beer that same year, dropping into bars with his dad on the way home from markets and ordering from tap handles he didn't recognize. One time it was Strongbow cider. David tasted it and said, "We could make this."

For Wenk, cider is an investment in the farm and the land. He is replacing Red Delicious trees that were planted in the mid-twentieth century with cider apples. Many of the family's new bittersweet and bittersharp trees are a few years from production, so most of their interim ciders are made from the farm's existing heirloom apples, like Esopus Spitzenburg, Stark, York, and Stayman Winesap. Wenk's newest experimental orchard is planted in calcium-rich quartz above the town that bears his family's name.

York Imperial

Discovered early in the nineteenth century in York, Pennsylvania, York Imperial was introduced commercially in 1830. This rotund and hearty apple's ease to grow and extended storage capacity made it a mainstay of orchards throughout the Shenandoah Valley in the Southeast and mid-Atlantic states. York continues the long tradition of apple juices and sauces from Adam's County processors.

CIDER PROFILE

Soft acidity and lightly fruity profile, backed by baking spices and green tea with a light, cotton ball-like tannin.

Several miles north along the foothills is Big Hill Ciderworks. Troy Lehman was getting burned out from the auto industry and started making cider and wine on weekends in the mid-2000s, and in 2010 he bought a farm, part of which used to be his grandmother's, two miles down the road from where he grew up. He convinced friend and fellow auto world exile Ben Kishbaugh to also purchase twenty-three acres of existing orchards in northern Adams County. The existing apples, like Winchester and Golden Delicious and crabs like Manchurian and Dolgo, supplied Big Hill's early ciders before their 2011 planting of cider apples was ready.

The Appalachian trail is located just a half mile from Lehman's farm, and he hopes that in the future both he and Wenk will have customer-facing places that will draw some of the visitors out of the valley and into the hills.

The high concentration of processing apples makes this region an ideal place for cider to grow in many spaces. Jack's Hard Cider and Reid's Orchard and Winery in Adams County and Hale and True Cider in Philadelphia have all tapped into this massive supply of apples to make easy-drinking ciders with additions of various fruits and hops that have found a fast market.

Delaware River

While Gettysburg and the surrounding areas were developing a market for processing apples at the turn of the twentieth century, orchards along the Delaware River watershed, between New Jersey and Pennsylvania, were focused on growing fruit for the greater Philadelphia area. Historically, these places could never compete with the Hudson Valley or points north for durable apples. Due to the mild climate and limited size of their orchards, they could not grow in-demand Baldwin or McIntosh. So they found their own niche instead, taking advantage of the region's early-ripening apple varieties that could go to market more quickly.

Growers specialized in apples like Yellow Transparent, Early

Ripe, and Wealthy that can ripen as early as mid-June. These first-of-the-year apples carried a real premium in the age before a global fruit market. But in the years after World War II, improvements to climate-controlled storage facilities eliminated the demand for summer apples, pressing apples firmly into the autumn of America's conscience.

Orchards that endured did so by turning directly to consumers. Kauffman's Fruit Farm, outside of Lancaster, has been supplying Dressler Estate since 2016. As with so many others, husband and wife Brian and Olga Dressler's hobby became a business as it slowly took over their garage in suburban Downingtown. Their Modern Still and Modern Sparkling ciders are crafted with care, highlighting the fresh fruit aromas of mid-Atlantic staples like Winesap, Golden Delicious, and Jonagold. The Dresslers have also begun working with several new, smaller orchards that are looking to build estate cider orchards.

Steve Frecon had the future in mind when he took his family's third-generation orchard in Boyertown, outside of Philadelphia, into the cider business. The 130-acre Frecon Farms in Berks County has been revitalized as Frecon tries to make cider with the farm's generations-old apples and new varieties they are testing every year. While the farm's cider continues to grow, they have run into significant boundaries in the form of Pennsylvania's unclear liquor control laws. They must be licensed as both a winery and a brewery: a winery if they want to sell at farmers' markets and state liquor stores and a brewery if they want to sell draft cider through beer channels like bars. Individual products are licensed separately, and those that enter into the beer channels need to be under 5.5 percent ABV, which is a near impossibility for anyone using ripe apples.

Washington, DC

While bureaucratic regulations challenge cidermakers in Pennsylvania, their flexibility has allowed one of the country's most dynamic cideries to flourish in the nation's capital. ANXO Cidery began as a Basque-inspired tapas bar in the up-and-coming section of Truxton Circle in the heart of Washington. Siblings Sam and Rachel Fitz, along with their partner Cooper Sheehan, had the first licensed winery in the District, taking advantage of a now-defunct wine pub rule that allowed them to operate the restaurant and sell alcohol for

Tom Oliver

No European cidermaker has had such a direct influence on American cidermakers as Tom Oliver. Before he started making cider in 1999, Oliver worked as a roadie for the Hawks, the Pretenders, and Van Morrison, and he has been the tour manager for Scottish pop-rock group the Proclaimers since 1988.

As a consequence of his touring days, few other European cidermakers are as tuned in to the changing preferences and demands of cider in the United States and what they might mean for his local market. His natural and often funky ciders from his small farm in Herefordshire are a must for any cider lover. While a staunch traditionalist, he released the UK's first hopped cider in 2014 after his first collaboration with Ryan Burk. Burk and Oliver continue to collaborate on their Gold Rush cider (contains no Gold Rush apples), a fresher and brighter style of cider than is typically found in Herefordshire. It remains a hit on both sides of the Atlantic.

both onsite and off-premise consumption as long as they also produced alcohol on-premise. After a long series of pop-ups across the city, they outfitted their restaurant with a 660-gallon former Barolo cask and started making Spanish-style cider.

After trying to sell 750-milliliter bottles, they realized that if cider was going to work, it had to be different. They reached out to Eleanor Léger of Eden in Vermont and Herefordshire cidermaker Tom Oliver for inspiration and collaboration. This new phase of ANXO was rooted in dry cider that used only apples, as a way to stand out from the rest of the canned cider hitting the market around the city. When they brought out their canned ciders in January 2018, they did so with the intention of breathing new energy and excitement into cider not only in the mid-Atlantic but around the globe. Fine European ciders from France, the UK, and Spain have enjoyed a following in the United States for years, but too often enthusiasm does not translate into sales. ANXO reaches across the ocean to build collaborative ciders that emphasize the value and quality of the apples and cider, packaging them for the new American cider consumer.

Newark, New Jersey

Newark cider's heyday of the early nineteenth century came in an era of geo-marketing, where the city was the brand more than the product. Newark—and New Jersey in general, with New York City on one side and Philadelphia on the other—has long been particularly poised to thrive in local markets. Early on, cider from Newark was often packaged as Newark Champagne and shipped across the Hudson, where it found its way into many of New York City's early fine-dining restaurants.

Historian Fran McManus, an expert on Newark's cider history and the cultural strategist for Ironbound Hard Cider, says the growing industrial landscape of Newark likely displaced its early orchards. She suspects the large cider mills that continued to turn out Newark Cider into the twentieth century were shipping dubiously labeled cider—made not from the historic Harrison, Campfield, and Graniwinkle but from apples grown outside Newark, and often beyond New Jersey. McManus has helped Charles Rosen, the founder of

Ironbound, weave historical stories into the brand's narrative. For McManus, there is a sense of pride knowing Newark was once a manufacturing powerhouse, a place that valued craftsmanship as part of its history.

Rosen named his Ironbound Farm after the Portuguese-Brazilian neighborhood in east Newark. He veered into cider with ambitions of creating a business born of place, with regenerative agriculture, urban renewal, and workforce development as its pillars. Rosen and McManus paint the picture of an early-nineteenth-century Newark as a time when coming into port was akin to entering a forest of apple trees. Today's mission is beyond recreating horticulture, though. It extends to job creation for the chronically underemployed in marginalized immigrant, formerly incarcerated, veteran, and special needs communities.

Ironbound's ciders are made from fresh eating apples grown throughout the larger region, but Ironbound has established a 108-acre biorestorative farm forty-five minutes outside Newark to grow the next generation of its cider. Urban ex-offenders and veterans work on the farm side by side with similarly overlooked rural employees in a shared effort to rebuild community as well as the land. Through Ironbound Hard Cider, Rosen is creating something that suburban New Jersey can enjoy, drawn from impoverished areas both rural and urban.

Core Takeaways

Although the mid-Atlantic shares or exceeds the infrastructure of the region's counterparts to the south and north, cider has been only a recent addition. The region has excellent terroir, apple varieties that make compelling cider, and farmers who have been growing apples for juice for generations. The expansiveness of the trees in Adams County is breathtaking, especially considering it was all built on applesauce. Industrialization of orchards has fostered colossal plantings and immense quantities of fruit that need large processors, packers, and cidermakers alike to keep pace with the rigors of fruit growing in the new economy.

The sleepy hills of Adams County lie within a quick drive of Philadelphia, Baltimore, and Washington, but few visitors to the area trek beyond the proverbial gift shop. Walking around modern Newark, it is hard to imagine that the entire area once made nationally heralded cider, or that southeastern Pennsylvania has a history that extends beyond 1863. But cider in the mid-Atlantic is, in many ways, a bridge between the present and past, and a vehicle that, once people pay attention, showcases the long-shadowed agriculture of the region.

ADAMS COUNTY, PENNSYLVANIA

- **Location and Geography:** Located in south-central Pennsylvania at the northern terminus of the Blue Ridge Mountains, the county is defined by rolling hills, with the historic battlefield of Gettysburg at its center. Within two hours of Baltimore, Philadelphia, and Washington.
- **Soil:** Limestone with quartz and flint.
- **Climate:** Humid continental climate with excellent air drainage off South Mountain. The area is uniquely sheltered, and the topography protects it from damaging frosts. USDA Hardiness Zone 6b.
- **Orchard Location:** Orchards cover the South Mountain Fruit Belt along the western border of the county. The rolling, apple-filled hills are about five hundred feet above the battlefield and the valley below.
- **Orchard Type:** Processing remains the backbone of the region, but large packing houses like Rice Fruit Company (the largest packer on the East Coast) and some direct retail orchards have brought innovation in both cash flow and varieties.
- **Significant Apple Varieties:** York Imperial, Golden Delicious, Stayman Winesap, Northern Spy, Winter Sweet Paradise, Honeycrisp, Kingston Black, GoldRush, Smokehouse, Gala, Fuji.
- **Cider Apple Plantings:** Adams County has some small plantings and estate cidermakers, but larger growers have not begun expansion into cider apples.
- **Producers to Visit:** Ploughman Cider (Gettysburg, PA).

DELAWARE RIVER

- **Location and Geography:** Rolling hills into the Delaware River water basin, with Philadelphia in the south.

- **Soil:** Well-drained loam soils over granite, with clay closer to the waterways.
- **Climate:** Humid continental with some air drainage. USDA Hardiness Zone 6b.
- **Orchard Location:** Orchards are mostly found in the hills on both the New Jersey and Pennsylvania sides of the Delaware River.
- **Orchard Type:** Most of the orchards are geared toward retail, fulfilling the local demand.
- **Significant Apple Varieties:** Winter Banana, Golden Delicious, Gravenstein, Winesap, Summer Rambo, Yellow Transparent, Harrison, Campfield, Poveshon, and Graniwinkle.
- **Cider Apple Plantings:** Cider apples are limited, but Ironbound Farm has invested in rebuilding the traditional Newark cider varieties.
- **Producers to Visit:** Ironbound Hard Cider (Asbury, NJ), Hale and True Cider Co. (Philadelphia, PA).

Orchards, Apples, and Temperance

In 1851, in the *Journal of Agriculture,* Massachusetts lawyer-turned-Unitarian minister Allen W. Dodge shared his thoughts on cider. His words represent the nation-wide attitude toward alcohol, and cider specifically, in the wake of temperance.

As to unsaleable apples, do you inquire what shall be done with them? Make cider? We say no, unless it is to be converted into vinegar. Of all the miserable drugs that were ever used for drink on a farm, cider, hard or soft, is about the most miserable. But our fathers and grandfathers used it, and they were wise and strong men. Yes, but no thanks to cider—that did not make them so. We have seen the long rows of barrels filled with October cider, horsed up in the cellar, as if planting, and hoeing, and haying, and harvesting could never be accomplished without their assistance. Aye, and not only the jug following the laborer, as closely as his shadow in the field, but the mug of cider at his side on the table morning, noon and night. But a new generation—and wiser we think in this respect—has sprung up, who have dispensed entirely with this muddling and peevish-making beverage. What shall be done with your unsound and unsaleable apples? Boil them—mix them with meal—and give them to your hogs. Depend upon it, they will thus do more good, than if ground up into cider. Our experience in this way of fattening swine has not been small, and we can bear the strongest testimony to the excellence of cooked apples for this purpose.

Nationwide, drinking alcohol was proclaimed an act of sin. States enforced stringent laws and regulations that laid the groundwork for national prohibition. Apples were no longer for fermenting and drinking, so the fruit began its slow descent to a sweet, homogenous monoculture for eating only.

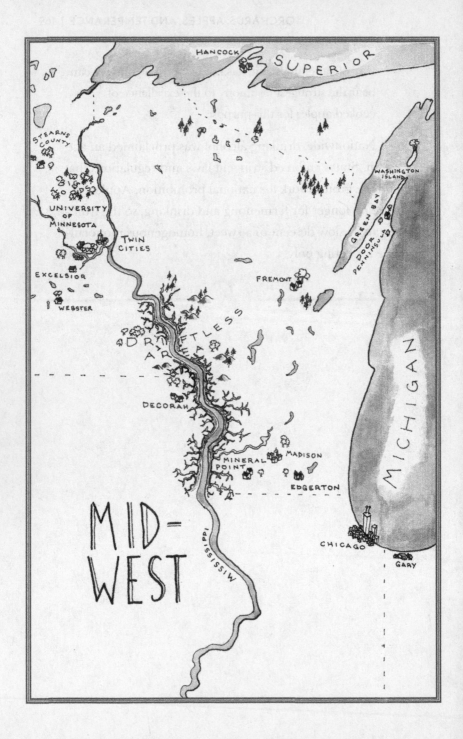

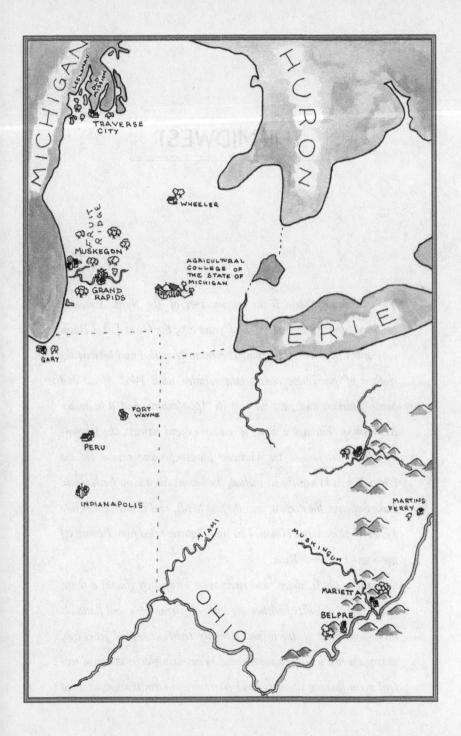

THE MIDWEST

The Canadian Shield is the original core of the North American continent. In its midst, millions of years ago, the Great Lakes Basin was afloat in a sea of magma. It eventually settled and became the seafloor of prehistoric oceans that collided with West Africa and South America and gave the east its Appalachian and Adirondack Mountains. Through a series of advances and retreats, the Laurentide Ice Sheet formed the Midwest landscape and carved out the Great Lakes. When the ice melted, the basins filled with fresh water. Lake Superior, the deepest, was the first to fill, and it spilled over into Lakes Michigan and Huron. Erie and Ontario filled from ice melt off the Saint Lawrence River.

Valleys, bluffs, slopes, and rivers were formed by glacial activity, and mineral deposits enriched the soils of streambeds and flatlands throughout most of the region. Roughly eighty thousand years ago, during the last ice age, a southbound Wisconsin glacier dammed several north-flowing rivers, causing reservoirs to form throughout what *became the lower Midwest. These reservoirs eventually carved out the Ohio River Valley, and in so doing paved the way for agriculture and settlement in the west.*

In the early nineteenth century, the Second Great Awakening spawned a host of new religions, trains of thought, social notions, and national customs. New ideas informing philosophy, religion, economics, industry, and trade came at a time when the nation's shifting boundaries encompassed a boundless frontier. Though the young nation was in the throes of the Industrial Revolution, initial frontier settlers were drawn by opportunities in agriculture. The frontier became equal parts land and concept, stitched into the American mindset as hopeful populations settled beyond the Appalachian Mountains.

Territorial expansion commenced immediately after the Revolutionary War. The newly established federal government set forth to expand the young republic from its coastal confines. Whereas Atlantic colonies had struggled for more than a century to establish civil societies, the Midwest experienced comparatively rapid growth over the span of a single generation.

The Northwest Territory, or Old Northwest, was established with the Northwest Ordinance in 1787. Defined as the land northwest of the Ohio River and east of the Mississippi River, it came at a time when eastern states were set on a path toward mercantilism and industry. Wage labor and immigration were on the rise, and the rift between the haves and the have-nots in the young nation was growing deeper. Spreading out, it was thought, would calm the country's bubbling social discord and divisive views on slavery.

The Northwest Territory was marketed as a bounty of agricultural opportunity for settlers, and five states were created under the ordinance: Ohio (1803), Indiana (1816), Illinois (1818), Michigan (1837), and Wisconsin (1848). Education was a foundational pillar in each state, as it had been among Puritans and the cultural elite on the Atlantic coast. Slavery was prohibited in the territory, but it remained a reality through the 1840s. Enslaved Africans and African Americans were made to work in U.S. Army camps and lead mines—mines that Indigenous people had been mining for centuries.

Dred Scott v. Sandford

The whitewashing of history suggests that the limited Black rights leading up to the Civil War and the years of Reconstruction that followed were *granted* by the white community. Rather, the Black, African, and African American communities *fought* for the acknowledgment of their rights—to voting, to education, to leadership, to public policy, to enfranchisement—which had been persistently neglected since the first forms of enslavement. Perhaps most notable is the 1843 Supreme Court case of *Dred Scott v. Sandford*, in which enslaved African Americans Dred and Harriet Scott unsuccessfully sued for their freedom, despite having lived in Illinois—a free state—for a decade. The ruling that enslaved and free African Americans were not citizens nullified the Northwest Ordinance and the Missouri Compromise, and it fueled the fire that sent a nation divided on slavery into civil war. The decision cemented white disregard for Black contributions to agriculture (including orchards and cidermaking), the economy, and beyond.

In order to efficiently transfer the new territory's federal land from public domain to private white citizens, whether by distribution or sale, it needed to be surveyed. The Public Land Survey

System was initially established to survey the land ceded to the United States after the Revolutionary War. Throughout the Northwest Territory, thirty-six-square-mile townships were created and divided into one-mile sections.

The mere consideration of pushing into the frontier arose from a bloodied past, one defined by European settlement at the cost of Native populations. The sun set over land that European settlers considered theirs for the taking. And take it they did. The Northwest Indian War (1785–1795), the Battles of Fallen Timbers (1794) and Tippecanoe (1811), and the Black Hawk War (1832) are among the bloody campaigns that expelled Indigenous Peoples from the Old Northwest—killing many and forcing survivors farther west or onto reservations—to make room for white settlement.

Marietta, in southeastern Ohio, where the Muskingum River meets the Ohio River, was the first settlement in the Northwest Territory. Settlers to the blossoming city and the greater territory migrated with an abundance of apple seeds, as was the early custom for westbound settlers and pioneers. Hopeful pioneers without access to established nurseries maintained the custom of growing trees from seed, guided by optimism that they might develop the next variety uniquely accustomed to the conditions of the region.

But the first generation of European settlers was not the first to introduce apples to the region. Indigenous Peoples' orchards were welcome sights for pioneers and land speculators who moved in after Native populations were pushed out. In Gnadenhutton, Ohio, in 1792—ten years after the massacre of ninety-six Delaware people at a Moravian Christian mission—Major William McMahon came across "the best apples he had ever tasted," seventy-five miles north of Marietta on the Tuscarawas River.

During the settling of the Northwest Territory, many seedling trees were valued less for their fruit and more for their rootstocks, onto which settlers could graft known, useful, and marketable varieties. Pioneers with means and know-how took scions from their kitchen orchards or purchased grafted stocks from the likes of Pell

Orchards and Prince Nursery in New York before moving west. William Coxe, the fruit explorer and nurseryman of Burlington, New Jersey, likewise furnished many settlers with scions and trees throughout the early Ohio territory. Some took trees from the East, and most took knowledge they acquired from the literature of the day. In doing so, pioneers were able to propagate sturdy, surefire varieties at comparable latitudes throughout the Midwest.

The Ohio Company of Associates, formed in 1786, required anyone who received land parcels to immediately plant apple, pear, and peach trees. These fruit trees with delayed bearing and long generational lifespans were a sign of permanence in a land with limited developing institutions. Apple seeds—and trees—became a symbol of land stewardship that encouraged homesteading and westward movement. The intent with planting them was to ensure settlement, not land speculation.

Israel Putnam III and his brother Aaron are credited as the first to graft apple trees in the Northwest Territory. Aaron and his father moved to Belpre, Ohio—the state's second settlement—shortly after the Ohio Company of Associates was formed. In March 1794, Israel set out to visit his Belpre family and brought scions with him. He arrived one month later and recorded in his journal on May 3 that he "walked about my brother's lots; engrafted a few trees with scions I brought on." Israel returned east shortly after and, from the Putnam family orchard, dispatched twenty-three scions protected with beeswax, packed in saddlebags, to Ohio, where they were grafted in 1796. Among the scions were known Northeast favorites— good for fresh eating and cider—like Rhode Island Greening, Roxbury Russet, Westfield Seek-No-Further, Newtown Pippin, Tolman Sweet, and Esopus Spitzenburg.

Israel eventually settled in Marietta, and each brother established a nursery with grafted fruit from the family's Connecticut orchard. Putnam's daybook records from 1810 show significant sales in bushels of apples and barrels of cider. In 1816, Aaron introduced Baldwin, England's Ribston Pippin, and Siberian

Crab. By 1821, the brothers were grafting sixteen thousand trees annually.

Rome Beauty

Rome Beauty's legacy begins in the hands of Israel Putnam III and the Ohio orchard he planted with New England varieties. Connecticut native Joel Gillett temporarily lived at Putnam's log cabin on his way downriver to settle in Rome Township in Lawrence County. Upon planting scions from Putnam's orchard, Gillett discovered a faulty graft throwing up a root sprout. He cut it off and gave it to his son, who planted it along the Ohio River in 1817. Rome Beauty was the result.

The tree was known locally as Gillett's Seedling for fifteen years. In 1832, George Walton, believed to have been a neighbor, named it Rome Beauty: "Rome" for the township and "Beauty" for the apple's stunning symmetry, vibrant red color, and generous size. Rome Beauty blooms late to boot, which helps protect it against late-spring frosts. It bears fruit within a few years and is a sturdy tree that can handle the weight of heavy crop years. The apples are prized for baking and good for cider. They are firm and durable, which made the apple a leading processing variety in the mid-nineteenth century.

Rome Beauty was one of the first marketed seedling apples to grow in the Northwest Territory. Into the 1850s and '60s, as more distant markets could be reached, the apple fetched double the price of many others. It showed growers that the region could produce fruit in its own right.

CIDER PROFILE

Accented with purple plums, roses, and rose hips. Moderate acidity and no tannin.

As settlements were established farther west, nurseries soon followed. Silas Wharton settled in the Miami River valley, two hundred miles west of Marietta, and opened a nursery. In 1824,

Wharton compiled a nursery catalog with six other nurseries that listed over ninety varieties of apples that ripened from early summer to late winter. Indiana had its first nursery thanks to Andrew Hampton, who furnished his orchard with grafted trees from Wharton's nursery. Hampton's nursery sold upwards of sixty-five thousand trees annually throughout the 1830s.

Ohio's population grew from 45,000 in 1800 to 1.5 million in 1840, and with more people came more demand for apples. Through grafting, apples were being produced with consistency in regard to size, shape, color, and taste. In 1859, Samuel Wood, addressing the

Wolf River

Found on homesteads across the northern United States, Wolf River's characteristic massive size is said to fill an entire pie with just one or two apples. A hard texture with little moisture makes it less than ideal for fresh eating but optimal for pie making and drying. In *Not Far from the Tree* (2007), author John Bunker says his neighbor calls it Wool Fiber because of its dry, pulpy texture, which some find closer to wool than fruit. Lee Calhoun and others attribute the apple's origin to William Springer, a lumberman from Quebec who bought a bushel of apples along the shore of Lake Erie on his migration from Canada to Wisconsin in 1856. The bushel is believed to have been Alexander apples, an imported Russian variety popular in cold climates. Springer saved seeds and planted them along the Wolf River near his new home in Fremont, Wisconsin.

This reliable cropping apple became very popular not only in the Upper Midwest, where its chilly Russian heritage thrived, but also in the mountains of North Carolina and New England, where old trees still dot Maine homesteads, planted there by migrating miners and lumbermen who moved east.

CIDER PROFILE

Fresh and distinctly appley, with tart fruit leather aromas. Usually used as a blending variety.

Ohio Pomological Society, recalled the early days of his nursery business and western settlement. "After the trees from my nursery commenced bearing," he said, "I could not furnish trees fast enough for the demand. Other nurseries sprang up around me, and I furnished them grafts free of charge." His experience with such high demand was not unique. And, because settlers had reliable access to grafted fruit, orchards in the Northwest Territory developed faster and with more specialization than their earlier eastern counterparts.

With settlement pushing into Michigan, farmers found thriving seedling orchards along Lake Michigan and the Ohio River that were planted by preceding generations of fur traders and missionaries. New settlers planted orchards and found their own success, and Michigan—specifically the southwest of the state along the shores of Lake Michigan—was soon recognized as a premium fruit-growing region.

In 1866, University of Michigan geology professor Alexander Winchell identified what he called the Fruit Bearing Belt of Michigan—the land along the eastern coast of Lake Michigan from the lake's head north to Muskegon—as a region unsurpassed by any other in the country. Growing seasons here were nearly three weeks longer than anywhere else on the lake, with mean average temperatures four degrees higher than western Wisconsin lakeshores. Growing fruit for the burgeoning cities of Milwaukee and Chicago, by the close of the nineteenth century, Michigan's orchard products valued nearly $4 million, or roughly $120 million today.

Great fruit and enthusiasm for it were reaped beyond the shores of Lake Michigan. Horticulturist and fruit grower Franklin Elliott opened a nursery outside Cleveland in the 1840s after moving from Connecticut with his family. He published *Elliott's Fruit Book; Or, the American Fruit-Grower's Guide in Orchard and Garden* in 1854 and wrote, "Orcharding and its profits pecuniary, as relating to the apple, has become well understood, and no one, who has land in anyway suited now hesitates to plant." Looking at information from the decade prior, Elliot estimated that more than six million trees were

German Immigration

To promote immigration from the newly unified German Empire in 1871, Alexander Winchell's isothermal charts were utilized in *Der Michigan Wegweiser*, a Michigan State–supported brochure published in Hamburg, Germany. The brochure and others like it called for help in clearing land, farming, and building cities in the Midwest, while noting the region's stark beauty, free education, and government by consenting citizens. With peaks of German immigration in the 1850s, '70s, and '80s, nearly three million German-born immigrants lived in the United States by 1890. Cities like Cincinnati, Chicago, and Milwaukee developed significantly Germanic neighborhoods.

German grain farmers also transformed the forests of Michigan into the leading producer of cereals in the second half of the nineteenth century. Kellogg's and Post were born from German grain-growing customs, earning Battle Creek, Michigan, its "Cereal City" moniker and subsequently quenching the new thirst for beer. German farmers bought expansive tracts of land, perfect for beer grains: grains that didn't spoil, could be easily shipped, and fermented readily with no concern for the season. The German practice of cold-, bottom-fermented beers (lagers) was a safer, more consistent practice than English ales, which are warm- and top-fermenting and expose yeast to the perils of air and bacteria. Beer soon became a commodity that reached large-scale commercial proportion.

propagated and planted annually throughout Ohio, Michigan, Indiana, Illinois, and Wisconsin.

With an abundance of marketable apples and propagated

orchards in the developing Midwest, taverns served a unique set of functions compared to those of the Atlantic states. In coastal states, taverns arose from the development of industries and the markets and trade that followed. In the rural Midwest, taverns were among the first buildings established in the wilderness, often doubling as the proprietor's farm and homestead. Before railroads and other transportation penetrated the region, farmers had little opportunity to transport their surplus. The tavern brought buyers to their door.

Taverns were built as places of exchange and locales to entice travelers to settle, so that towns might develop around their presence. In some instances, early territorial roads were diverted through towns where a well-operated tavern existed. With the exception of reform hotels that sprang up in the temperate decades leading to the Civil War, cider flowed freely in all Midwest taverns. Many were farm-based operations, in that they grew much of what filled their larder, and cider was a common beverage made from nearby orchards.

As farmers began to understand the science of their craft, they called for government support in agriculture and scientific education to improve their industry. In 1855, the Agricultural College of the State of Michigan, now Michigan State University, became the first university in the United States dedicated to scientific agriculture, and it would become the template for land-grant universities across the country.

Nationwide momentum for government support of education and scientific agriculture culminated when President Abraham Lincoln signed the Morrill Act of 1862. This statute granted federally controlled land to states, which states could sell, using the proceeds to establish universities that promoted agriculture and engineering. President Grover Cleveland then enacted the Hatch Act of 1877, which provided federal funds to land-grant universities in each state to create agriculture extension programs to improve farming through academic and scientific research by communicating and sharing directly with the farmers.

The American government was also a major contributor to the development of commercial agriculture. In 1862, Lincoln also signed an act of Congress that established the United States Department of Agriculture—a bureau dedicated to improved means of farming through science, resource conservation, and economic development. Lincoln called it "The People's Department," as it catered to the half of the American population that was then living on farms. It was the department's responsibility, among other things, "to procure, propagate, and distribute among the people new and valuable seeds and plants."

Lincoln signed the Pacific Railroad Act the same year, financing the Union Pacific and Central Pacific Railroad companies to construct the transcontinental railroad. Completion of the First Transcontinental Railroad in 1869 shortened the east-west journey from six months to two weeks. As more rail was laid late in the nineteenth century, railroads started catering to growing commercial production by carting immense loads of farmed goods back and forth between Midwest markets and those on the Atlantic coast.

Chicago became the nation's intersection, where East meets West and North convenes with South. Land values nationwide rose in proximity to rail lines. In the Midwest, prairies were filled with tracks and towns grew alongside train depots. With a distribution network in place, farmers were able to expand their orchards to previously unforeseen scope and ambition. Small players without means to develop commercial operations perished.

As the frontier pushed into Minnesota, which became a state in 1858, pioneers were faced with a new set of challenges. The collective agricultural knowledge and wisdom borrowed from previous generations was not enough to stave off the severe cold of the state's northern reaches. Regardless, people came. One of them was Peter Gideon, who arrived in Minnesota from Illinois in 1853 with a group of New England farmers to make their own way upon the land. He brought grafted and seedling fruit to his new farm in Excelsior, along the banks of Lake Minnetonka. His early apple experiments were unsuccessful, leaving the homestead family nearly penniless until he bought a collection of seeds and scion wood from a nursery in Maine.

This collection included imported Russian apple varieties specifically bred to withstand the harsh northern winters. In 1868, Gideon crossed Duchess of Oldenburg, a Russian variety, with a native crab apple to develop the Wealthy apple, named after his wife, Wealthy Hull. The apple's success signaled a dramatic change in the family's fortune—and in the progress of cultivating apples in some of the coldest weather found in the country. Growers who adapted the new variety took advantage of river markets and the high demand for fruit. They built flatboats in the fall and took thousands of barrels of apples to Chicago, where they fed the growing industrial workforce, and as far south as New Orleans, where French immigrant communities distilled the fruit into brandy.

Gideon's individual triumph was part of a larger network of amateur and professional fruit breeders across the state, all of whom worked in relative isolation. In 1873, these breeders built an association, which developed informally from the Minnesota State Fair into the Minnesota State Horticultural Society, with a goal of concentrating the state's fruit breeding efforts. In 1878, Gideon was named superintendent of the State Experimental Fruit Farm. This government- and university-supported project bought land close to Gideon's existing farm on Lake Minnetonka. Gideon retired on poor terms from the program in 1889, at age seventy, and the farm was sold. Before his death, he sold off much of his own lands and his experiments were uprooted for housing. In 1907, Minnesota reestablished an experiment station, today known as Minnesota Landscape Arboretum, southwest of Gideon's first attempts.

Wealthy joined Rome Beauty and other notable Midwest apples like Wolf River and Haralson, which all thrived in local and national markets. Reliable transportation, persistent commerce, and significant support from government agencies set farming on a commercial trajectory from whence it would not return.

Modern Cidermakers and Apple Growers

The Midwest was the first American frontier, but its original diversified homesteads have largely given way to consolidated fields of soybeans and corn. Apples continue to be a key part of agriculture in Michigan, where the apple industry remains one of the few growing sectors. But their importance has diminished in Ohio, where the Rome Beauty belt along the Ohio River was once as famed as any orchard-intensive area of New England. Each Midwest state has its own distinct agricultural legacy, storied with its own peaks and valleys that have ultimately helped shape contemporary cider as it thrives throughout the region.

Cider in the Midwest has grown by leaps and bounds, fueled by the large processing orchards of Michigan and supported by passionate growers and cidermakers. It has moved from farm stands and fall weekends to fine dining restaurants and pint glasses. As craft beer has empowered consumers to drink locally, cider has risen with the tide, adopting many of the beer practices, including heavy use of used spirit barrels, hops, and cans. Orchards dedicated to cider are springing up as interest grows and a new generation takes over old orchards.

CHARACTERISTICS OF MIDWEST CIDER

Western Michigan processing apples like Rhode Island Greening, Idared, and Northern Spy that were once valued for their ability to translate into applesauce and pie have found a new outlet as world-class refreshment. Fresh and vibrant, many of these ciders are meant to be drunk young, capturing the best of the orchard's aroma and flavor. Midwest cider is generally acid-forward, as tannic apples have been adopted at a slower rate than other cider-centric places on the coasts, but the results are a fascinating study in blending the old and new of Europe and North America.

Ohio and Indiana

Ohio and Indiana, the first two states cut from the Northwest Terri tory, have been slow adopters of cider compared to the rest of the Midwest. The Rome Beauty belt has been replaced with soybeans and corn, which dominate the agricultural resources of the states. Small orchards along Lake Erie and the Ohio River have begun planting for cider, but most of the orchards there are built as retail outfits serving local communities and nearby cities, dwarfed by larger orchards in Michigan.

Growing interest has led small and midsized orchards in both states to start making cider. McClure's Orchard and Winery in Central Indiana added cider to its other agricultural retail offerings, while The Winery at Spring Hill, along Ohio's Erie lakeshore, started planting cider apples to supplement its grape harvest.

Dedicated cider operations in Ohio remain sparse, but a decided few are hoping to change that. Matt Moser Miller, in

Grimes Golden

Grimes Golden hails from Wellsburg, West Virginia, from a seedling planted along the Ohio River by pioneer settler Edward Cranford in the 1790s. From 1870 on, the apple was listed in nearly every southern nursery catalog. Old orchards throughout the South are littered with productive, slightly russeted Grimes Golden apple trees. Its flavor is deeper and richer than its more widely planted offspring Golden Delicious, and its high potential alcohol once made it the favorite of distillers.

CIDER PROFILE

White raspberries and peaches in maple syrup. High alcohol potential, often reaching 9 percent ABV.

Richland County, left academia and apprenticed at Eve's Cidery in the Finger Lakes before adapting those techniques to the rolling hills of central Ohio. In Martins Ferry, along the Ohio River, Josh Klatt is repopulating his uncle's old farm with heirlooms like Black Oxford and Grimes Golden—a native from just across the river in Wellsburg, West Virginia—that are primed for cidermaking.

Hostetler Farms, located outside Indianapolis, is the brainchild of Dustin Hostetler, whose initial cider orchard of two thousand trees, grafted in 2012, grew into a nursery operation. This growing enterprise specializes in heirloom and cider apples not typically found alongside commercial varieties at mom-and-pop roadside orchards. As the trees have begun to bear, he is able to conduct juice analysis to better understand how his Indiana apples might translate into cider. Whereas some growers in more established Midwest states are able to focus on a handful of varieties that thrive in their regions and have proven to make great cider, Hostetler continues to experiment with more than forty varieties as a pioneer for Indiana cider. He plans to put his family's fields—two hundred acres of

GoldRush

Introduced in 1994 by the PRI breeding program—a collaborative program between Purdue, Rutgers, and the University of Illinois—GoldRush quickly became a favorite for cidermakers and growers. It is a late-blooming, disease-resistant apple that avoids threats from spring frosts and is often the last variety to be harvested, typically remaining on trees into November. GoldRush is loaded with high sugars and acid, and it stores incredibly well for months after harvest, making it a valuable multipurpose apple.

CIDER PROFILE

Carries notes of peach, sugarcane, anise, and cantaloupe. High sugar content means ABV can creep above 9 percent.

soybeans and corn that were farmed two generations ago—back into production with apple trees. In 2019, Hostetler and his son set out fifty thousand trees, and they are also working with the University of Ohio and other apple-breeding organizations to grow new trademarked apple varieties.

Mississippi River Valley

The great northern plains of Minnesota, like the whole of the United States, are bisected by the Mississippi River. From glacial lakes in northern Minnesota, the river begins its meandering course through the state and terminates at the humid bayous of Louisiana in the Gulf of Mexico. The upper reaches of the Mississippi acted as the first superhighway in this part of the country, providing access to every town, farm, and community along its 2,320-mile stretch. The river not only framed the western reach of the Northwest Territory but came to play a central role in frontier migration and the economies and cultures that developed along its banks.

Saint Paul and Minneapolis, collectively known as the Twin Cities, are split by the Mississippi River in the great northern plains. When Europeans first arrived, they encountered land and a climate—defined by brutal, frigid winters and unexpected frosts—unlike what they had left behind on the East Coast and in Europe. Many of the East Coast apples settlers brought, along with some berries and cereals, were not able to take root during the shorter growing seasons and untimely frosts, leaving larders sparse in times of early settlement. Horace Greeley, newspaper publisher and apple enthusiast, said in 1860 that he "would not live in Minnesota because you can't grow apples there."

But the river valley's slightly warmer temperatures and rich, alluvial soils slowly fostered a fruit culture akin to that in the East. Many growers today, in fact, have to fight the fertile, prosperous growth throughout valley orchards, where vigorous trees require heavy pruning. From the fledgling efforts of Peter Gideon to formal university-led research, a century and a half of Minnesota infrastructure today supports eighteen cideries, when there were none as recently as 2009. And the number is quickly growing, as nearly a dozen cideries are in the planning stages.

Following Gideon's work, the state legislature, in 1907, established the modern fruit-breeding farm under the direct supervision of the University of Minnesota. The Haralson apple, a cross of Wealthy with Malinda (a little-known Vermont apple that was introduced by its originator's son to Minnesota in the mid-nineteenth century), was released in 1922, the first of eighteen apples released by the program over its hundred-year history. Each variety takes decades to develop, test, and troubleshoot, and today, the university plants between three thousand and six thousand seedling apples in its orchard each year. Fruit from these trees can be assessed three or four years later, as the trees begin to bear. The university tastes through the thousands of trees in the fall and begins making its decision as to which apples move to the next phase.

Minnesota's fruit breeders have stringent criteria for their apples, as the fruit needs to prove economically viable and delicious and survive a growing list of climate-related problems, from frosts and hail to polar vortexes and −40 degree Fahrenheit winters. Apples that make the cut, so to speak, are transplanted to grower partners around the country so their viability as a commercial apple can be explored, which may take decades.

The University of Minnesota's most famous apple is the Honeycrisp. The first crosses that would eventually birth Honeycrisp took place in 1964, but the apple was not released until 1991. Honeycrisp's signature crunch and sweet, tart flavor captured the minds (and mouths) of the populace at a time when apples were either green or red. Many seasoned orchards were initially skeptical of the new multicolored apple, but consumers loved the crunch, and growers found buyers willing to pay a premium for it. Developed to thrive in the Minnesota cold, Honeycrisp initially did not do well in the

Honeycrisp Lineage

Honeycrisp changed apples in the United States, and many of the subsequent commercially successful apples from the University of Minnesota, like First Kiss and Snow-Sweet, are descendants of Honeycrisp. The apple is widely regarded as a poor cider apple, but its forebears do have some interesting cider qualities. Frostbite, for example, first came into bearing in 1921. Its small size and distinct sugar-cane and pineapple flavors, reminiscent of rhum agricole, make it one of the most divisive apples and a real oddity within breeding trials. It remained obscure, known only as MN 447 until 2008, when it was given the official moniker and finally released for propagation. In 1937 Frostbite was crossed with Northern Spy and officially selected in 1950 as Sweet Sixteen, an apple that shares Frostbite's wild fruitiness and high sugar without the funkier flavors, and one that is used by cidermakers in northern climes. The open pollination of Sweet Sixteen led to the creation of Honeycrisp, which retains the fruit and sugar with the signature snap.

humidity of Virginia or in the high deserts of Washington. But the apple was a game changer for orchards from Minnesota to Maine that could finally give competition to western orchards.

Honeycrisp revitalized Midwest and Northeast orchards and earned the University of Minnesota a seemingly endless supply of funds at the right time. Competition from China had driven apple prices to all-time lows, but Honeycrisp created a marketable mainstream premium apple for U.S. growers. Until the patent expired in 2008, the university received royalties for every Honeycrisp tree that went into the ground. Honeycrisp, the most valuable fruit patent in the history of the country, provided a cushion for the university that allowed it to withstand the waves of funding cuts similar programs saw in the 1990s.

Since its teetotaling roots with Peter Gideon, the U of M program has been focused on fresh table fruit. But recent changes within the university and Minnesota's cider industry have brought cider to the forefront of conversation. The existing collection of cold-hardy apples in the university's orchards are being assessed for cider potential, and new breeding trials are under way to explore the next great northern cider apple.

Minnesota orchards largely grow university-developed apples. A majority of the state's orchards are between thirty and sixty acres, sustained by selling directly to consumers. Equipped with proprietary apples like SweeTango, Zestar!, and First Kiss, growers command some of the highest prices per pound in the nation for their crunchy, sugar-rich, snappy apples. But this can be a double-edged sword. While it fosters a sense of pride and earns growers uncharacteristically high prices, it also deters growers from planting cider apples not fit for market, which—void of a significant cider community—would bring in a significantly lower price per pound. There are also no large processors in the state, and excess apples are typically shipped to Michigan.

Peter Gillitzer, who runs Milk & Honey Ciders with Aaron Klocker and Adam Theis, attributes the state's interest, support, and passion for apples to the ongoing connections Minnesotans have with agriculture. The 3.6 million residents of the Twin Cities account for over two-thirds of Minnesota's population. Many city residents come from farming towns across the state and beyond, and many still have family on a farm or families that own agricultural land that they rent to others. Gillitzer, a sixth-generation Minnesotan, notes that while Minnesota has a global draw, many Minnesota-born residents stick around.

Located an hour and a half north of Saint Paul in Stearns County, Milk and Honey's orchards are planted on an old dairy pasture along a glacial moraine unfit for row crops. Stearns County is the number one dairy county in the state, a result of Minnesota's history of German and Scandinavian farmers. But its modern cultural landscape and that of the greater Twin Cities area draw not only from across the state, but from East Africa and Southeast Asia, evidenced in their significant Somali and Hmong communities. The diverse array of food has informed the greater upper Midwest community, in a sense creating room for new products in the realm of food and beverage.

Milk and Honey's orchards are in a part of Minnesota colloquially known as the Big Woods. It was never a large apple-producing region, but it remains home to countless small homestead orchards with Wealthy and Haralson trees. While larger growers are ripping out old heirloom varieties to plant market-premium university varieties like Honeycrisp and SweeTango, Haralson remains among the most widely planted trees in home orchards. The rest of Milk and Honey's Minnesota fruit comes from the state's larger fruit-growing regions to the south, where there is less rain and more alkaline limestone soil. Their own gravelly, rocky ground covers rich soils, stressing the trees in a positive way and ultimately improving the flavors imparted in cider.

Gillitzer began grafting trees from Fedco in 2011, intent on seeing which varieties could survive Minnesota winters. Years later, he is doubling down on hardy European and American varieties like Kingston Black, Ellis Bitter, Wickson, and Golden Russet. Milk and Honey also sources Chestnut Crab and Northern Spy from the Driftless Area along the Mississippi, as well as Wickson, Kingston Black, and Yarlington Mill from eastern Washington State and New Hampshire. Sourcing from the national landscape brings a unique expression and character to their ciders, and the approach creates a conversation about the differences in where apples come from and the traits they impart to cider. It has also helped Gillitzer home in on the traits of a majority of Minnesota apples—what he describes as a briny, salty, oyster-like minerality.

For Milk and Honey, differentiating cider from the established wine and beer communities in Minnesota has been a challenge, so education has become an integral facet of the brand. Milk and Honey's tasting room, which opened in the summer of 2017, is as much a classroom as it is a place to engage with their product. Before there was a cider community in Minnesota, Milk and Honey followed the lead of the beer market, where sour beers proved to be a gateway to high-acid beverages, wild yeasts, and the nuances of cider.

Just south of the Twin Cities, in Webster, Minnesota, Sweetland Orchard was home to unique apples long before 2010, when Gretchen Perbix purchased the orchard with her husband, Mike Perbix. Fifty varieties of apple trees, planted by the previous owner, were thriving on the loamy soils. The orchard is home to many University of Minnesota varieties, and it pushes the northern boundaries of where hardy winter apples like Northern Spy are able to grow. Perbix has found that many of the university-developed apples, like Centennial Crab, Chestnut Crab, Keepsake, and Sweet Sixteen, make excellent cider. The apples are loaded with acid, sugar, and body, which lend a unique balance of bracing structure not found in European varieties.

Perbix's previous work as an academic grant writer has empowered her and the rest of the Minnesota Cider Guild to obtain cider-related grants for the University of Minnesota. Now the university conducts research into the needs of the cider community, assesses cold hardiness of cider varieties, and delves deeper into cider fruit growing and the analysis of fermented juice.

Minnesota's cider production has already outpaced wine production throughout the state. Perbix has come a long way since her days of fermenting Haralson apples from neighborhood trees, and her community leadership and grant writing have made an undeniable impact on Minnesota cider. In conjunction with the university, she is planting tannic varieties at Sweetland Orchard, which is up to three thousand trees and counting, to see if they can survive the threat of polar vortexes and unforgiving changing climate. With the developing cider industry, Perbix sees a fast-approaching opportunity to inform growers of the economic benefits of growing cider fruit.

Drawn by the oscillating hills, Nate Watters and his wife, Tracy Jonkman, traded a CSA farm in the Connecticut Valley in 2009 for an orchard perched above a Mississippi tributary in Rice County, south of the Twin Cities. A northern New York native, Watters set out to make distinctive cider that could only come from Minnesota. This meant using only Minnesota fruit, so Watters has partnered with eight local growers. He relies on native, wild yeasts for fermentations, and lets those fermentations carry out until there is no residual sugar, which he says can mask the nuances of apples.

Watters credits his New York days as the inspiration for starting an orchard. He lived in Plattsburgh, just south of Canada "near the Mac capital of the world," he says, in reference to Lake Champlain McIntosh apples. While his Minnesota orchard is filled with tannic apples he planted in 2014, his Keepsake Cidery produces cider that is full of heirlooms and university-developed apples, including the cidery's namesake. Keepsake is a university cross of Northern Spy and Malinda, an obscure New England apple, from the same breeding trials that developed Sweet Sixteen in the 1930s. Watter says he chose the name because Keepsake is not the prettiest or biggest apple, it does not catch your eye, it comes in late, and there is no big ad campaign behind it. But, in his eyes, it is one of the most delicious apples to ever come from Minnesota.

Watters has been eager to experiment with fermenting the university-bred apples. Some, like Keepsake, have been inspirational discoveries. Others, like Frostbite and Honeycrisp, have not translated well into cider, where the process of fermentation leaves little more than saccharine sweetness and flavors of lemon and caramel. In the case of Honeycrisp, though, with its high sugar content, Watters sees potential for producing ice cider.

Minnesota's changing climate creates a host of challenges for growers, who continue to battle invasive and native pests as well as hotter summers and later frosts. Late-blooming European cider apples are a recent addition to the state's orchard landscape, and January 2019 was the real test for many infant orchards, when temperatures dropped to −40 degrees Fahrenheit. But the freeze does not scare Watters. For him, as the trees leave dormancy and bloom in the spring, it is a chance to learn which varieties are able to bounce back from the extreme cold. For now, Watters considers his orchard not one full of cider fruit, but a petri dish under close observation, from which he can glean the varieties that will be viable in Minnesota for future cider orchards.

Driftless Area

As the Mississippi River flows over Saint Anthony Falls in Minneapolis, the gentle inclines of the riverbanks grow into a dramatic limestone canyon with the meandering river at its floor. Furiously draining glacial lakes created a torrent of water that pierced through the Driftless Area and formed the valley gorge. This area earned its Driftless moniker because it is one of the few reaches of the northern states that was never conquered by glaciers. Jagged outcrops and narrow river-dug ravines cut through the rolling hills, creating unique microclimates that have enabled orchards to dot the hillside and plateaus since early European settlement.

Although there is no formal boundary, the Driftless Area is centered along the Mississippi River, beginning in southwestern Wisconsin and running from southeast Minnesota, through Iowa, and into northwestern Illinois. As the river courses onward past the Driftless Area, the walls of the river valley recede and the floodplain widens for the rest of its course toward the Gulf of Mexico. Pioneers to the area—then and now—quickly learned the benefits of airflow through the valley, as they had seen in the Hudson and Ohio River valleys.

Despite the growing apple and cider industry, Wisconsin remains a dairy state, a course set largely by early Norwegian and German farmers who found that cows and cranberries sustained viable industries through fierce winters. Iconic large red dairy barns dot the hills as the Driftless Area begins to soften, where rock protrusions round into gentle hills before settling into flat lakeshores.

Deirdre Birmingham worked for years in agricultural development nonprofits before she and her husband, John Biondi, bought a farm in Mineral Point, Wisconsin, with no business model in mind. No one had lived on the old dairy farm for decades, but there were wild apple trees everywhere. Research led them to English and French cider apples, and they saw cider as an opportunity to implement their farming philosophy of working together to make a farm-based, value-added product. They started planting in 2003, and now the Cider Farm orchard has nearly ten thousand trees, planted mostly with tannin-rich varieties, intermixed with acid-driven, disease-resistant apples like Liberty and Priscilla. In March of 2019, after operating for eight years in a borrowed facility, they opened their own Cidery and Tasting Room in Madison.

Tannic varieties were hard to come by when Birmingham was first getting started, so she sourced most of the trees from Dan Bussey, who started collecting tannic apples in the early 1980s on a four-acre orchard in Edgerton, Wisconsin, southeast of Madison. Bussey, who worked in the restaurant equipment business for forty years, became intrigued by the diversity of nineteenth-century apples when he started reading old pomological texts in college. He grew up on a farm in rural Wisconsin, surrounded by cold-hardy apples like Duchess of Oldenburg and Fameuse (aka Snow), and he recalls hearing stories from his grandfather about a lost Perkins tree, a Minnesota variety with a convoluted history that led him to place a want ad in a local paper. After he got a call from someone with a Perkins tree, it set him on the course of tracking down old trees. Once he had the bug, Bussey collected and cultivated 350 varieties, focusing on lost heirloom apples from the nation's past.

He bought a Mount Gilead apple press that was made in Ohio at the turn of the twentieth century, and in the mid-1980s, after a trip to a Madison homebrew shop to buy equipment, he ended up selling his pressed juice to the burgeoning home cidermaking community. When laws changed to reflect the growing risk of *E. coli,* he was unable to sell cider from the farm, but locals continued to bring their fruit to press for their own use.

Bussey was drawn away from his orchard to the other side of the Mississippi River, to Decorah, Iowa, to manage the growing orchard for Seed Savers Exchange. The nonprofit organization— a network of plant enthusiasts who cultivate, collect, and spread unique plants across the country—was created in 1989 to preserve many of the homestead varieties found throughout the upper Midwest. Bussey expanded the orchard from five hundred varieties at the beginning of his tenure to around fifteen hundred, including nearly a hundred cider varieties, by the time he departed in 2017. Bussey assembled his decades of cumulative, comprehensive research into *The Illustrated History of Apples in North America and Canada,* an invaluable seven-volume resource of catalogs, history, and descriptions of sixteen thousand of the continent's apples.

Golden Russet, one of Bussey's favorite russeted apples, is scattered throughout old orchards across the Driftless Area. Many of the trees were planted by the previous generation's struggling dairy farmers, looking to secure some extra income by diversifying and establishing reliable perennial crops in lean times. Marie and Matt Raboin, who operate Brix Cider in Mount Horeb, Wisconsin, supplement their thousand-tree orchard in nearby Barneveld with apples from some of these old orchards. Like Deirdre Birmingham, the Raboins both returned from nonprofit agricultural work in Africa intent on growing apples. They, too, saw that the only way to make their small orchard successful was to create a final product, so they started planting in 2014 and released their first commercial cider three years later. Their taproom in Mount Horeb celebrates their grower partnerships by offering a rotating selection of single-orchard ciders made from each of the orchards they source from.

The Raboins also work with Bussey, picking from his orchard and fermenting his fruit. If an apple's juice stands out when fermented, they will then plant it in Barneveld. The couple is committed to making an American cider, so instead of forcing European apples to grow in Wisconsin, they propagate wild apples in addition to planting domestic varieties, to learn what ferments to their liking and grows well in their climate.

In December 2012, Elizabeth Griffith left her acting career in New York City to return to her family's Door Creek Orchard just outside of Madison. Her parents, former schoolteachers, purchased the old Norwegian homestead in 1984 from the last generation that was interested in farming. They focused on biodiversity and soil regeneration, so not all of the farm's eighty acres are planted with trees. Much has been left as prairie woodland and marsh, and orchards are rotated with sheep in the fall to facilitate soil health. The animals eat dropped apples, some of which may carry or develop disease that would otherwise work its way into the soil and next year's crop.

Since they purchased the farm, the family has slowly uprooted Red Delicious and Rome Beauty trees to make room for heirlooms like Grimes Golden, Esopus Spitzenburg, Wolf River, Chestnut Crab, and nearly a hundred other varieties. Wisconsin has very few commercial wholesale growers, which Griffith attributes to the colder climes and lack of lake moderation, but it leaves her more room to experiment with heirloom apples and disease-resistant trees like their U-Pick favorite: Pixie Crunch. While Griffith does not make cider commercially, juice from her late-season russets is a perennial favorite for home cidermakers, and, when there is time and surplus, her husband is able to squirrel away a few carboys for basement experiments.

Western Lake Michigan

In contrast to the carved, hilly landscape of western Wisconsin, the state's eastern lakeshore along Lake Michigan is filled with mementos from its glacial history. Deep loamy soils are speckled with teardrop-shaped hills of sandy glacial deposits called drumlins. Underground ice pockets melted as glaciers retreated, soil collapsed, and kettle lakes formed as a result. Because of its depth, Lake Michigan rarely freezes and generally maintains steady, yearly temperatures around 45 degrees Fahrenheit. Air temperatures drop well below zero in winter, but the lake's depth helps protect against some of the worst temperature fluctuations.

Wisconsin's orchards are dwarfed in scope by their counterparts across the lake in Michigan, which is warmer than the Wisconsin side, but the lake does make eastern Wisconsin warmer than the western part. In northern Wisconsin, the temperate Door Peninsula juts into the lake—creating Green Bay—and has historically been home to many of the state's apple and cherry orchards, where fruit thrives in the well-drained limestone and glacial loam soils. In addition to sharing the moderating effects of the lake, Wisconsin and Michigan both benefit from university work and have a diversity of apple cultivars. But Wisconsin falls behind Michigan in total production. Whereas Michigan quantities and cold-storage facilities enable that state to sell apples year-round, Wisconsin lacks both, so the market is all harvest-driven in the fall.

Yannique and Bob Purman of Island Orchard Cider rely on fruit from their orchard on Washington Island, five miles northeast of the Door Peninsula. The peninsula's beauty draws 2.5 million visitors a year, and the Purmans first came to the island as a vacation destination during the summer, to escape Milwaukee.

Settled by Icelandic and Scandinavian immigrants, the island's year-round population of six hundred swells to four thousand during the summer. While Bob had always been interested in fermentation, the Purmans first started to look at cider more seriously in the early 2000s, inspired by visits to Yannique's father in Brittany, France. The weather in Wisconsin is much more severe, despite sharing a similar latitude, but the Purmans began to see similarities between Brittany's maritime climate and rocky shores and the old farm they owned on Washington Island. They planted an orchard there in 2006, and it has grown to include thirty-five varieties of French, English, and American cider apples. The Purmans also draw from existing Door Peninsula orchards, where many growers have a mix of old, cold-hardy varieties like McIntosh and Cortland in addition to modern varieties.

More and more orchards across the region are pursuing cider, but the push has been shackled in part by entrenched industry. Powerful tavern leagues and distribution lobbies have had a disproportionate say in the future of craft beverage producers across the state. Rather than seeing cider as an extension of local agricultural endeavors that have potential to draw tourism, a spike in cider sales, some argue, threatens a dip in beer sales. Efforts from small producer organizations have fallen on deaf ears, as Wisconsin has been slow to adopt many of the progressive farm laws that have enabled growth in places like New York and neighboring Minnesota. While this may change as the cider industry continues to gain momentum, it has been an unfortunate reality for cidermakers in Wisconsin.

In the mid-1990s, cider-curious Illinois-based chemist Charles McGonegal called every orchard located within sixty miles of Chicago. He was on the hunt for Ribston Pippin, a multipurpose English variety he had come across only in literature. Brightonwoods Orchard, just north of the Illinois border near Milwaukee, did not have Ribston Pippin, but McGonagall learned that they did have other unique heirlooms. Brightonwoods was started as a hobby farm in the 1950s and has since grown to include two hundred varieties on 18.5 acres.

After years of making award-winning amateur cider, McGonagall took ÆppelTreow Winery and Distillery commercial in 2001, when he and his wife, Melissa, partnered with Brightonwoods and leased a decades-old animal barn on the property. ÆppelTreow, which translates to "apple truth" in Old English, has proved an elusive concept, as they work to perfect their craft and style and adjust to the demands of the climate and market.

Lake Michigan's southern tip extends to Gary, Indiana, where Stan Wash planted Overgrown Orchard with trees from Cummins Nursery in the Finger Lakes and Virginia's Albemarle CiderWorks.

The orchard, which sits on a fallow soybean farm where loamy river soils once helped feed industrial cities around the lake, has grown to four hundred trees comprising sixty different varieties. Wash oversees it with three friends. Where many orchards are defined by sweeping landscape and rolling hills, Overgrown is at the intersection of highways and abandoned rail lines. But it is still able to contribute to cider's presence in Chicago.

While waiting for their orchard trees to bear fruit, Wash and his friends work with Nichols Farm and Orchard northwest of Chicago. Wash first learned about Nichols at a farmers' market. He was making cider vinegar and came across a number of varieties he was unfamiliar with at the Nichols stand. A consistent farmers' market vendor for years, Nichols Farm's mature trees and supply of heirloom apples gave Overgrown Orchard the raw materials to enter the natural wine and craft beer bars in Chicago. They have found particular success at their modest size, producing 2,500 gallons a year while everyone maintains their respective day jobs. In addition to Winter Banana, a late-season apple native to Indiana, Overgrown uses wild crab apples sourced from the metro area and relies on a juice base from Cox's Orange Pippin, striking a balance between local fruit and European structure.

Southeastern Lake Michigan

Southwest Michigan grows around 70 percent of the apples for the entire state, which ranks third nationally, behind Washington and New York. The number of orchards in Michigan declined as mid-twentieth-century innovations consolidated orchards close to cities and processing facilities, but the state's orchard products valued $122 million in 2019.

Orchards in southwest Michigan were built for processing, as these apples do not have the crunch or other qualities desired for fresh eating. Michigan-based operations like Tyson and Gerber turn millions of tons of apples into frozen pies and applesauce each year.

These old processing varieties also have high acids and sugars, which translate magnificently to bright and crisp ciders.

On Lake Michigan's eastern shore, Virtue Cider is the brainchild of Greg Hall, former brewmaster of national beer brand Goose Island—which his dad, John, grew and sold to Anheuser-Busch. Greg's goal was to make European-style cider for a national audience. Redstreak, Virtue's first cider, was scaled from basement carboys to a winery in Michigan and then quickly lapped up by Chicago bars and restaurants.

Investments poured in after Redstreak's initial success, and Hall financed a massive ciderhouse in Fennville on fifty acres in the heart of Lake Michigan's premier fruit farms. Entering 2012, Virtue was equipped to sell the hundreds of thousands of gallons of cider being processed at the cidery, drawing apples from local orchards and cider apples from Mineral Point's Cider Farm as well as Poverty Lane Orchards in New Hampshire.

Hall adopted many of the practices that made Goose Island successful, crafting a quality product that sold at premium prices: twenty-five dollars for a 750-milliliter bottle. But while cider fans liked the dry, European-style cider, it couldn't penetrate the larger general market. The high-priced bottles languished on shelves, leaving the whole system in disarray. In 2015, the orchard, two massive ciderhouses, and Virtue's large debt were bought by Anheuser-Busch. Since the sale, many of the original intentions of the brand have changed: bottles are supplemented with cans, and rosé ciders with more residual sugar have joined the ranks of the dry cider that launched the brand.

Virtue's problems have been a learning experience for many within the industry, and there has not been a national brand with their vision to sell cider at that price, on that scale, since. Still, Michigan orchards continue to plant more tannic apples, and cidermakers continue to open their doors, albeit with different business models informed by Virtue's launch.

By volume, the densest area for fruit growing in this part of

Michigan is known as the Fruit Ridge. Located near Grand Rapids in Kent County, glacial deposits of clay loam rise up over two hundred feet above the lakeshore twenty-five miles east of the water's edge. With excellent air drainage and frost protection from the moderated lake, the area was a large supplier of fruit to a growing nineteenth-century Chicago. Peaches were the primary crop then, but in the early twentieth century a devastating winter forced many growers to convert to later blooming apples.

In the last decade and a half, the ridge has undergone another dramatic shift in the orchard landscape. The declining price of processing apples has moved many growers to plant higher-valued fresh eating apples like Honeycrisp and Gala. Today, apples arrive at packing houses and are put through optical sorting machines that can do the job seasonal workers once did. Top-grade fruit ends up in grocery stores, while other apples are destined to be sliced for pie filling, where the size and shape of the apples is still very important. If apple size falls outside the prescribed norms of the market, they are deemed juice apples. These blemished apples have helped shape the cider industry in Michigan, allowing once-small operations like Vander Mill to become large, significant regional producers.

When Paul and Amanda Vander Heide opened Vander Mill in Spring Lake in 2006, the couple did not expect to be selling throughout the Midwest and Kentucky ten years later. The plan was to have a small retail cider operation that catered to the local community. But a handshake partnership with nearby Dietrich Orchards, a family operation in Michigan's Fruit Ridge, has provided Vander Mill with the resources to find consistent growth. After selling most of their cider from their small taproom, Vander Mill began selling to Chicago in 2011, funding the first stage of their expansion.

Despite setbacks, including particularly rough weather in 2012 that destroyed 90 percent of Vander Mill's crop, cider continues to grow throughout Michigan. Local hometown cider brands from outside Detroit in the east to Grand Rapids in the west, and from the southwestern fruit belt north to the Upper Peninsula, all have their own devoted followings. Michigan is the state with the most members in the American Cider Association, and together, efforts are made to educate the Michigan consumer on what Paul Vander Heide says is a grassroots scale: local people making local products and talking to their respective communities about it. Vander Heide believes that state pride in local products stems from the automobile industry and the heyday of the Motor City of Detroit.

Vander Mill's success was built on the eating apples of the Fruit Ridge, but Vander Heide and Dietrich Orchards also planted twenty acres of bittersweet apples in 2016, the same year Vander Mill expanded their operation from the original Spring Lake location to Grand Rapids. While planting bittersweet varieties is generally considered a risk for growers, Dietrich is large enough that the small acreage will not pose a threat to the overall operation. But both parties understand the gamble in tannic fruit. For Vander Mill, even if the apples prove successful, it remains unclear whether the cider made from the apples will enjoy the same success the brand has found with their cider produced from eating apples.

For Vander Heide, it is important for cider to be available at multiple price points and in various formats—from costly 750-milliliter bottles to cheaper six-pack cans. With help from other Michigan cider producers, he was able to transform the Michigan Wine Council—which initially refused membership to cideries— into the Michigan Craft Beverage Council to represent cider and craft beer as well as wine. It is another step in making cider a beverage for everyone.

While the Fruit Ridge dominates Michigan's contemporary apple industry by volume, the state was once filled with small orchards that catered to local markets. Orchards like Uncle John's Cider Mill, in central Michigan, sustained the shift to large processing plants by positioning themselves as an agricultural experience as early as the 1970s. John Beck, the fourth generation to operate the farm, bought it from his parents and turned barns into gift shops that drew people off the highway and into the orchard. Their parking lot spans thirty acres, and every spot gets filled over Columbus Day weekend.

For generations the family stored cider for themselves. But in 2003, Beck's son Mike made it part of their growing business. Uncle John's semidry canned ciders are made mostly with Rhode Island Greening, while their other ciders take advantage of processing favorites like Northern Spy, Winesap, and Jonathan. Beck's own ten acres of bittersweets add additional complexity to their ciders, and their Melded cider brings together the varieties of Michigan's past with the newly introduced tannic apples to build something that is proudly Michigan. As consumers become increasingly familiar with the nuances of their ciders, Mike continues to tweak by fermenting them drier year after year.

Great Lakes International Cider and Perry Competition (GLINTCAP)

Every spring, cidermakers from around the globe descend upon Grand Rapids, Michigan, to taste, scrutinize, and judge their colleagues' previous year's work. GLINTCAP is the largest cider competition in the world, having eclipsed England's Royal Bath and West Show in 2016. Sponsored by the Michigan Cider Association, the contest has retained its strong emphasis on home cidermakers even as it grows. The awards list reads like an up-and-coming scouting report for who is making the best new ciders in the United States.

Thirty miles north, Eastman's Antique Apples was started in the late 1970s on a century-old family farm in Wheeler. It grew to nearly a thousand varieties on three thousand trees over fourteen acres. Rafe Ward's uncle started the farm as a hobby that morphed out of control. His parents bought the property when Ward graduated from college, and duties were split between his family and the family of his wife, Nicole. They began selling apples at farmers' markets, where they often had in excess of fifty varieties on offer, each with its own story.

After ten years as part-time orchardists, Rafe and Nicole stepped up to take over the orchard full time. Today some of Eastman's Forgotten Ciders are among only a handful of ciders in the country made from red-fleshed apples like Redfield and Hidden Rose (aka Airlie Red Flesh and Mountain Rose). The rising tide of rosé cider across the country has been great for business, but the Wards have to remind people why theirs is so special in a sea of adjuncts. Early rosé ciders made by Virtue and Uncle John's both featured Eastman's apples.

Red-Fleshed Apples

Red-fleshed apples have been a novelty of the apple community for generations. Niedzwetzkyana, a red-fleshed apple from the mountains of Central Asia that has produced many other red-fleshed progeny, first arrived in North America at the end of the nineteenth century, and later passed into the hands of breeders and university programs. Many of these apples are tart, astringent, and certainly not ideal for eating fresh, but apples like Redfield have been embraced by the cider community for decades. Geneticists at Michigan State University are looking for the next great red-fleshed cider apple and finding promise in Cranberry and Otterson.

Grand Traverse Bay and Northern Michigan

Traverse City, in northwestern Michigan, has been a prized fruit-growing region for over a century. Grand Traverse Bay, to the north, is separated from the rest of Lake Michigan by the Leelanau Peninsula, then further bisected into the East and West Bay by the smaller Old Mission Peninsula, named for the Native American reservation established there in 1836.

Located hours from any major city, Traverse City farms have focused on processing fruit for decades. Peterson Farms, one hundred miles south, is the largest processor east of the Mississippi, providing apple products for the likes of McDonald's and Subway. While the counties around the bay represent roughly 25 percent of the state's apple crop, the area is the tart cherry capital of the country.

With the bay's moderating effects, apples in this part of the state emerge from winter after their southern and midstate counterparts. In devastating years, like 2012, delayed bud break in Traverse City has protected trees from the catastrophes that unfold in other parts of the state.

Nikki Rothwell serves a dual role in this community. She is a Michigan State extension agent—coordinating researchers with farmers—and co-owner of Tandem Ciders with her husband, Dan Young, who was a partner and brewer at the People's Pint brewpub in Greenfield, Massachusetts, where he had been serving West County Cider since day one. In 2004, after they moved back to Rothwell's home state of Michigan, the couple started looking at the glut of apples left behind by the processing industry. They called West County's Terry Maloney, who offered invaluable advice on how to move forward.

Tandem Ciders was built on the earlier generation of processing apples like Rhode Island Greening and McIntosh, which make up their Greenman and Smackintosh ciders, respectively. Young pays growers above market value for apples to dissuade them from tearing out their old trees for newer apples or land developers, and Rothwell informs them about what cider varieties grow well in Michigan.

Tandem benefits from both tourists visiting Traverse City and Chicagoans who identify with the area. In the 1890s, Chicago residents took excursion boats across the lake to destination spots along Michigan's fruit belt, informing future generations of the cultural exchange along the lake.

Today, dozens of wineries dot the hillside and bluffs of former cherry orchards along Traverse Bay. Left Foot Charley started as a winery in 2004 but, within a few years, winemaker Bryan Ulbrich expanded to apples alongside his Riesling and Blaufränkisch. He doubled down on the label's cider efforts in 2014 after a devastating grape harvest left many of his tanks empty. Inspired by the state's— and nation's—tradition of apple growing, opposed to its more adolescent efforts with grapes, he began planting an experimental orchard for more tannic apples. The orchard has begun to bear, with interesting results that are mostly served on-premise alongside cider made from Otterson apples Ulbrich receives from the university research program.

Left Foot Charley's taproom experience has something for everyone, from tannic, unfiltered cider to Cabernet Franc and their best-selling Cinnamon Girl cider, which keeps the lights on throughout the year. Many wineries and breweries have looked to Left Foot Charley for guidance on how to add cider arms to their operations. Since Left Foot introduced cider in 2008, it has surpassed wine production by 150 percent, something Ulbrich attributes to cider's approachability. Their wine tends to sell to more established restaurants that serve premium glass pours, while their cider is served at the local bowling alley.

Farther north in Michigan's Upper Peninsula, Phil Kelm and Tom Adolphs forage wild apples on the Keweenaw Peninsula for their Gitche Gumee Ciderworks. The Upper Peninsula makes up almost one-third of the state's land area but only 3 percent of its total population. Homesteaders, drawn by the massive copper mines, etched out farms in the dense woods. Commercial orchards were never a success in the unforgiving winters and short growing season. Instead, Kelm and Adolphs collect community-sourced wild apples, paying by the pound for what shows up at their door. Like other feral apples, these tiny, untended, acidic, and tannic apples are survivors. They deliver a unique sampling not only of Gitche Gumee's small production, but of greater Michigan.

Core Takeaways

The Midwest was the first frontier for the United States after independence, and it became the first testing ground for agricultural innovation and invention as techniques from the coast came west. Educational institutions remain a vital resource as farmers grapple with an ever-changing set of challenges and pave the way for growth. Large farms growing cash crops have dominated the landscape since the nineteenth century and only grew more consolidated in the twentieth century. These tottering giants began to crumble as prices dropped and farmers looked to diversify into new markets. Cider has filled the void left behind by sagging applesauce sales, as old orchards are being redirected into the glass rather than the jar. Over the centuries, research centers and their extension agents have found ways to propel the region's growth in the face of frost, climate change, and economic downturns, helping not only to grow fruit but also to find an audience for the region's bounty.

MISSISSIPPI RIVER VALLEY

• **Location and Geography:** Large amounts of agricultural lands in the Upper Midwest, centered around the Twin Cities of Saint Paul and Minneapolis.
• **Soil:** Stony gravel and glacial till are found in the big woods north of the Twin Cities, with more alluvial and clay soils south along the Mississippi River.

- **Climate:** Continental climate with few to no climate moderators, extremely cold winters, and hot summers. USDA Hardiness Zone 4a–4b.
- **Orchard Location:** Orchards are found south of the Twin Cities above the Mississippi River gorge and north of the cities in the Big Woods, a former dairy heartland.
- **Orchard Type:** Most of the orchards in the state are direct retail operations selling cold-hardy cultivars developed by the University of Minnesota, fetching some of the country's highest prices per pound.
- **Significant Apple Varieties:** Honeycrisp, Zestar!, Haralson, SweeTango, Sweet Sixteen, Keepsake, Hyslop Crab, Frostbite, Golden Russet.
- **Cider Apple Plantings:** Limited to estate cideries and university experiments.
- **Producers to Visit:** Milk and Honey Ciders (Saint Joseph, MN), Keepsake Cidery (Dundas, MN), Sweetland Orchard (Webster, MN), Number 12 Cider (Minneapolis, MN).

DRIFTLESS AREA

- **Location and Geography:** Unlike the rest of the Upper Midwest, this area—consisting of western Wisconsin and the immediate areas in Minnesota, Iowa, and Illinois—was never covered in glaciers. Instead, the terrain is a series of oscillating hills and valleys.
- **Soil:** Windblown loess and eroded silts are found throughout the often steep terrain.
- **Climate:** Humid continental climate, with excellent air drainage through the hills and into the Mississippi River. USDA Hardiness Zone 4b–5a.
- **Orchard Location:** Old orchards can be found throughout the old dairy country, from the western bank of the river to the suburbs of Madison, WI, with some larger operations near Gay Mills, WI, and in the areas immediately near the river.
- **Orchard Type:** Some are involved in fresh packing, but most are geared toward direct-to-consumer sales.
- **Significant Apple Varieties:** Wolf River, Prairie Spy, McIntosh, Northwest Greening, Haralson, Honeycrisp, Wealthy, Chestnut Crab, Geneva Tremlett's, Dabinett, Yarlington Mill.
- **Cider Apple Plantings:** Some estate cideries have cider apples, with increasingly more homestead and smaller plantings going in the ground.
- **Producers to Visit:** The Cider Farm (Madison, WI), Brix Cider (Mount Horeb, WI), Restoration Cider (Madison, WI).

WESTERN LAKE MICHIGAN

• **Location and Geography:** The lake-adjacent areas of Illinois and Wisconsin.

• **Soil:** Largely pocketed with sinkhole lakes and drumlin fields left behind from centuries of glacial activity. The Door Peninsula has more limestone and gravel, as one of the western extensions of the Niagara Escarpment.

• **Climate:** Humid continental climate, with strong moderation from the lake, though less so than on the eastern shore, where the prevailing winds do not pass over the lake. USDA Hardiness Zone 5b.

• **Orchard Location:** Orchards are found in both formerly urban and suburban communities, with the greatest concentration along the warmer Door Peninsula.

• **Orchard Type:** Most of the orchards are geared toward fresh eating or retail, with no processing on this side of the lake. Much of the fruit goes to hungry markets in Milwaukee and Chicago.

• **Significant Apple Varieties:** Cox's Orange Pippin, Frequin Rouge, Honeycrisp, Northwest Greening.

• **Cider Apple Plantings:** The area has some established estate cideries, with other small plots in production.

• **Producers to Visit:** ÆppelTreow Winery and Distillery (Burlington, WI), Island Orchard Cider (Ellison Bay, WI), ERIS Brewery and Cider House (Chicago, IL).

SOUTHEASTERN LAKE MICHIGAN

• **Location and Geography:** Extending from North of Grand Rapids, MI, to Indiana, Lake Michigan is 922 feet deep and 118 feet wide at its widest point.

• **Soil:** Deep, rich clay soils left behind from when the lake was larger.

• **Climate:** Temperate climate severely moderated by the lake. USDA Hardiness Zone 5b–6b.

• **Orchard Location:** Most of the orchards are located near the lake, except, notably, those in the Fruit Ridge. Located just north of Grand Rapids, this intensely cultivated rise in the terrain runs eight miles wide and twenty miles long and produces nearly two-thirds of Michigan's apples.

• **Orchard Type:** Formerly focused on processing apples, since the 1990s orchards have moved increasingly toward fresh eating apples.

• **Significant Apple Varieties:** Honeycrisp, Idared, Cox Orange Pippin, Northern Spy, Crispin, Braeburn, Jonagold, Paula Red, Rome Beauty, Rhode Island Greening.

- **Cider Apple Plantings:** A growing number of cider apple trees are going in the ground, as both large growers and smaller businesses seek to innovate. Many are looking to sell apples rather than make cider themselves.
- **Producers to Visit:** Vander Mill (Grand Rapids, MI), Uncle John's Cider Mill (Saint Johns, MI), Virtue Cider (Fennville, MI).

GRAND TRAVERSE BAY AND NORTHERN MICHIGAN

- **Location and Geography:** At nearly the northern tip of Michigan's Lower Peninsula, the Grand Traverse Bay area is very hilly, with what were once islands that became connected to the mainland as the water level receded.
- **Soil:** Complex glacier soils, with clay and sand over limestone and granite.
- **Climate:** Lake Michigan and the bay, enclosed by the Leelanau and Old Mission Peninsulas, help moderate the climate. The area's unique microclimates create a long growing season for such a northern latitude. USDA Hardiness Zone 5b–6b.
- **Orchard Location:** Orchards are found on both the peninsulas and in the surrounding areas.
- **Orchard Type:** With urban markets hours away, this area has largely concentrated on processing apples. Wine tourism has been a part of the community since the 1970s and has helped establish the area as a beverage tourist destination.
- **Significant Apple Varieties:** McIntosh, Rhode Island Greening, Jonathan, Northern Spy, Honeycrisp, Red Delicious.
- **Cider Apple Plantings:** Some of the larger growers have begun experimenting with cider apples, and several estate producers have them in the ground, though few have reached maturity.
- **Producers to Visit:** Tandem Ciders (Suttons Bay, MI), Left Foot Charley (Traverse City, MI), Townline Ciderworks (Williamsburg, MI).

Apples and Myths in the American Frontier

In the quilt of American folklore, Johnny Appleseed takes ample cloth. He is often touted as a barefoot hugger of trees and planter of seeds, who wandered the new frontier on a mission for orchards. But his portrayal has been spun from mythic yarn, with an idealized narrative taking the place of the man's actual life. Descriptions of Johnny Appleseed are almost intentionally loose and elastic: He is a relatable, shapeshifting character who fits into any and all counterculture movements that have surfaced throughout the nation's history. Funny enough, he has not been painted as a pomologist, horticulturist, or agrarian, but as a transient recluse who wept for the tyranny of humanity and shed apple seeds as tears.

Many stories have been woven into the fabric since John "Appleseed" Chapman's birth in Leominster, Massachusetts, in 1774, but they serve the imagination and silver screen better than they do seekers of history. What is known is that Chapman moved west and planted countless apple seeds along the way, mostly in Ohio; ultimately settled in Fort Wayne, Indiana, where he died in 1845; and then became a dramatically misrepresented cultural icon in 1871, when writer W. D. Haley published an embellished history in *Harper's New Monthly Magazine*.

The nickname "Appleseed" was not used in association with Chapman until May 1821, when he was forty-six. Any documentation of a John Chapman—or any nameless apple seed planter—before that point may or may not have been him.

Chapman's legend is tied less to record than to an American people trying to understand the shifting social notions of their mercantile future by looking to their agrarian past. By the end of the nineteenth century, the seemingly limitless, expanding frontier had reached the Pacific and, for the first time, the nation had to grapple with the confines of boundaries. Cultural diversity prevailed, and it permeated the entire country. The legend of Johnny Appleseed became a relic and symbol, the story of a distant era marked by opportunity and endless potential.

Chapman is rarely, if ever, mentioned in the celebrated texts and specific works of horticulture and pomology from his time. While little is known of his New York path, he ended up in Venango County, Pennsylvania, having moved southwest from Warren, just north of what has become Allegheny National Forest. Chapman found little success with his first planted seedling trees in Pennsylvania, where grafted trees were taking hold and beginning to produce superior fruit. So he went west, into the frontier.

Chapman crossed the Ohio state line and moved southwest toward Columbus, arriving in Licking County around 1801. To the southeast lies Marietta, where George Washington had his land office and where veterans seeking their land grants were required to go for the deeds. Veterans were sent on their way from the land office with apple seeds, which were to be planted and cared for, to prevent land speculation.

Chapman dedicated the first quarter of the nineteenth century to central Ohio, where he traveled, planted, and tended trees between Mansfield and Licking County. His approach was to scatter seeds, loosely enclose them with brush piles, and return some years later to sell any surviving saplings for a meager gain. In some instances, Chapman borrowed from known techniques of the Wyandot people, who had orchards along the south shore of Lake Erie and into Ohio, down the Sandusky River. He, like the Wyandot, planted seeds at the confluence of two rivers, leaving two sides of the future orchard somewhat protected by water. The third side would be guarded by a makeshift fence of whatever brush resulted from the lightly cleared wood patch.

Chapman dabbled later with leasing government plots, and he ultimately bought land outright in western Ohio and eastern Indiana, near his final resting place of Fort Wayne. His nomadic tendencies favored his early reputation. Guided by wanderlust, Chapman occasionally set forth to establish nurseries on new land that was not largely populated—difficult to get to and removed from navigable waterways. In this regard he was well intentioned, but he remained a bit player in the grander scheme of homesteading and orcharding in the nineteenth century. He had completely settled in Fort Wayne by 1836, and, in the years before his death, purchased close to two hundred acres from Fort Wayne to as far west as Wabash Township, about thirty miles from the Illinois border. His death was sudden, brought about by late-winter illness in March 1845.

In an era when internal improvements and increased transportation enabled national communication for the first time, it is no wonder the words "Johnny Appleseed" went from lip to lip, county to county, and state to state. Transportation was changing the very notion of pioneering and going west, and Chapman entered American folklore as the frontier was becoming a myth unto itself. His eccentricities and projected kindness distracted Americans from the genocide and displacement of Indigenous populations that defined the country's expansion. Chapman's story championed white settlers and their journey into new, untouched land while ignoring the realities of displaced communities.

Chapman scattered thousands of apple seeds, but none of his trees ever bore documented commercially viable fruit. The seeds Chapman planted, which were gathered almost exclusively from cider mills, spawned new varieties of apples at a time when established nurseries in the Midwest and on the East Coast had already begun planting grafted trees of named varieties. While breeders cultivated the next generation of eating fruit, Chapman's seedling apples would be useful only for the cider press. It is likely that those who knew how chose to graft over his fruiting trees with scions of reliable, reputable fruit they traveled with or purchased from established local nurseries on their way into the frontier.

Chapman's journey is disconnected from the cultivated apple culture that grew up in his romping ground in future generations.

By the dawn of the Civil War, the seedling apple culture that had been the backbone of cider in North America was being replaced with grafted orchards. Later observers of Chapman firmly assign him to the dominant culture, rather than the last throes of alternative cultivation. In that way, his horticultural anarchism was yoked by the dominant market-driven culture. Chapman's lifestyle and the feral trees he harbored are eulogized by Henry David Thoreau in his 1862 essay "Wild Apples." Writing a generation after Chapman, Thoreau bemoaned the loss of his beloved, unpredictable, mouth-watering, fleeting wild apples that were succumbing to an urban America. His seedling cider orchards did not have a place among the apple pie, apple fritters, and applesauce of the twentieth century. Instead, the culture was largely forgotten about until 2001, when Michael Pollan's book *The Botany of Desire* brought cider back to the seedling, and Chapman into the popular narrative.

Chapman came to personify the frontier as a rural hero and farming pioneer who embodied the American spirit. His story remains deeply rooted in the pastoral landscape of the American frontier, and he has become a peg from the past that forever finds a hole in present narratives. Chapman's seeding legacy is incongruent with the tidy rows of vast orchards that have sprung up over the past century but more attuned to the new generation of cidermakers exploring seedling fruit again. This nomad was part of a millennium of people who grew apples from seed rather than graft, but during his time he was the outcast. Had he been born a hundred years before, his seedling apples would have blended into the frontier. He was a man out of time, practicing a dying way of life that did not fit with the market-driven lifestyle that took hold in the development of the Midwest.

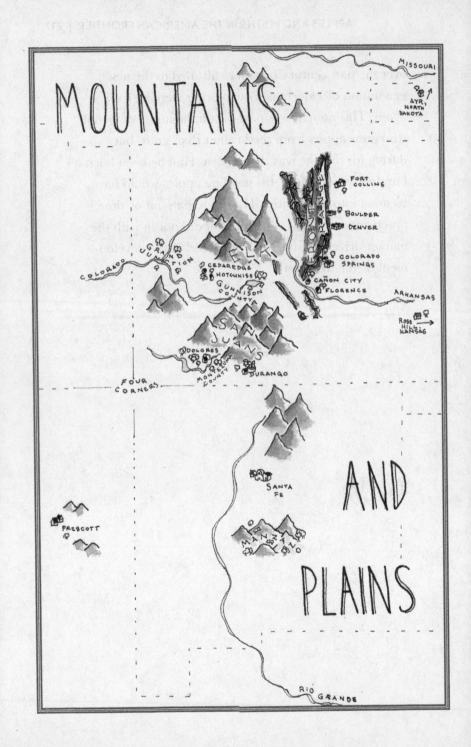

MOUNTAINS AND PLAINS

As primitive reptiles and amphibians crept along the line of mammalian evolution millions of years ago, trace minerals oxidized and formed brilliantly colored red rocks throughout western North America. Ancient ranges that predate the Rocky Mountains succumbed to millennia of rain and erosion from streams. Sedimentary rocks deposited during the Paleozoic Era formed the Colorado Plateau in the heart of the American Southwest. Sand and sediment left behind on the flat plain slowly hardened into rock. Softer stones settled to form valleys and gorges, while the hardest rocks formed ridges that framed the valleys below.

Ensuing sand and mud created sheets of rock up to four hundred feet thick during the Mesozoic Era, which includes the Jurassic period. Swampy plains were born from the shifting geology, and mired reptiles from the era became petrified fossils in the hardened rocks. Seawater flowed into the murky plains and connected the Arctic Ocean with the Gulf of Mexico. The Cretaceous period followed the

*Jurassic, and with it the Rocky Mountains rose from the ocean floor
as seawater sank to the ocean basins. Rain, streams, frost, and ice
formed the Rocky Mountains in the same way they came to define
cultivation in the western states millions of years later.*

By 1853, the frontier boundary reached all the way to the Pacific, and miners, ranchers, and farmers flooded the territory. But the new landscape challenged the cultivation practices and institutions of coastal society. As settlers arrived beyond the Mississippi, across the Great Plains, and into the shadows of the majestic Rocky Mountains, they faced severe weather, arid landscapes, and new obstacles in irrigation and water rights. The first settlements in the Southwest grew throughout Colorado when gold was discovered in the Rockies, and orchards flourished in tandem. The territory that became Colorado in 1876 served as the launchpad for frontier settlement.

The Rocky Mountains stitch peaks throughout the United States and run 3,200 miles from Alaska to New Mexico. Rising up from the high prairie, the Front Range is followed by a series of river valleys, a multitude of individual ranges, countless microclimates, and numerous peaks and canyons that presented stunning topography to settlers on their course west.

Colorado had long been the homeland of Nuutsiu (Ute) and Diné (Navajo) people before European invasion, which began in the sixteenth century with Spanish excursions from Spain and Mexico. Some of the first orchards in the Southwest were planted in the seventeenth century by Spanish missionaries in Santa Fe. They built their mission sites in the Manzano Mountains, named for the abundance of apple trees they planted (*manzana* means "apple" in Spanish).

Trade developed between Spaniards and Indigenous Peoples, whose animal hides and cured meat were of great value to Spanish explorers. But Spaniards also kidnapped Indigenous Peoples for slave labor at their homes and in their fields, marking the start of the displacement and forced assimilation of Indigenous communities. Europeans traversed paths first trod by Indigenous Peoples, and these footpaths evolved to become the arteries that opened passage through the Rocky Mountains.

Fresh from his stint as an army officer in the Northwest Territory, Captain Meriwether Lewis was enlisted by President Thomas Jefferson on an expedition west along the Missouri River, to find an as-yet-unknown stream and follow it "toward the setting sun." In their journals, Lewis and his partner, William Clark, documented sightings of wild crab apples as well as cultivated domestic European apples. They found apples in the plains and learned that the Cheyenne dried and pounded them into flour. The duo made botanical descriptions of apples, observed blossoming apple trees in April, and ate dried apples throughout the winter.

Knowledge spread of the new trail Lewis and Clark cut through the Rockies. First fur trade and then gold brought scores of settlers farther west. By 1860, more than five thousand miners a week came to the Rockies with their gold pans and rockers, founding towns like Aspen and Colorado Springs. They traveled with seeds or seedling trees, and Colorado apple culture developed on the Front Range from the widespread establishment of kitchen orchards.

Stark Bro's Nurseries and Orchards

In 1816, twenty-four-year-old James Stark, an avid horticulturist who was given land in Missouri for his service in the War of 1812, migrated from Kentucky to the western banks of the Mississippi. Stark traveled on horseback equipped with scions from his family's orchard. When he arrived in Pike County, he set out grafting scions onto native crab apple trees. Those few trees grew to roughly fifty acres and became the foundation for Stark Bro's Nurseries and Orchards, the first commercial nursery west of the Mississippi River.

Many settlers who set out west traveled through Saint Louis and visited Stark Bro's, buying fruit and trees to carry with them. At the time of Stark's death, his son William—one of seventeen children—took over the business. William's sons Clarence and Edgar took the business into the twentieth century and developed a relationship with Luther Burbank, a horticulturist and leader in agricultural science living in California. Upon Burbank's death in 1926, Stark Bro's bought the rights to propagate and distribute many of Burbank's cultivars.

The biggest impact Stark Bro's had on American orchards came through popularizing Red and Golden Delicious apples. These revolutionary apples set commercial and home orchards alike on new paths, and their pristine appearance came to dominate national and international markets. But in their early days, they were splotchy and streaked, with a depth of flavor that older generations recall fondly. Their sweetness, monochromatic skin, and ease of growing—thanks to chemical innovations—supplanted many of the country's distinctive apples.

Rocky Mountain peaks reach over fourteen thousand feet—stunning altitudes that initially sank farming spirits. Many of the early orchards, albeit planted at half that elevation, faced triple-digit summer temperatures, erratic spring and fall frosts, deep winter freezes, and three-hundred-plus days of clear skies that threatened trees and crops with sunburn. As in the East, orchards were still a fixture of homesteading and pioneer culture, but farming the unforgiving altitudes of the Rockies was a particularly arduous task.

Jesse Frazier is believed to have planted the first orchard in Colorado. As one of the first settlers in Florence, along the banks of the Arkansas River on the Front Range in Fremont County, Frazier came to be known as Uncle Jesse. He arrived from Missouri in 1859 with a bundle of apple trees in an ox-drawn carriage, and he mined coal near Coal Creek while those trees matured. But grasshoppers—accidentally introduced to the West by settlers—took out the majority of his trees. Frazier went back to Missouri for replacements and, armed with an understanding of his new environment, set out planting two thousand apple, pear, and peach trees late in the 1860s to cater to pioneer traffic. His second-attempt orchard grew to nearly 130 varieties of apples on close to thirty acres, proving that the Arkansas Valley was indeed a fruit district. Frazier's efforts and seedling plantings spawned the Colorado Orange apple, the first commercial variety native to the early orchards of the eastern Rockies.

When the Mexican-American War ended in 1848, the United States gained what became California, Nevada, Utah, and parts of Arizona, New Mexico, Wyoming, and Colorado. Settlers to Colorado's southwest Montezuma Valley, chasing silver and gold in the San Juan Mountains, found the valley's climate beneficial for fruit growing. Jasper and Norman Hall moved there from Cañon City, in Fremont County, and introduced fruit to the region in McElmo Canyon. The northern mountains and lack of transportation in Montezuma County were barriers to trade, but those same mountains protected orchards from winter's worst winds and catered to rudimentary market development west along the San Juan River and south to Texas and Mexico.

By the late 1850s, rapid extraction of gold and silver began to exhaust mineral resources. As a means to continue enticing white settlers west, President Lincoln's 1862 Homestead Act offered relatively easy access to 160-acre plots of farmland. Homestead claims were quickly staked, and northern farmers moved in large quantities to the Great Plains, often forcing Indigenous Peoples off their land.

In an attempt to lure settlers, alter the landscape, and promote the planting of trees, Congress passed the Timber Culture Act in 1873. Homesteaders were offered an additional 160 acres if they cultivated and planted trees on one-quarter of the acquired acreage. Tree groves would provide fencing, fuel, and building materials, while orchards and tree fruit would supply sustenance. But these acts, along with Lincoln's push for the first transcontinental railroad, did not have the immediate impact on western expansion the government had hoped for. Great Plains land and the Rockies were too marginal and mountainous. Potential settlers and investors in the transcontinental railroad feared the ongoing hostility between Europeans and Indigenous communities. But the railroad remained a vital pursuit for the government, as evidenced by the ratifications made to the original act in 1864, in the midst of the Civil War. New laws doubled initial land grants to twenty miles and gave railroad companies rights to sell their own bonds and collect government loans quicker.

When the transcontinental railroad was completed in 1869, it hastened the decimation of the Indigenous populations and the Plains buffalo. As hostility spiked between Americans and Indigenous Peoples, the new rail line facilitated transportation of troops and weapons that enabled utter devastation of Indigenous communities and cultures. When Ulysses S. Grant assumed the presidency in 1869, he called on Major-General Phillip Sheridan to expel Native Americans from the Great Plains. During this time, tens of thousands of buffalo, a sacred and vital species to Native Plains cultures, were killed for sport with .50 caliber rifles by hunting parties outfitted by the U.S. Army, leaving surviving Cheyenne and other tribespeople no choice but to relocate to reservations.

In addition to the transcontinental railroad, the 1860s saw charter acts and land grants for rail lines that would connect Lake Superior with Puget Sound; Springfield, Missouri, with Albuquerque, New Mexico; and eastern Texas with San Diego. With soldiers home from the Civil War, the government enlisted its army to force

Indigenous Peoples onto reservations and dispel them from projected rail lines. Between 1850 and 1880, the number of counties crossed by a railroad grew tenfold, from roughly two hundred to almost two thousand. The thirty thousand miles of track laid before the Civil War grew to two hundred thousand by 1900.

With orchards and markets developing on the Front Range and in southwest Colorado, Gunnison County—between the Elk and San Juan Mountains—became another prime fruit region, with its slightly warmer—and longer—growing season. The Arkansas

The Long Walk of the Navajo

Christopher "Kit" Carson entered Navajo territory in Arizona during the Civil War with government orders to starve out the Native tribe and force them to surrender. Carson coaxed the Utes to help execute his "scorched earth" policy—burning crops and housing in order to leave residents starving and homeless—as they were familiar with Navajo customs and geographic strongholds. Painfully echoing the expedition led by John Sullivan and James Clinton in western New York, Carson smashed century-old orchards and irrigation systems, crippled Navajo agriculture, and left them starving. Over the course of two years, a series of marches known as the Long Walk of the Navajo forced the tribe from their ancestral homelands in Arizona to the Pecos River valley, three hundred miles east in New Mexico. Southwest history became likewise marred by violence and the pillaging of settlements, agriculture land, and orchards as Indigenous cultures continued to be whitewashed and displaced.

River valley and its many tributaries poised the area for irrigation and orchard development. Colorado's unique climate grew fruit of unrivaled quality that sold for premium prices from the time it was introduced. James Giles planted an orchard in Montezuma County that came to be known as the Gold Medal Orchard in 1904, after some of the fruit won awards at the World's Fair in Saint Louis.

Markets also developed north of the San Juan Mountains, along the western slope of the Rockies in Mesa County, around thousands of trees that were planted with the surge of mining towns in the 1880s. William Pabor was among the first to plant apple and other fruit trees in the county, in what is known as Grand Junction or Grand Valley. He wrote about the possibilities of cultivating fruit throughout the Grand Valley in *Colorado as an Agricultural State*, claiming the state's fruit industry could potentially go unrivaled in the country: "In a word, take care of the orchard, and some day not very far distant, cider will be sold at ten cents a gallon in Colorado."

With irrigation readily available from the Colorado River, apples and peaches were quickly regarded as viable crops, and people started investing in the fruit industry late in the nineteenth century. By 1900, the Orchard Mesa Company had 300 acres of trees planted while Cross Orchards covered 240 acres. In the first years of the twentieth century, twenty thousand acres of trees were planted throughout Mesa County.

As more farmers claimed their 160-acre plots, water rights became a central issue. Farmers and state governments developed a system of canals that brought deep snowpack runoff to farmers, opening millions of acres to cultivation in Colorado and the arid West. In 1886, Colorado had an estimated forty thousand miles of canals. Dr. Alexander Shaw, the first to push the quality of Colorado's fruit to national acclaim, acknowledged, "So far as the scope of apple culture in the future of Colorado is concerned, it will be bounded only by an extreme altitude and water supply." Shaw took samples of Colorado fruit to the New Orleans World's Fair in 1884, and he presented *Apples of Colorado* during the 1886 Northern Colorado Horticultural Society meeting, showing 150 varieties of apples from fifty different orchards throughout Colorado.

Orchards in Colorado magnified what was developing on homesteads throughout the Southwest. Apples with a strong commercial following in the country's eastern regions were carried across the Mississippi, the varieties representative of settlers' former homes. Colorado's multitude of microclimates and influx of settlers fostered a uniquely diverse inventory. Shaw's 1886 presentation of Colorado apples included the South's widely grown Winesap and Ben Davis apples; Northeast apples like Roxbury Russet, Spitzenburg, Northern Spy, and Maiden's Blush; and Midwest varieties like Wealthy, Pewaukee, and Haas. All had found their place in frontier orchards and local markets.

Modern Cidermakers and Apple Growers

Whether nestled in amber waves of grain or the steep slopes of the Rockies, apples remain an essential feature of agriculture in the United States. The fruit has never rivaled cereals or grains, but apples are scattered across homesteads from North Dakota to New Mexico. Farmers grew cold-hardy Haralson in the north and adapted Jonathan and Stayman Winesap in the central plains and arid mountains, where frigid winters morph into a sunbaked desert. Throughout the central continental United States, the lack of large climate moderators like lakes or oceans can mean extreme temperature fluctuations that wipe out entire harvests in their most vulnerable times. Contemporary orchardists and cidermakers across the plains and mountains are on the front line of fighting increasingly unpredictable changes in climate.

Rockies orchards are relatively small due to extreme terrain and a difficult growing environment, leaving growers unable to take advantage of economies of scale. Most apples growing in the mountains and plains serve local markets, but even then long distances between isolated mountain valleys and consumers challenge the definition of local.

The lack of natural barriers in the plains means orchards can be rocked by sudden, unexpected weather that quickly sends the mercury dropping and humidity spiking, meaning fruit may not set or ripen properly. Apple scab and other fungi can set in to any tree under the humid sun in Nebraska or Kansas, defoliating trees and denying the fruit any chance at ripening, all this while trees struggle to stave off chemical drift from neighboring corn and soybeans.

Meanwhile, in the high desert of the Southwest, old orchards are fading into the landscape as the climate continues to burden trees. Orchardists across this tough terroir persist because of the value their fruit—fresh and fermented—brings to local patrons. While most of the cider in the state is made from out-of-state apples, there is an increasing amount made from local fruit. Cider-specific orchards are on the rise as orchards big and small invest in a fermented future.

CHARACTERISTICS OF CIDER IN THE MOUNTAINS AND PLAINS

Rockies apples grow at high elevation and under a near-constant mountain sun, so they are comparatively high in sugar and acid. Acids and sugars develop from dramatic shifts in nighttime temperatures, and the results are ciders that tend to be hyperexpressive, with aromas that seemingly jump out of the glass. The brawn, freshness, and depth of mountain apples is undeniable, and the quality of certain ciders coming from the Rockies reflects the legacy of premium fruit grown there centuries ago.

Cider from the deserts in the Southwest is intensely rich, textured, and powerful, from apples soaking up the heat during the day and getting a break as the mercury plummets at night. Look for ABV north of 9 percent. Tannic fruit is limited to higher elevations but, generally, the maritime European apples are pushed to the limit and very hard to grow in deserts. Plains fruit does not have the same intensity or weight found at the high elevations, but it does have a depth and texture from ripening under the sweeping sun.

The Plains

Stacy Nelson-Heising's family has been growing grain on the North Dakota prairies for generations. A chef by training, she returned to the farm after her father retired from farming soybeans and wheat. With the equipment sold off and most of the land leased to larger operations, Nelson-Heising sought to try her hand at something different on the sixty-five acres closest to the house. Her dad had planted it over to alfalfa—which grows with relative ease and requires little intervention—to keep chemicals away from the yard. It was prime orchard land, so Nelson-Heising planted one hundred eating apple trees in 2012 and nine hundred more in 2013.

The family had always been innovators. Nelson-Heising's father, Chuck Nelson, had the first certified organic farm in the county, and he even tried to grow grain biodynamically but found it nearly impossible at the scale of their large operation. Her experimental planting quickly multiplied over the years after she and her husband, Dan Heising, sought counsel from the local university's business students. They saw that the relatively unknown category of cider was prone for growth, so they launched Cottonwood Cider House a few years later and started planting cider-specific varieties.

North Dakota is an unforgiving place to grow apples. Brutally long winters can kill off less tolerant apples, while near-constant wind across the plains presents challenges for pollinators and can easily blow over trees that are not staked or thoroughly supported. The upside, though, is that the general lack of orchards throughout North Dakota means there are fewer endemic pest pressures that come with larger apple cultivation. Cottonwood's experimental ciders embrace their full spectrum of apples, employing common local North Dakota apples like Haven along with Harrison and

Roxbury Russet. Nelson-Heising's culinary background comes in handy when blending from the diversity of eating varieties and cider fruit on their orchard, and those nuances are celebrated in every bottle and glass they sell to their still deeply tied agricultural community.

A few states south, in Kansas, the plains prove both fruitful and challenging at Meadowlark Farm Orchard and Cidery. Owner Tom Brown worked in Pakistan and Afghanistan for almost two decades, developing projects for NGOs and contractors pertaining to the business of fruit and seeds. Finding himself ill suited for the corporate world, Brown returned to Kansas, outside of Wichita, and planted a U-Pick apple and peach orchard in 2011. While not a central part of the initial business, cider had been in the back of Brown's mind since 1984, when—after a year in Pakistan—Brown and his wife, Gina, found themselves pitching their tent on a farm in

Stayman Winesap

The Stayman Winesap is a seedling of Winesap that first bore fruit in 1875 for Dr. Joseph Stayman of Leavenworth, Kansas. The name is the cause of much confusion, as it is sometimes listed as simply Stayman and often cited as the offspring of Winesap and Stayman. The problem is amplified by the countless offspring of Winesap that include its parent's name in its own. The confusion over the variety began when Dr. Stayman mailed several scions from his experiments in Leavenworth to nurseries across the country, as his system was confusing and details were lost in adaptation. Its popularity exploded, though, when it was listed in the Stark Bro's catalog in 1895. Fairly disease resistant and somewhat easy to grow, Stayman Winesap surged throughout the country, especially in the Southeast.

CIDER PROFILE

Moderate body. Gently floral, with cedar, buckwheat honey, and golden raspberry.

western England, having backpacked all the way from Turkey. The farm's proprietor offered them cider drawn from a wooden barrel in the barn. Rough and crude, the cider shocked and delighted Brown, who took up making cider for himself while working in alcohol-scarce Muslim countries.

The learning curve was steep when Brown started planting, but the number of people he saw drinking mass-market cider made him think it would be worth it. Agriculture in Kansas is primarily wheat and beef, which can withstand the unpredictable prairie climate, so there are limited resources or local expertise on growing apples. Brown acquired trees from Stark Bro's and Cummins Nursery and found that the hot Kansas climate develops flatter, oblate apples and kills off many of the northern European cider varieties and American eating apples, like Honeycrisp. But he's had success with multi-purpose apples like Wickson, Arkansas Black, and Golden Russet. Since receiving his farm winery license in 2016, he's seen exponential growth, proving his foresight and faith in a community willing to support a growing agricultural-based beverage category.

Colorado's Front Range

Denver lies in the shadow of the Rockies at the terminus of the Great Plains. The city that was once a vital supply link into the looming mountains has grown by leaps and bounds since World War II. In the late 1980s, empowered by legislation and inspired by traditional European beers and pubs, the Front Range cities of Denver, Fort Collins, and Colorado Springs were hotbeds of home-brewing and microbreweries. This beer-brewing legacy—along with rapid urban development and competition from Washington—pushed apples, orchards, and cider to the forgotten fringes of Denver culture.

Brad Page opened Coopersmith's Pub & Brewing in Fort Collins in 1989, seeking to emulate the offerings and styles he found in England—which always included a token cider tap. Cider was not included in the brewpub laws at the time, so Page got government permission to make it, with the caveat that it include 25 percent grain malt. The added malt powder had little effect on the flavor of the cider, but it boosted the alcohol beyond the norm for the apple juice he sourced from west of the mountains. Page attributes some of his cider's original popularity to its significantly higher alcohol content than the rest of his English-inspired offerings.

Page stayed in the brewing world, opening other breweries and pubs, until he and his wife, Kathe, started Colorado Cider Company in 2011, bringing loads of juice from the mountain valleys to a warehouse outside of Denver and tinkering with hops and fruit with the same enthusiasm that has defined American craft beer. The couple planted their first block of cider varieties in 2013. But as the business grew, Page moved from local Colorado apples to Washington apples, largely because of the unpredictability of Colorado's crop, which can be unsettling to a business of any size.

Fruit growers along the mountains are constantly challenged by their elevation, climate, and isolation. Devastating frosts are a regular occurrence. Springtime temperatures can swing over sixty degrees in 24 hours, which threatens to bring out fruit buds and then freeze them. In 2017, most growers in the Rockies lost close to 90 percent of their crop from untimely weather events.

While the mountains present many challenges, they also create microclimates that can foster successful orchards for those willing to try. Page and other cidermakers are using this practical information to educate local growers on the value and practicality of planting multipurpose and cider apples, even on the Front Range, where hardier varieties have a strong chance at survival. Working with Colorado State University, Page received a grant to study the local industry and show growers the marketplace potential for apples and new plantings that they might view as risky.

Colorado's amateur cider community was thriving decades before its new generation of cidermakers. Dick Dunn has been fostering and supporting cider since 1994, when he took over an

email-based newsletter called *Cider Digest,* which has been addressing the nitty-gritty of cidermaking since 1991. Its 1,400 members
have received over 2,100 editions of the newsletter, which reaches
around the globe and helps make the cider world a smaller place.

Dunn was among the first in Colorado to plant cider varieties,
which he did on an acre-and-a-half plot near Boulder alongside
existing Northern Spy, Cortland, and Baldwin trees. He was driven
by a quest for knowledge that was not available. Dunn has been a
constant advocate for cider, from helping to shape judging standards
in the 1990s to aiding in the formation of the Rocky Mountain
Cider Association, the precursor to the Colorado Cider Association,
which stretched from Montana to New Mexico. By fostering an
outlet that questions all facets of cidermaking, from motives and
philosophies to genetics and fermentations, Dunn has made communication a facet of the cider community that is as integral as
the apple.

Old trees—vestiges of the agricultural past—dot the suburbs of
Boulder. In the nineteenth century, migrating settlers from New
England and Appalachia planted diverse orchards on the Front
Range and Western Slope with apples like Limbertwig and Wolf
River. This diversity diminished with twentieth-century monoculture planting and cheap transportation for apples from Washington.
Many of the remaining commercial operations were wiped out in
the 1950s, when bitter subzero temperatures froze trees of all types
at the end of fall. Faced with massive reinvestment, many farmers
tore up their remaining trees in favor of barley or hay. Others sold
their land in the post–World War II housing boom, and acreage
turned to subdivisions and neighborhoods.

When University of Colorado biology and ecology professor
Katharine Suding moved to Boulder from Berkeley, she was drawn
to an old tree in her field and others just like it that she had found
near abandoned coal mines. Contemplating the growth of Boulder
around these old trees inspired her to create the Boulder Apple Tree
Project, which seeks to bridge the often-tenuous gaps between

college students, nature, and the rest of the Boulder community through the universal language of food and apples. First-year biology students go into backyards around the city to learn tree genetics, grafting, pruning, and landscape ecology. The project has mapped trees across the city and hopes to identify dozens of unique heirlooms and forgotten apples.

Cider is a natural fit for many of the long-neglected, aesthetically challenged apples scattered throughout the city. Brant Clark shared many bottles of cider with his neighbor Eric Johnson before the friends started making cider at home, which set them on a quest for cider apples. They started Widespread Malus as an avenue to explore local apples, imported cider varieties, and imported Kazakh seedlings from the USDA collection at Geneva. Their cidermaking quest evolved into a community restoration project that teaches people how to tend and manage their own old trees.

After collecting apples from Boulder's forgotten trees, Clark and Johnson met Amanda Scott of 63rd Street Farm, and she agreed to plant the first of their experimental orchards in 2015 on land she leases from the city of Boulder. In the arid foothills of the Rockies, great awareness of the resources spent transporting food long distances gives credence to the premium of local fruit. Boulder has been proactive about connecting farmers with vacant land while rebuilding and empowering local food systems. Apples and orchards have taken an integral role in these efforts as local farmers have begun planting trees for their CSA inventories. In coming years, these trees will cater not only to Scott's CSA, but also to local restaurants and Widespread Malus's forthcoming cidery.

Not all orchards on the Front Range were plowed over for grain or housing. Several thriving orchards around Fort Collins and Canyon City, along the Arkansas River, grow unique premium varieties like Akane and Esopus Spitzenburg for discerning farmers' markets. Daniel Haykin's cider fire was stoked by the diversity of apples he found every week at the market. His curiosity led him to purchase a refractometer so he could measure the sugar of the juice and apples he was discovering. His hobby quickly outgrew his basement, and as the venture turned pro, he and his wife, Talia, set themselves apart with two goals: to win at Franklin County CiderDays and GLINT-CAP, both of which they achieved their first year in business.

Daniel and Talia launched Haykin Family Cider in suburban Aurora in early 2018. Thanks to connections and partnerships built from years of farmers' markets visits, Daniel now has access to 250 apple varieties. Their first year producing commercially unfurled at the same time as one of the worst recent harvests in Colorado. With local orchards nearly depleted, Daniel turned to Bill Lyon, fellow Colorado resident and partner at CiderView Orchard (part of Tieton Cider Works in Yakima, Washington), to supplement his crop. Many of the varieties from Yakima were the same heirloom apples found locally, but Daniel says he had to relearn how to make cider because of how differently the apples behaved during fermentation. While Fort Collins, Hotchkiss, and Yakima are all arid, high-elevation growing regions, Colorado-grown apples, he says, are consistently higher in sugar, and—even across the mountains—the same apple can taste radically different both fresh and fermented.

Daniel throws out the traditional method of blending apples in favor of a wide set of single-varietal ciders that local restaurants, retailers, and his own tasting room guests sip and savor in search of the next new thing. He hopes to capture some of the same excitement that has people lining up for IPA releases nearly every weekend at breweries across the country.

Another big player in Front Range cider, Eric Foster and Phil Kao took Stem Ciders from a ramshackle tasting room in the heart of Denver's River North Art District to start Acreage Ciderhouse and Eatery, their new production space, restaurant, and tasting room just east of Boulder in Lafayette. Their success has dramatically changed the cider conversation, as massive crowds visit their facility throughout the year. Many of the greater Front Range's estimated six hundred new residents a day come to Acreage to recapture childhood memories. Foster and Kao, both from Michigan, hope fellow transplants can bring old farming and apple-adjacent traditions to their new home. Like Colorado Cider, Stem relies mostly on Northwest apples for their flavored ciders, while Michigan and local apples round out their diverse inventory. Stem aims to make cider accessible to everyone, and Acreage Ciderhouse and Eatery, a pomme temple of sorts, pushes boundaries and conventions while drawing many of the new Colorado residents to the cider community.

Colorado's Western Slope

Colorado's Western Slope has been the center of fruit growing in the Rocky Mountains since the end of the nineteenth century. Extended sunlight hours, coupled with rising warm air from the valley floor that helps moderate cold alpine nights, makes western Colorado fruit some of the most dynamic in the country. At the turn of the twentieth century, before the invasion of codling moth and other alien pests, fruit grown here was considered unparalleled for its flavor and aesthetics, and pristine apples from the Western Slope were shipped across the country. That legacy is carried today by Palisade peaches that fetch nearly twice the price of their California or South Carolina counterparts. In the Grand Valley, along the Colorado River, larger growers like Williams Orchards have held on through decades of innovations. In the mid-twentieth century, that meant transitioning to dwarfing rootstock, improved frost protection, and peaches. Today, that means cider.

Spending money on hail netting, microspray irrigation, and in-ground propane heaters might be considered over the top in other growing regions, but it has proved essential for Dan and Ty Williams in the face of inclement weather on the Western Slope. Moreover, balanced by the price fetched by the Williamses' organic apples, peaches, and cherries, the investments pay for themselves many times over. In years like 2017, when neighboring orchards lost most of their crop, Williams Orchards was able to bring 80 percent of its crop to market.

Operating under its fifth generation, Williams is the largest apple grower in the Western Slope. With 1.1 million trees on six hundred acres, the farm has been a leader in the market since its beginning in 1921. Williams was among the first to plant dwarfing trees in Colorado in the 1970s, and the orchard removed many of its older Jonathan and Winesap trees to make room for Fuji, Gala, and then Honeycrisp, when the family foresaw shifts in market demands.

Williams has also been growing wine grapes along the Western Slope for decades. Their leap into cider in 2014 was a bulwark against future uncertainty. They plant thousands of cider apples each year, and while Medaille d'Or and Dabinett are not as lucrative as their lip-smacking Honeycrisp, these trees may become an important asset for the farm. Their Snow Capped Cider brand is sold throughout the western part of the state and has won several awards at GLINTCAP.

Since arid mountain valley orchards often receive less than ten inches of annual rainfall, Williams captures and diverts mountain runoff in the spring. On the bright side, minimal rainfall also translates to less humidity, decreased mildew, and almost no fire blight. Centuries ago, long before the arrival of Europeans, Indigenous Peoples built diversion ditches and irrigation systems to combat the lack of rain.

Today, changes in precipitation levels are pushing old water use agreements and rights to their limit. Large reservoirs on the mesa and mountains above the Williamses' orchards, diverted from the Colorado River, have kept them quenched in the driest years, but unusually low snowfall in the winter of 2017–2018 left farmers scrambling as their pools dried. As the dry season progressed, Williams was forced to install cameras and hire security around its water reserves after they were broken into and water was diverted to other properties. The following winter normalized the water level and the crisis subsided, but water access remains a tense issue up and down the arid mountains.

The future of growing fruit in the mountains is tenuous, but the result is some of the greatest tasting fruit grown in the country. Brad Page bought an orchard in Hotchkiss, just south of Grand Junction, shortly after starting Colorado Cider in Denver. His experimental planting of perry pears and bittersweet apples has been something of a trial by fire, as declining snowfall at high elevations leads to limited access to water for his orchard. In some years, water is depleted before the fruit is ready to harvest. In others, late frosts can erase entire sections of the orchard in a single night. But when the stars align and the youthful orchard bears fruit, the lush tannins and juicy bittersweets show great potential.

Page learned to grow bittersweets in Hotchkiss from aerospace engineer Shawn Carney. Carney bought an old fruit farm in nearby Cedaredge in 2003, originally set on tearing out the many old Red Delicious and few Rome Beauty trees to plant a vineyard. But once he discovered the diversity and possibilities of apples, he was hooked. In the early days of his Blossomwood Cider, which launched in 2006, Carney would drive to Poverty Lane Orchards in New Hampshire multiple times a year and occasionally up to Washington's San Juan Islands in search of high-quality bittersweet apples. His orchard soon bloomed as he top-grafted nearly five acres of old Red Delicious trees into heirloom and cider apples. He was particularly enchanted by the intoxicatingly aromatic French bittersweets, which he made into naturally sweet keeved cider.

Intensely sensitive and challenging to make, Blossomwood's signature French-inspired keeved ciders easily reached 7 percent ABV, with a generous amount of stable sweetness that subtly balanced the tannin, acid, and alcohol. Carney credits clear skies and the hot Colorado sun with boosting sugar levels, which translate to higher brix, more alcohol, and a wider foundation to manage keeving.

Keeving

Keeving is a process unique to cider that has its debated origins in France and England. Apples, unlike grapes, are high in pectin, a soluble carbohydrate that is released during maceration before the fruit is pressed. A successful keeve sees the formation of a jelly-like membrane called *le chapeau brun,* or "the brown hat," on the top of the liquid. While this process may occur naturally, most cidermakers in the United States and Europe who practice keeving add calcium chloride and pectin methylesterase to increase the viability and speed of the keeve.

The brown hat, besides acting as oxidation that protects the unfermented juice, traps large amounts of nitrogen in its jelly embrace. The cider is then transferred to another vessel and separated from the jellied cap and the particulate matter that sinks to the bottom. With the nitrogen—an essential component for fermentation—stripped from the brilliantly clear cider, the juice slowly ferments over the course of months. Starved yeast will continue to ferment but cease before all the sugar has been consumed. These "stuck" fermentations are not dead but simply slowed. Traditionally in France, these farmhouse ciders are bottled in early spring, when cold cellars and creeping fermentation are at their quietest. The cider continues to ferment in the bottle and naturally carbonates. Keeving was once an oddity in North America, but a number of producers big and small are perfecting the technique to make more complex and naturally sweeter cider.

Sadly, his signature style ended in 2014 after an expansion deal that saw the cider business end up in the hands of a brewery in Fort Collins. Carney's messy exclusion from the brand he spent years building stained the cider industry in Colorado, but the orchard at Cedaredge continues to thrive under Carney's hand, with the most recent addition being new Spanish cider varieties. It now covers nearly eight acres, three of new trees and five atop the old-growth Red Delicious. While Carney has stopped making cider, his cider fruit is all under contract, being bought by Colorado cidermakers.

Montezuma Valley

In the greater southwest region of Colorado that borders Utah, Arizona, and New Mexico, making up the Four Corners, Montezuma Valley has thousands of forlorn trees that have been waiting for revitalization since the late nineteenth century. While Grand Valley growers in west-central Colorado innovated and evolved to keep their fruit competitive, orchards in Montezuma County, which is one of the poorest in the state today, remained stagnant and have become a record of a past agricultural time.

Orchards in the heyday of Montezuma County were like those in the rest of the state: hundreds of diverse varieties growing together to minimize the impact of weather events and maximize crop yields throughout the seasons. Exceeding six thousand feet in elevation, these alpine orchards were particularly sensitive to late-season spring frosts. In the past, trucks from Texas and Mexico would make the trek into the valley for apples, but the oil crisis of the 1970s made exporting Montezuma fruit cost-prohibitive. With major cities six hours away in any direction, and isolation from nearby highways, the lack of demand for apples meant that orchardists never invested the time or money in replanting their large old trees with modern varieties or improved rootstocks. Fed by spring snowmelt, the trees have survived anyway. Large, barely irrigated trees of the Montezuma Valley produce rough, small, high-acid, astringent apples that are excellent for making cider.

In 1975, Bill and Denise Russell established Mountain Sun Juice in the Montezuma County town of Dolores. Apples were processed and nationally distributed as organic juice—the last large use of Montezuma Valley apples. Faced with increasing competition, the plant ultimately closed in 2001 and was sold for parts the following year. Not long after, wildfire responders Jude and Addie Schuenemeyer decided to settle down and buy a local tree nursery. They inherited a stock of trees and, to their surprise, a multigenerational string of loyal consumers with volumes of stories about their old trees. Intrigued, the Schuenemeyers set out to record and map the history and biodiversity of homestead orchards. Their nursery business morphed into the nonprofit Montezuma Orchard Restoration Project (MORP), with the goal of saving the genetics of the valley by rebuilding the economic value of the trees. Cider has become a leading segment of their mission.

MORP has mapped 120 of the estimated 250 historic orchards in the region, many dating back to the original nineteenth-century mining settlements. Ongoing DNA testing has revealed nearly two hundred unique varieties growing throughout the valley that are not found anywhere else in the world. Through this unique gene pool, MORP has begun distributing thousands of trees back to the community, establishing eight educational orchards at area schools in addition to selling trees to people for their own use.

Preservation is only part of MORP's vision. The project aims to build a successful orchard economy in the economically depressed communities throughout Montezuma County. Many of the orchards MORP works with are smaller than eight acres, planted to supplement families' incomes. In the years since Mountain Sun Juice closed, some of the apples are picked for local food banks, but most end up rotting on the orchard floor, where they serve only the deer. U-Pick and farmers' markets are not feasible, due to the county's remote geography, so MORP is looking to build a different use for their fruit.

Following in the footsteps of Mountain Sun, the future of the valley might lie in apple juice. The low pest pressures at these elevations mean that orchards do not have to spray, especially when growing for juice, where appearance hardly matters. MORP has piloted programs to bring mobile juice pressing equipment to the old trees. The project is connecting cidermakers with orchardists looking to recapture some of the gold in the mountains, marking the first time in generations that such quantities of Montezuma County fruit have been brought to market.

In 2009, Martha and Dusty Teal came upon fifty forgotten trees while rambling through knee-high grass in Dolores. Seduced by the orchard and the land, and having sold their bookstore and bakery in town, they made the jump and found themselves on the original board of MORP. Teal Cider emerged as a passion, born to justify the purchase of the land, whose trees are at least eighty years old. The forgotten orchard contains mostly an old strain called Double Red Delicious, but it is scattered about with unknown—though excellent—cider apples. In 2012, the Teals began planting a neighboring parcel with a hundred semi-dwarf heirlooms and cider apples grafted by MORP.

Another estate-driven cidery, Fenceline Cider was started by Sam Perry and Neal Wright out of collaborative efforts through MORP. Driven by Perry's passion for horticulture, Fenceline taps into the wealth of the experimental orchard plantings he started in college and the thousands of underutilized trees spread across the county. Even the legacy McIntosh, Jonathan, and Rome Beauty apples, Perry notes, have more complexity and higher acids than today's commercially grown strains, which translates to more character and flavor in cider.

Fenceline's high altitude allows them to control temperatures easily and keep cooling costs low. Just opening the doors to their production facility at night is enough to regulate fermentations, keep them slow, and retain apple phenolics and nuances that can burn off at higher temperatures.

Fenceline's riverside taproom has become a perfect venue for the community to share stories about their experience with the history of apples and orchards in the region. Wine has an undeniably rich culture, Perry says, but not many people grew up with a vineyard in their backyard. Apples are an integral facet of many American experiences, especially in Montezuma County, and flavors in Fenceline's ciders have proven to spur a time warp at the tasting room that facilitates memory and perpetuates legacy.

Montezuma County is home to Fort Lewis and its century-old terraced orchard, with ditches dug along the roots and trees to maximize floor irrigation. The fort originally served as a cavalry base in the late nineteenth century to control local Indigenous communities. When Fort Lewis outgrew its initial military function, it aimed its oppression beyond the local Jute, Navajo, and Apache and brought young men from Indigenous communities across the country for an assimilationist education. Programs like Fort Lewis crept up throughout the country at the end of the nineteenth century seeking to "reform" Native people by educating them as white students. After the assimilationist school closed in 1910, it became an agricultural high school and then a public liberal arts college. Now it is the source of one of Fenceline's most interesting ciders.

Perry's vision has come to encompass a rich, community-focused program that infuses education, business, and agriculture into its mission. Because alcohol-adverse Jute and others are an important part of the local community, Perry makes an unmatched nonalcoholic sparkling apple juice for his taproom.

The Southwest

Perry's interest in apples was seeded by his college roommate and colleague, Kanin Routson, who started Stoic Cider with his wife, Tierney, in northern Arizona in 2017. Without access to the hundreds of acres of trees found in the Montezuma Valley, they sought fruit from local seedling trees to supplement limited Arizona high-country apples.

With scarce water, seedling trees are a rare occurrence in the arid Southwest desert—a stark contrast to the bountiful apple forests in the Northeast. It can be seventy degrees Fahrenheit in February and freezing in May, and September monsoons are not uncommon. With no surge of prospectors, mineral booms, or early industry, this portion of the Southwest remained largely on the fringes of western settlement. Fewer homesteaders made land claims, and so there were historically fewer orchards. Stark Bro's pushed an orchard campaign late in the nineteenth century and early in the twentieth century by offering trees to the region via mail, but their push was mostly for Red Delicious. Surviving trees tend to grow close to water, and they are often a combination of late flowering, early harvest, and drought and sun tolerant.

The Routsons have been tracking down the wild and forgotten seedlings across the Four Corners region, driven by Kanin's earlier academic research. For his PhD thesis on apple genetics, Kanin collected DNA samples from across the greater Southwest in an effort to understand the history and diversity of the region and where its apple trees came from. Glimpsing into the past, he cataloged and identified trees that might have been planted by Indigenous Peoples and Spanish, Mormon, and other European settlers. Stoic Cider now hopes to capture some of that diversity in the bottle for future generations by propagating unique seedling apples on their farm, at 4,600 feet of elevation. The couple has begun to trial the first generation of seedlings from some of their favorite apples, local feral trees, and Kazakh seeds acquired through the USDA.

Acequias—community-managed irrigation channels built upon earlier Indigenous-laid networks by the Spanish in the seventeenth century—remain an important feature of agriculture in the Southwest. Orchards north of Santa Fe still draw off the Rio Grande for fruit destined for the growing cities in the valleys below. Cidermakers are beginning to look at these orchards for opportunities, as local producers like Sandia Hard Cider, Santa Fe Cider Works, and New Mexico Hard Cider are all opening taprooms.

Core Takeaways

The central interior of the United States is a difficult place to grow apples. Growing fruit here is a balancing act among water, heat, frost, and the market that is amplified by the extreme elevation and the great distance between orchard and consumer. The orchards that have managed to hold on for this long have been able to do so because of the community's work and values alongside the trees' bounty, whether that be a tree-ripe Kansas peach, a desert Golden Delicious, or a mountaintop cider. Cideries both large and small continue to mature, drawing in more and more curious drinkers. As orchards and apples come under more pressure to sacrifice their individuality to conform to the national supply chain, cider offers an avenue that marginal growers can take to help establish something that their community—both locally and around the country—can appreciate.

THE PLAINS

• **Location and Geography:** Expansive stretches of prairie that have been cut by water and pocketed with hills.
• **Soil:** Sandy, semi-arid, with limestone and clay.
• **Climate:** With no large bodies of water or other natural protection, weather can come fast and furious, often leaving inexperienced growers with dead trees and a failed crop. USDA Hardiness Zone 4b–8a.
• **Orchard Location:** Orchards are mostly located near cities. Areas around Lawrence, Kansas, along the Missouri River have a long tradition of tree fruit.
• **Orchard Type:** Orchards are mostly retail operations selling to restaurants.
• **Significant Apple Varieties:** Stayman Winesap, Winesap, Jonathan, Rome Beauty, Arkansas Black.
• **Cider Apple Plantings:** While there are more cider apples in the plains than there were a decade ago, they are still scarce.

- **Producers to Visit:** Meadowlark Farm Orchard and Cidery (Rose, Hill, KS), Cottonwood Cider House (Ayr, ND), Jefferson County Ciderworks (Fairfield, IA).

COLORADO'S FRONT RANGE

- **Location and Geography:** The Rocky Mountains tower ten thousand feet over the plains below.
- **Soil:** Eroded hillsides and alluvial plains shaped by mountain runoff.
- **Climate:** Semi-arid climate subject to extreme temperature shifts. The mountains and foothills create unique microclimates. The area immediately closer to the Rockies is warmer than the plains farther east. The mountains famously provide three hundred days of sun. USDA Hardiness Zone 5b–6a.
- **Orchard Location:** Today most of the orchards are found in the Boulder and Fort Collins areas of Colorado and south along the Arkansas River in Canyon City. Foothill orchards lie at 5,300 to 6,000 feet above sea level.
- **Orchard Type:** Orchards are mostly geared toward retail, with most of the larger orchards in Boulder and elsewhere being replaced by housing.
- **Significant Apple Varieties:** Stayman Winesap, Winesap, Jonathan, Rome Beauty, Arkansas Black.
- **Cider Apple Plantings:** Few cider-specific orchards exist, but more are going in the ground, and there are many heirloom apples for the lucrative farmers' markets.
- **Producers to Visit:** Haykin Family Cider (Aurora, CO), Colorado Cider Company (Denver, CO), Stem Ciders (Denver, CO).

COLORADO'S WESTERN SLOPE

- **Location and Geography:** The Western Slope is defined by a deep river valley carved by the Colorado River in the midst of the high peaks of the Rocky Mountains.
- **Soil:** Porous alluvial soils, with clay deposited from the snowmelt every year.
- **Climate:** The high desert climate makes orchards heavily dependent on snowmelt throughout the year. Hailstorms and other extreme weather and frosts are a major risk factor. USDA Hardiness Zone 6a–7a.
- **Orchard Location:** Most of the orchards are around the Colorado River and its tributaries around Grand Junction and upriver in Cedaredge and Hotchkiss. Orchards are at 4,000 to 6,300 feet in elevation.

- **Orchard Type:** Large orchards are fresh packers for urban markets on the Front Range and in neighboring states.
- **Significant Apple Varieties:** Honeycrisp, Jonathan, Red Delicious, Gala, Fuji, Golden Delicious, Jonagold, Pink Lady (aka Cripps Pink), Granny Smith, Golden Russet, Pitmaston Pineapple.
- **Cider Apple Plantings:** Until recently, cider apples were contained to smaller and homestead orchards, but several larger orchards have begun planting cider apples at scale—some for their own production and others for sale to cideries in other parts of the state.
- **Producers to Visit:** Snow Capped Cider (Cedaredge, CO), Jack Rabbit Hill Farm (Hotchkiss, CO).

MONTEZUMA VALLEY AND THE SOUTHWEST

- **Location and Geography:** High mountains and deep valley throughout southwestern Colorado extending into New Mexico, Arizona, and Utah.
- **Soil:** Wind-deposited loess and alluvium soil, with clay in the river valleys.
- **Climate:** Arid alpine climate with rainfall concentrated in the winter. Prone to extreme weather but better protected than the plains to the east. USDA Hardiness Zone 4a–6b.
- **Orchard Location:** Montezuma County is the former apple heart of the region, where orchards sit along ridges and mountain runoff.
- **Orchard Type:** Far from large markets, most apples are raised for processing, though there was a brief time when fresh fruit was exported to distant markets in the Southwest. Homestead, small, and retail markets have been a fixture of the area since the Spanish intrusion in the 1500s. Orchards are located at four thousand to eight thousand feet in elevation.
- **Significant Apple Varieties:** Red Delicious, Double Red Delicious, Colorado Orange, Arkansas Black, Autumn Strawberry, Rome Beauty, Nickajack, Grimes Golden, Jasper Hall Jelly Crab.
- **Cider Apple Plantings:** While there are many old heirloom and seedling trees, there is limited new planting dedicated to cider.
- **Producers to Visit:** Fenceline Cider (Manco, CO), Santa Fe Cider Works (Santa Fe, NM).

Prohibition and the Reverberations of Temperance

Most popular cider stories cite Prohibition as the root of cider's demise. But the Eighteenth Amendment—which was enacted in 1919 and prohibited the manufacture, sale, transportation, importation, and exportation of "intoxicating liquors"—was the culmination of a century of social movement that demonized alcohol as the root of all social ills.

Colloquially known as the Great Experiment, Prohibition had a profound impact on the alcohol industry in the United States. Across the country, regional breweries shut their doors and wineries began cranking out fresh, unfermented juice, while the few remaining cidermakers looked to vinegar to hold off insolvency. Prohibition did not kill off any sense of a thriving cider industry; when it was ratified in 1919, cider had been a marginalized cultural beverage for decades, largely removed from the public consciousness as populations developed around urban centers. Into the 1920s, cider enjoyed a brief revival as bootleggers supplied it and brandy to Chicago and New York. Sparkling cider was often passed off as fine champagne once the first few rounds had been poured, and in the days of unscrupulous underground alcohol, few questions were asked and fewer palates educated.

Setting aside cider's short popularity among bootleggers, the rising tide of temperance had swelled mostly from those Americans who had been most likely to drink cider. Tales of vast cider orchards being cut down by axe-wielding Prohibitionists are greatly exaggerated. For generations before cider sales were outlawed, orchards across the country had given up growing apples for cider and had instead developed the infrastructure to support marketable eating apples. Compared to any other orchard products, cider had the lowest return on investment. Late in the nineteenth century, during pomology's golden age, it made no sense for growers to invest in cider when other, more lucrative opportunities lay within their grasp. The fruit needed to make good cider all but dried up.

When the Twenty-First Amendment repealed the Eighteenth and legalized alcohol again in 1933, the drinking landscape had irrevocably changed. While many breweries pivoted—Coors had invested in ceramics and Yuengling ventured into ice cream—hundreds of others never reopened their doors. There were over four thousand breweries in the United States before Prohibition, a number that was not reached again until 2016. While a few commercial cidermakers, like Mott's, did make hard cider after the repeal, few invested the necessary resources, and the category fizzled.

Prohibition did not solve the social ills that the temperance movement had blamed on alcohol—including domestic violence, childhood poverty, and unemployment—but it did successfully ruin alcohol for decades. Spirits, once viewed as an unsavory transaction with the devil, gained popularity because of their high potency in a small package. Cocktails, vital in making poorly made spirits bearable, were ascendant at the expense of wine and beer, because of the poor quality of both during the period. Cider and apple brandy were made fairly easily under the watchful eye of Prohibition agents, and barrels were smuggled from rural orchards to cities, but, after repeal, few urban dwellers returned to cider.

So while the Great Experiment set the American drinking culture back by decades, cider had been stuck in history for generations. The beverage, and the rural lifestyle it represented, vanished amid Gilded Age advancements, urbanization, and the mechanization of commodity and industry. Ensuing legislation surrounding Prohibition did little more than advance urban conveniences and push cider further back in time.

As Americans returned to legal alcohol in the 1930s and after World War II, cider—with its rural trappings and production—faced a new suburban America that was quickly paving over farmland.

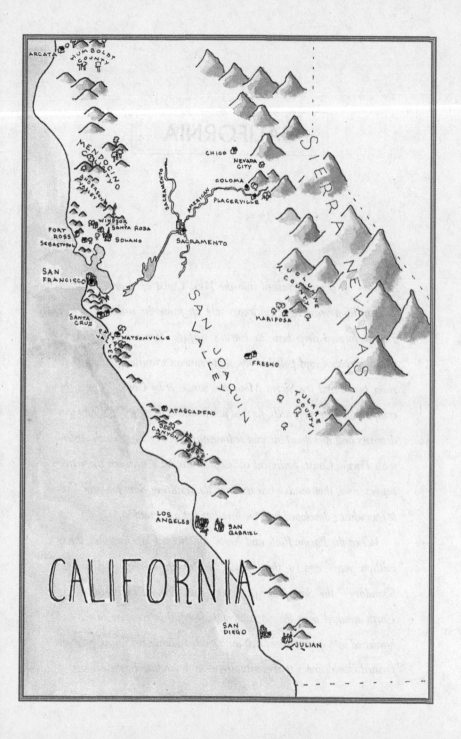

CALIFORNIA

A chain of islands crashed into the West Coast of North America 150 million years ago. Volcanoes rose up from the collision, while granite formed deep beneath Earth's surface. Erosion and glaciers slowly exposed and polished the subterranean granite, giving rise to sheer peaks and the Sierra Mountain range. The Coast Ranges, by comparison, are mere hills, formed just millions of years ago from ash deposits and metamorphic and sedimentary rocks along North America's Pacific Coast. Sediment collected at the base between these two ranges, and, thousands of years later, the resulting San Joaquin Valley would be developed into the breadbasket of a nation.

When the Pacific Plate and North American Plate first met, thirty million years ago, a third plate was disappearing, and a new boundary—the San Andreas Fault—was formed in its place. As Earth quaked over the years, metal-rich fluids were released and hardened into quartz veins rich with gold. In other instances, gold ore formed in volcanoes that eventually went dormant. In the middle of

the nineteenth century, discovery of these shimmering gold deposits
turned the frontier into a superhighway and became the foundation of
California.

Settlers to California had the entirety of the frontier behind them. When gold was found near Sacramento in 1848, the ensuing rush of prospectors quickened the need for civil government, and California entered statehood in 1850. With no continental land remaining on the horizon, the federal government met its goal of a widespread, bicoastal population. Thousands of Europeans and Asians left their struggles at home for mining camps, farm fields, and the dynamic economy of California. They brought sundry plants and new industries that coalesced with Spanish and Indigenous cultures that had been in place for three centuries and shaped the agriculture and social structure of California.

Before the gold rush, one of the country's most diverse Indigenous communities had been cultivating the land for fifteen thousand years. The region's high Sierra peaks, Coast Ranges, and deserts isolated Native people, who developed small autonomous groups with unique dialects, cultures, and organization, and subsisted on a largely foraged diet. Subsistence agriculture was made challenging by the dry growing season, and the bountiful landscape encouraged a mobile lifestyle. Permanent settlements were not a Native practice until Spanish colonization imposed them in the eighteenth century.

Apples were first introduced to California through Spanish missions, which were built throughout Alta California—as the region was then called—from 1769 to 1823. The resource- and land-hungry Spanish monarchy sent Franciscan missionaries with military support to build missions roughly every thirty miles throughout Alta California, from southern San Diego (1769) to Solano (1823) in the Bay Area. Twenty-one missions were built as self-sustaining outposts where residents grew their own food. After Monterey became the capital in 1777, passing ships docked there for inspection, and manifests from the time show stores of fruit tree seeds and seedling trees, most of which came from South America. Mission sites were within close proximity to water as well as to Indigenous Peoples, who were forced into labor, Christianity, and assimilation. Promises of steady food lured the Indigenous population, but death tolls were high as European diseases and massacres rampaged the Indigenous workers. In the century following Spanish colonization, California's estimated Indigenous population dropped from around three hundred thousand to twenty thousand.

Mission growers found success with temperate and semitropical fruits. In addition to apple trees, olive, citrus, nut, pear, peach, quince, plum, and fig trees (hence the Mission fig) were planted to provide sustenance in *huertas,* or food gardens. Mission orchards spread up to forty acres, often protected by adobe walls or cactus hedges. One of the largest, planted by Padre José Zalvidea at San Gabriel outside present-day Los Angeles, had over 2,300 trees. Orange groves at San Gabriel mark the beginning of California's orange industry (which would go on to form grower cooperatives and become Sunkist Growers in 1952), and the state's wine industry grew from grapes introduced by Spaniards at mission vineyards, which often exceeded a hundred acres.

As Spain continued to build missions and push north, the monarchy was met by a current of Russian exploration down the Pacific coast. Russia was in search of a maritime fur trade, so the tsar sent trappers and Orthodox Christian missionaries looking for riches and souls. Russian efforts were concentrated through the Russian-American Company, which by 1812 had made it as far south as modern-day Sonoma County, where Fort Ross was built as an agricultural base to supply Russia's Alaskan settlements. The orchards at Fort Ross—consisting of cherry, peach, pear, quince, and apple trees—were the first in Sonoma County and the first non-Spanish attempt at organized agriculture in California.

Alta California became part of newly independent Mexico in 1821, and after the Mexican War of Independence (1810–1821), without vital regular support from Spain, the mission system was largely abandoned. Orchards and gardens suffered, goods became scarce, and enslaved Native Californians fled. In a last-ditch attempt to fend off encroaching Russians, Luis Argüello, California's first governor under Mexican rule, supported construction of Mission San Francisco Solano, the twenty-first and final mission, built in 1823.

Mission San Francisco Solano and the twenty other missions were closed a decade later when the Mexican Congress issued a secularization act. Under the act, missions were to become secular *pueblos,* or villages, and land was to be transferred from the Catholic Church to the Mexican government. Pío Pico, the last governor of Alta California, auctioned off numerous missions in 1845, but their general disarray failed to draw buyers. Much of the acreage was given to individuals as land grants that established *ranchos*—huge plots of excellent land along the coast that catered to ranching— and the seeds for California's commercial agricultural endeavors. Twenty years before the gold rush, Spanish, then Mexican land grants drew the first American settlers to California. They went seeking wealth in trade and trapping and established the earliest homestead orchards with fruit trees from Mexico, Central America, and the eastern states. By 1846, under the land grant system, eight million acres were owned by only a few hundred *rancheros.*

Fort Ross became irrelevant as new trade arrangements developed to supply Imperial Russia's Alaskan adventures and overhunting displaced trappers and Indigenous Peoples. With its prime purpose as an agricultural station rendered moot, it went up for sale. German-born Swiss pioneer John Sutter, who had settled sixty miles east in the Sacramento Valley, made the purchase in 1841. The bill of sale includes twenty-four houses, "nearly every one having an orchard," the largest of which contained more than two hundred trees.

Sutter had arrived in Alta California when it was a Mexican territory. At the time, Governor Juan Bautista Alvarado gave Sutter permission to establish a colony near Sacramento with the express purpose of staving off interests from the Indigenous, Russian, American, and British communities. In an effort to do so, Sutter enslaved members of the Nisenan tribe and forced them into labor and protection of his territory. In 1848, shortly after Mexico ceded a large part of its territory to the United States, one of Sutter's employees uncovered the first shimmers of gold in Coloma while constructing a water-powered mill. Sutter tried to keep it quiet, but Samuel Brannan, a Maine-born Mormon newspaper publisher and owner of a general store living on Sutter's property, publicized the gold discovery in the *California Star,* a paper he debuted in 1847. His store and other services reaped the benefits of the influx of treasure seekers many times over.

Gold rush pioneers and farmers introduced premium apple varieties to California. Coloma and Sacramento became boomtowns seemingly overnight. In the four years following the first discovery of gold, California's population spiked from under 10,000 (excluding Indigenous Peoples) to 250,000, a particularly impressive number considering that the first passenger railroads did not arrive from the east until years later. Slavery had been illegal under Mexican rule since 1829, partly to deter American settlers in Texas, but it became a reality in California as Americans poured into the territory. California became a free state in 1850, largely because (white) state delegates believed slavery to be an unfair advantage in the gold mines. Early photos depict Blacks and whites seeking gold side by side, but civil rights were not extended to the Black or Indigenous communities. The perversely named 1850 Act for the Government and Protection of Indians perpetuated Indigenous servitude and supported the continued kidnapping and killing of Indigenous people.

While the nation debated over slavery, in California, orchards came just as quickly and spread just as widely as settlers did, as the allure of gold drew migrants from all over the world. Plants and fruit trees were brought from North America's Atlantic coast, across the Pacific from Asia, up from ports in Central and South America, and from islands in the southern seas. By the end of the 1850s, nearly two million pounds of gold were extracted from within the state—and fruit trees seemingly replaced every pound.

Wharfs were built in San Francisco's Bay with haste in response to the steady arrival of passenger ships, increased sea trade, and the blossoming fruit industry. The influx of wealth created high demand, with large budgets for luxury items like fruit and alcohol. In boom-towns at the peak of the gold rush, in the early 1850s, apples sold for $3 each and bottles of various forms of alcohol for $8—roughly $100 and $270, respectively, in today's dollars. Dozens of ship inventories—published in the 1850s in *Daily Alta California*, which descended from Brannan's *California Star*—reference barrels of apples and cider arriving in California from eastern ports.

By steamboat from the Atlantic coast, the cheapest and most common route to California was around South America's Cape Horn, despite unpredictable weather that often dragged the trip out to ten months. Two routes went through the Central American isthmus—one through Panama (before the canal) and one through Nicaragua—but apple seeds and seedling trees subject to the tropi-cal climate fared poorly. Thousands of young apple trees were brought to California via the Cape Horn route, and, in an effort to ensure safe arrival, it was common practice to pack the trees in dried moss.

Numerous merchandise brokers and general commission mer-chants sprang up, acquiring ship cargoes for resale, often on con-signment or through auction. In addition to tin, zinc, boots, candles, and provisions like molasses, butter, cider vinegar, and apples (both dried and fresh), 1850s advertisements include multiple references to cider, cider brandy, and "Champagne cider"—believed to be from Newark, New Jersey.

The growing local demand was met by orchards in all directions around the Bay: to the south in Santa Cruz and Watsonville, north in Sonoma and Mendocino Counties, and southeast in Tuolumne County. Each area became a hotbed of fruit growing that catered to developing settlements and San Francisco, in addition to prospectors in the Sierra foothills. Coastal proximity enabled growers to access markets along the Pacific and beyond, and provisioning towns were quickly established as the likes of groceries, hotels, and fruit tree nurseries catered to the needs of growing communities.

In its first twenty years of statehood, 85 percent of California's population lived in the northern portion of the state. Northern counties in the interior and along the coast were established close to gold mines. These communities were either at high elevation with cooler nights or protected from coastal breezes, and they produced superior apples in greater abundance than the hotter southern counties. A. P. Smith established the first commercial nursery in California in 1848, on sixty-five acres he bought in Sacramento from John Sutter. Smith set out fruit trees, shrubs, ornamentals, and vegetables that soon catered to the rush of immigrants, and he irrigated his nursery with water drawn from the Sacramento River by a ten-horsepower steam pump. Others quickly followed suit.

James Lloyd LaFayette Warren and his son John Quincy Adams Warren established a transcontinental business to benefit California's early fruit industry and agricultural efforts. James was a nurseryman in Massachusetts, but he set off with the rush to California in 1849 and established a nursery and stores in Sacramento and San Francisco, focusing on farm equipment, seeds, and plants. John remained in Massachusetts and brokered the shipment of goods to California wharfs, where his dad received and sold them through his stores. In 1853, Warren and Son published California's first descriptive nursery catalog of fruit and ornamental trees. By the following year, Warren and Son was a firmly established nursery business and farm store, and the company established the weekly *California Farmer*, which became a leading publication and an invaluable resource for agriculture and farming in California into the twenty-first century. It published its last issue in 2013.

The earliest apple growers planted mostly winter varieties from the Atlantic states like Esopus Spitzenburg, Rhode Island Greening, and White Winter Pearmain. As settlements were established in the valleys of Southern California, where temperatures were significantly higher and sunburn a greater threat to trees, varieties with larger leaves, like Red Astrachan and Duchess of Oldenburg, were better protected against the sun and able to withstand the winter chill hours. But the market remained concentrated in the northern counties. Newtown Pippin and Yellow Bellflower—both yellow-hued varieties—were so revered for their quality that they maintained a market premium in the face of increasing fervor for red apples.

California growers catered to local and distant markets, to which they shipped apples in fifty-pound boxes. Barrels and barrel-making—cooperage—remained the standard for apple packing east of the Rockies, but the custom fell out of favor as the craft was impeded by a lack of coopers and hardwood trees, and the need to import staves and hoops for casks in the West. Rising demand for fresh fruit supported a growing box-making industry that also catered to dried and canned fruit, canned fish, soap, candles, sugar, cigars, and jewelry. The need for case boxes

Yellow Bellflower

New Jersey pomologist and author William Coxe wrote of the age and size of an old Yellow Bellflower in his county of Burlington, claiming, in 1817, that the original tree was by then "very large and old." Others cite the apple as originating in 1742. Yellow Bellflower became a staple of orchards from Maine to California, where it played a supporting role to Newtown Pippin. Its rich flavor and long storage ability made it an ideal companion, but relatively few trees exist today, as the variety was swapped for Golden Delicious and Mutsu to fit a similar fresh profile.

CIDER PROFILE

Herbaceous. Ripe peach. No tannin but generous acidity.

increased as goods were shipped during the Civil War, and the opening of the transcontinental railroad led to immense growth in box exports of fresh fruit from California—which grew to fifty million pounds in 1888.

Many of California's earliest nurseries were started on apple roots imported from France as seeds or seedling trees. The first trees in Watsonville were planted on rootstocks from mission gardens, but as the commercial industry there took off, growers switched to the same French rootstocks that found favor in California's Mediterranean climate. Early settlers in Sonoma County planted seeds from Fort Ross fruit to start their orchards.

Toward the end of the 1850s, French-born barber turned nurseryman Felix Gillet arrived in Nevada City, California, sixty miles northeast of Sacramento. Inspired by California's booming apple trade, he established Barren Hill Nursery in 1866 and became the nation's leading pioneer in perennial crop agriculture. He introduced dozens of fruit, nut, and grape varieties to California by making multiple visits home to France, importing plant species, and propagating them at his nursery. The stock Gillet created went on to establish multiple agricultural industries throughout California and the Pacific Northwest, including apples, almonds, walnuts, strawberries, and wine and table grapes. Among Gillet's most notable contributions are the introduction of Cabernet Sauvignon, Chardonnay, Syrah, and Merlot grapes.

Cider was part of a larger drinking culture persisting in California despite broader national abstinence and temperance. It was consumed alongside porter and ale, a myriad of fruit brandies, whisky, absinthe, port, Madeira, Cognac, Claret, Sauternes, and Champagne. Gold rush pioneers were largely young, unmarried men who left the temperate ways of their parents' generation and went west in search of wealth. According to the 1852 census, there were seven times as many white men as white women in California. Many left their old homes permanently, while others aimed to return home flush with riches. Whatever their intentions, the early days of the gold rush were far removed from the evangelical values of the Second Great Awakening.

Inhabitants of Northern California replaced the old Puritan values of home with a new social culture. Most of the population followed work in the gold mines and lived in any one place for only a short period of time. Numerous saloons opened, and by 1854 there were nearly six hundred in San Francisco alone. Gaming was legal and common throughout the city, and gaming houses flowed with cider and spirits. Life in the mines was hard and cutthroat, and those who stepped out of the mines dropped into saloons or took to the old mission grounds to bet on horses.

Demand for apples in the early years of California bred a black market of fruit trees that established growers fought to suppress. In 1858, the first California nursery convention was held in San Francisco "to regulate prices and sale of trees," as less-than-amateur growers—referred to as tree peddlers—were hawking mislabeled varieties and trees in poor health. Misrepresentation challenged the viability, profitability, and quality of California fruit, but the combined strength of multiple nurseries was able to dissuade the peddlers. By 1860, there were an estimated 670,000 apples trees in California, and twice as many peach trees. The state's estimated value of fruit products for the year was upwards of $4 million, or more than $120 million in today's dollars.

In 1860, some thirty-five thousand Chinese immigrants made up 10 percent of California's growing populace. Chinese prospectors fled civil war and famine for opportunities in California mines, and they settled throughout the length of the Sacramento Valley. The new immigrants were met by racism and exclusion, as exemplified by foreign miner taxes and legislation sanctioned by the federal government that denied Chinese immigrants admission to schools, hospitals, and municipal jobs. Anti-Chinese sentiments culminated in 1882 with the Chinese Exclusion Act—the first immigration law passed by Congress—which prohibited further Chinese immigration to the United States.

Prior to the exclusion, the Central Pacific railroad company recruited twelve thousand Chinese immigrants—who made up 90 percent of the railroad's workforce—to build the transcontinental railroad. When the transcontinental line opened in 1869, California produce diversified—not just from the newly accessible markets, but from Chinese irrigation science, levee building, land reclamation, and centuries-old sustainable farm practices, as well as foodstuffs from the Chinese pantry that were sown throughout the Sacramento Delta in the second half of the nineteenth century.

The Chinese Exclusion Act gave license for discrimination as gold diminished. In 1890, 75 percent of California's agricultural labor force was Chinese, but this number dropped as racist policies persisted. Fires were set in Chinese neighborhoods by the white community, and the Geary Act, passed in 1892, extended Chinese exclusion into the twentieth century, when Congress declared exclusion indefinite. The gap in California's agricultural workforce was filled with Japanese workers, who arrived as eager wage earners free from the tumult surrounding the 1904 Russo-Japanese War.

Japan was in the midst of a cultural, political, social, and economic shift in the late 1860s, which opened the country to global trade and international influence. Japanese immigrants fulfilled labor contracts on sugar plantations in Hawaii and sailed to the mainland in the 1870s. Claus Spreckels, a German-born brewer-turned-sugar-magnate living in San Francisco, made a fortune in Hawaii's sugar business. He purchased a former Mexican land-grant rancho in Santa Cruz, invested in the Santa Cruz Railroad to Watsonville, and, in 1889, came to operate the nation's largest beet sugar operation there. A price war with the American Sugar Refining Company in the 1890s left Spreckels unwilling to match market price to growers. Many of them converted their acreage to apple orchards, and by the turn of the century, Watsonville produced nearly two-thirds of California's apple crop.

Into the twentieth century, ports of entry in Seattle, Portland, and San Francisco welcomed a rush of Japanese immigrants who went to work for rail, cannery, and logging companies and contributed to the mining and salt industries. Excluded from the growing manufacturing and urban jobs, many Japanese laborers sought opportunities throughout the fertile Sacramento and San Joaquin Valleys in orchards and agriculture.

Apples, as well as hops, strawberries, and grapes, were widely farmed by Japanese farmers, who leased and managed existing orchards in Sebastopol, in Sonoma County, and eventually started their own early in the twentieth century. In addition to sugar beet acreage, apples and orchards were replacing wheat fields and grain, which suffered diminishing prices with the advent of the transcontinental railroad. Refrigerated railcars were introduced in 1888, fresh fruit was shipped nationwide, and California canneries—which excelled at production, dehydrating, packing, and shipping—facilitated a boom in the dried fruit industry.

Takeshita Kametaro, from Japan's Kumamoto prefecture, was the first Japanese farmer to establish himself in Sebastopol's apple industry, and he did so with a sixty-acre orchard. Despite land laws that made it difficult for Asian immigrants to own agricultural land, or even lease it for any considerable length of time, Japanese farmers were able to acquire farmland from white owners who viewed their tenants as a means to a reliable workforce and high returns.

As Japanese workers found success and implemented mechanical improvements in Sonoma County orchards, a new scientific approach to plant breeding was under way. In 1875, New England native and horticulturist Luther Burbank began experimenting with plants and seeds on an acre plot in Santa Rosa. Inspired by his early successes with potato varieties in Massachusetts, Burbank started a small nursery and published his first catalog in 1880. The rising demand for dried fruit in California turned Burbank's eye to fruit trees, and by the turn of the century he had developed a stock of five hundred thousand fruit and nut trees that were sold for a premium to developing nurseries throughout California, the nation, and the world. Burbank introduced more than eight hundred new varieties of fruits and plants and played a seminal role in establishing the Plant Patent Act in 1930, which granted patent protection to plant breeders for the first time in history.

Plant breeder Albert Etter was on a similar path in Humboldt County, where he was working to establish an apple industry. Etter was born in Colorado but grew up in Humboldt, learning how to cultivate fruits and plants from his mother. He started an orchard in the 1890s with five hundred apple varieties—many from the University of California extension program founded in 1868—to graft and see which would thrive in the county's loamy soils and rainy, coastal climate. In addition to the proven prosperity of Esopus Spitzenburg, Newtown Pippin, and Rome Beauty, Etter found success with numerous other seedlings and was among the first to see commercial value in crab apples for breeding purposes. Etter also bred the Ettersburg family of strawberries, which were developed to withstand California's heat, drought, and manual picking and canning, and the new fruits revolutionized the state's strawberry industry.

Wickson

In 1944, Albert Etter developed the Wickson apple and named it for his mentor, leading pomologist and author Edward Wickson. Wickson's high acid and generous sugar has made it a favorite variety among cidermakers from California to Maine, but its cherry-like size makes harvesting it difficult. The origins of Wickson are unclear, as Etter's records show it was a cross between Spitzenburg Crab (which today is totally unknown) and Newtown Pippin. Regardless, Wickson is one of North America's truly distinct and great cider apples.

CIDER PROFILE

Rose, lemon verbena, bright acidity, and balanced light tannin.

By the dawn of World War I, policies aimed at restricting immigration imposed literacy tests and head taxes (essentially an entry fee) on immigrants. The Immigration Act of 1917 allowed temporary migrant workers but upheld the ban on contracted labor. Migration from Europe declined, and California farmers asked the federal government to waive the tests and taxes affiliated with Mexican immigrants for one year, thus beginning California's relationship with Mexican farm labor. Between 1917 and 1921, during the first of two Bracero programs (the second of which lasted from 1942 to 1964), some seventy-five thousand Mexican workers were allowed into the United States.

At the conclusion of the First World War, with much of the national economy entrenched in industrial efforts, Japanese farmers owned or leased over 450,000 acres, a majority of which were in the northern counties. Acreage deemed undesirable by white farmers was made fertile with intensive, high-yield Japanese farm practices, and orchards were planted beyond Sonoma County and throughout the central valley and Tulare County, once considered too hot and arid to support fruit trees and perennial crops.

The Immigration Act was amended in 1924, placing severe restrictions on Japanese immigrants entering the United States. Anti-Japanese land laws made it increasingly difficult for Japanese farmers to own land, and many of them left orchards, hop fields, and vineyards for the fruit-drying business and chicken farming, which could be done with significantly less land. Before the United States entered World War II, established Japanese farmworkers still produced over 40 percent of California row or "truck" crops and managed thousands of fruit and nut trees. They dominated the trucking, distribution, wholesale, and retail businesses, and controlled nearly all of the strawberry, tomato, and celery crops and markets.

While agriculture thrived along the Pacific Coast, the American prairies and high plains of the Midwest faced severe circumstances caused by exploitative and destructive farming at the hands of previous generations. The ensuing Dust Bowl and drought years fortified the national depression and brought a rush of desperate families and farmers west. Congress repealed all former Chinese Exclusion Acts during World War II—China was an ally—and President Franklin Roosevelt signed an executive order that forced 120,000 people of Japanese ancestry, most of whom were American citizens, into concentration camps. After Japan bombed Pearl Harbor, Japanese expulsion was sold as a necessary evil to sustain national safety, and it left thousands of suitable farmland acres open to the arrival of white Midwest farmers displaced by the Dust Bowl.

Internment left the Japanese community in social and economic despair. What was intended as an attempt by the federal government to secure land for the country's growing commercial farm endeavors proved to be a virulent error that led to food waste and a dismantled community, and harmed economic welfare throughout the nation. Farming had provided surplus for a national market and the economic foundation for a majority of Japanese living in California, but their forced displacement from more than six thousand farms irrevocably changed that. In addition to the racist injustice, labor was lost, commodities were shorted, food intended for U.S. troops was not available, and prices skyrocketed.

The Japanese-American Evacuation Claims Act, signed by President Harry Truman in 1948, was the first civil rights–associated law of the twentieth century, and it intended to compensate those interned. In its report, Truman's Committee on Civil Rights called Japanese internment "the most striking mass interference since slavery with the right to physical freedom." The committee urged the abolition of racist legislation, but it did little to make up for the hundreds of millions of dollars in income and property that was taken from people of Japanese descent. The majority of internment camp survivors did not have their property returned to them, nor did they receive fair wages when they returned to the workforce. Industrial improvements made during the war were now being applied to small farms and came to define domestic agriculture, but

California's once-thriving apple industry was left shadowed by a more temperate Pacific Northwest.

Modern Cidermakers and Apple Growers

California's orchards run from the arid mountains above San Diego, north to the great irrigated San Joaquin Valley, and into Redwood valleys and hillsides. In Sonoma County, Gravenstein apples are planted next to world-renowned Pinot Noir grapes, while in Fresno, Fuji and Gala grow alongside walnuts and almonds. Orchards expanded as California emerged as an agricultural behemoth and then receded as technology, communications, and media became ascendant. Since the 1990s, California's orchards, similar to others around the country, have undergone tremendous changes as processing centers have given way to fresh-packed apples.

California cider has grown by leaps and bounds, as evidenced by the surge in small, local cideries alongside large regional and national brands. The state's wineries and breweries have increasingly adopted cider as the beverage grows in popularity. California cider often relies upon nineteenth- and early-twentieth-century apples, vestiges from the prime of California orchards. New plantings of heirloom, tannic, and cider-specific apples are on the rise throughout the state's diverse terroirs, and unique ciders are emerging whose full potential is only just beginning to be explored.

THE CHARACTERISTICS OF CALIFORNIA CIDER

California's cider community, like its orchards, runs the entire gamut of the industry, from mineral-driven ciders in forested Humboldt County to full-bodied bruisers along the Mexican border to probiotic, health-conscious versions in the heart of Los Angeles. Ciders throughout the state are generally more tannic and higher in alcohol and have savory dried and candied fruit flavors.

Southern California

The town of Julian, in San Diego County, was once the apple capital of Southern California. At an elevation of over four thousand feet, it began as a gold mining town and, thanks to automobiles, became an alpine extension of Los Angeles and San Diego. As these cities grew, their new residents recreated the agricultural traditions of their Midwest and East Coast pasts by making annual treks into the mountains. Located within two hours of twenty million people, Julian balloons every fall with people chasing their apple fix. At its height, the town had only about seven hundred acres of apples, all dry farmed—no irrigation or watering of any kind—with nearly fifty feet of space between each tree. The fruit was destined for grocery stores in the local urban markets or for tourists' preferred apple delivery system: pie.

Dry-farmed Blacktwig, Northern Spy, and Winesap captured the imaginations of Brian and Kathleen Kenner who, for a number of years, operated Julian Ciderworks. The Kenners first came to Julian for horses after careers in the dot-com arena, and when an interest in the history of apples and cider surfaced, Brian Kenner approached it the only way he knew how: through data analytics. He believes there are two paths for cider companies: either high production or mass specialization. Before Julian Ciderworks closed in 2019, Kenner had mapped and plotted large parts of the hills to better understand the unusual orchards.

Kenner developed software to monitor nearly every aspect of cidermaking, from the first sign of green tip through harvesting and the fermentation process. His orchard programs collect and compile vast amounts of data on everything from the weather's effect on pollination to bloom times, acidity, and sugar levels and put it in a database. It remains to be seen how Kenner's database will fully benefit the greater community, but his belief that the right technology will help lead to more boutique cideries may define the future of cidermaking.

In Julian's extreme growing conditions, on the edge of the Anza-Borrego Desert, trees bloom in February and get harvested as late as November. The long growing season gives the fruit a chance to develop high sugars, and juice ferments to more than 16 percent ABV, more than twice the average of cool-climate ciders. Lack of water has historically meant wide spacing in orchards, which keeps the trees from competing with one another for limited resources. Throughout the century, the orchards that once made Julian the envy of Southern California have declined. Pies that continue to draw thousands of visitors a year are now usually made with Washington apples, and most of the local fruit drops to the ground from benign neglect. But the area still makes some of the most distinctive ciders in the country thanks to its extended growing season.

Hot and dry Santa Ana winds in autumn have been the scourge of farmers throughout Southern California for generations. They blow through the mountains and valleys at over forty miles an hour and bring desert air from the Great Basin and Mojave Desert to the coast, fueling forest fires and destroying crops. Dave Carr of Raging Cider and Mead Co., about fifty miles west of Julian, hypothesizes that the Santa Anas dehydrate the apples and drive sugars up while they are still hanging on the tree.

Carr, like Kenner, monitors Southern California's challenging climate, zooming in on everything from chill hours and water levels to the adaptability of promising seedling rootstocks. He started experimenting with cider in the post-industrial warehouse town of San Marcos in 2007. His wife, Kerry, developed a gluten intolerance, so he turned his experiences with homebrewing and drinking cider while visiting family in England toward the potential of Julian fruit. In 2015, the Carrs formed Raging Cider as a three-generation family affair with their children and grandchildren. By working with local fruit, rejuvenating abandoned orchards, and using native yeasts for fermentations, Raging Cider's goal is to produce cider reflective of San Diego County's unique growing conditions.

Cider has found a market north of San Marcos in the sprawl of Los Angeles County. Toronto native Mark McTavish moved to Los Angeles equipped with Spanish *sidra* and a mission to push the boundaries of cider and show that it is a category—not a singular beverage. His tart, unabashedly assertive Spanish ciders quickly grew a solid fan base and bolstered McTavish's belief that the large Los Angeles County population just needed to get cider in its collective hand. He began distributing other brands of cider from New York, Ontario, and parts of Europe to his favorite bars and restaurants. With a finger on the pulse, McTavish's portfolio of cider grew and shrank as the market ebbed and flowed, and he began learning market nuances and the different styles of cider.

McTavish's years peddling cider and stressing education built him the perfect platform to start his own cidery, uniquely adapted to the Los Angeles market. Drawing from the health-centric culture of Southern California, 101 Cider House uses vocabulary like "cold-pressed" and "probiotic." Their messaging is backed by its naturally fermented apples, used in conjunction with a host of different fruits and botanicals for ciders that steer toward sour and are reminiscent of kombucha. The low-carb and low- to no-added-sugar beverage was introduced just as people were looking for an alternative to beer, wine, and cocktails but wanted something more than the rising tide of hard seltzer. Early success with 101 Cider House enabled McTavish to launch a more traditional brand, Stoked Cider Co., which will hopefully make room for the rest of McTavish's imported favorites.

Central Coast

North of Los Angeles on California's central coast, where oak-roasted tri-tip steak is preferred over avocado toast, apples are still being grown in coastal valleys and mountains. In See Canyon, south of San Luis Obispo, eating apples like Jonathan and Gala were planted for the growing communities nearby before orchards like Gopher Glen Organic Apple Farm began looking at cider as a path for the future.

John DeVincenzo, a central coast orthodontist and amateur horticulturist, had a hobby of buying up farms, including what would become Gopher Glen in See Canyon's Avila Valley in 1970. Its remote location quickly made the forty-acre farm his favorite, and his breeding efforts were concentrated there. Because it is a trial orchard, trees are planted seemingly at random. Today, Fernando Martin, who started working for DeVincenzo when he was fifteen and is now in his fifties, is the only one able to identify each of the farm's 112 varieties.

When DeVincenzo passed away in 2009, Raven and Jake Smith—whose family worked at Gopher Glen—purchased the farm to maintain its legacy, and the couple introduced Gopher Glen Cider Co. in 2016. Fermentations have been a learning process for the Smiths, but the juicing aspect has been easy. Gopher Glen is one of the few orchards left in California that has been grand-

Jonathan

First discovered as a seedling of Esopus Spitzenburg in the Hudson Valley and named for Jonathan Hasbrouck, who was instrumental in drawing attention to the apple, Jonathan has been frequently used in breeding programs worldwide and is the parent of over ninety cultivars, such as Jonagold, Akane, Jonamac, Mutsu, and Idared. While cultivated in New York, it found greater success on the West Coast.

CIDER PROFILE

Often very full-bodied, creamy, and textured, with fresh fruit balanced by dried leaves and scrub grasses.

fathered in for secondary ag processing, meaning they are allowed to sell unpasteurized apple juice, which is otherwise illegal. They use a century-old press to do so and have supported local home-cidermaking ventures for many an amateur looking for unique juice from rare and heirloom varieties.

After visiting New York and New England cideries, where estate-grown fruit and private orchards are more commonplace for cidermakers, the Smiths realized that Gopher Glen was a potential treasure trove, as no other cideries in San Luis Obispo County have their own orchards. Each year since their first production, the couple has made a single-varietal cider. Arkansas Black was first, in 2017, and Gravenstein followed. As a means to accentuate the farm's terroir, each single-varietal cider is fermented with wild native yeast. The Smiths make a handful of different ciders, but their single varieties have drawn increasing interest from the central coast's enthusiastic wine industry, leaving the future for Gopher Glen wide open.

Trees of Antiquity, California's leading nursery and contributor to antique and heirloom apples, is some forty miles north of See Canyon on Highway 101 in Paso Robles. Along with Cummins Nursery in New York, Trees of Antiquity ranks among the first nurseries in the country to cultivate cider varieties. Terry and Carolyn Harrison started the project as Sonoma Antique Apple Nursery in Northern California in 1980. When they retired, Neil and Danielle Collins took over. They expanded with eighty acres in Paso, not far from California Polytechnic State University, where the two met. After college, Neil worked under A. G. Kawamura, who later became California's secretary of agriculture. Collins's efforts have begun to seed both commercial and home orchards with relics of the past that cidermakers nationwide can draw upon.

Many of the central coast cideries have roots in the region's wineries. In the 1980s and '90s, many of them began making wine from Pinot Noir and Rhône grape varieties like Syrah and Mourvedre that drew attention away from the lauded Cabernet and Merlot of Napa. Tablas Creek Winery, founded in 1989, has been a champion of the region's Rhône movement since day one. Its longtime winemaker, coincidentally also named Neil Collins, hails from England's West Counties. He started making cider and selling it from the tasting room at Tablas Creek before forming his own winery, Lone Madrone, as well as a cider company, Bristols Cider House, named for his hometown in the UK.

Collins has been able to champion the crossover between winemaking and cidermaking, utilizing much of the same equipment for each process. He sources apples from across California for ciders to be sold in the county or at Bristols' taproom in Atascadero, an under-the-radar city in San Luis Obispo County that is great for apples and relatively untouched by the wine industry's surging land values just north. Atascadero has limited cider fruit, but Bristols takes advantage of access to Newtown Pippins in Watsonville and other heirloom varieties from the Sierra Foothills and Sebastopol. In the same way that southern Rhône wines are made predominantly from blends, Bristols will often ferment more than forty varieties in a year, to find balance and strike personality in their ciders.

The momentum of the central coast's wine industry has also elevated cider. Mikey Giugni first discovered cider while making Pinot Noir and Chardonnay in Tasmania, where a neighboring winery was making cider as part of its sparkling wine program. When he moved back to the central coast, he partnered with friend Mike Brughelli to build Scar of the Sea, focusing on the highest-quality locally sourced Pinot Noir and Chardonnay from some of the best vineyards in the Santa Maria Valley. Giugni began experimenting with cider out of little more than curiosity; like Neil Collins, he finds more freedom and flexibility with cider than wine.

While Scar of the Sea wines have found national acclaim, Giugni believes that his ciders, especially those made from Newtown Pippin, are his best products. His cidermaking approach mimics winemaking, and his ethos translates to rich, full-bodied ciders suggestive of his finesse with Chardonnay. After aging for over a year in a barrel, the ciders are blended with a small amount of fresh juice from the new harvest to kick-start a secondary fermentation before being bottled. Juice is a natural supplement that fits well with Giugni's philosophy: it prevents him from needing sugar, additives, or yeast in the final product. The cider's extended maturation in old Chardonnay barrels develops characteristics that are rarely found in a market focused on immediacy.

California's unpredictable climate has deterred Giugni from betting on cider varieties, so he focuses instead on the legacy orchards and heirloom fruit he is able to find throughout California. As with vineyard work, Giugni believes that certain orchard practices have a direct influence on his ciders. As a means to celebrate the works of growers the label deals with, transparency of sourcing has come to play a vital role in Scar of the Sea's messaging. Giugni lists his fruit sources on every bottle. Quality, he feels, is the key to success and longevity in such a new and competitive market. Giugni's apples are from Bear Valley Ranch, owned and operated by the Theroit family. Mike Theroit farmed the orchard in the Santa Cruz Mountains' Pajaro Valley for nearly forty years, and like many others throughout the valley, Theroit grew apples for Martinelli's, located in Watsonville along the Santa Cruz Bay.

Santa Cruz

For over 150 years, Martinelli's has sustained an apple industry centered on Newtown Pippin, the key component in their ubiquitous juice. The company was started in 1868 by Stephen Martinelli, an Italian-speaking Swiss immigrant. As a teenager, Martinelli came to the Pajaro Valley in 1859 to join his brother Louis, who had arrived nine years earlier during the peak of the gold rush. With no luck prospecting, Louis began growing apples in the valley. At age seventeen, Stephen started bottling sodas and other beverages in one of the barns on his brother's farm, and soon began experiments fermenting some of his brother's crop. Formed in 1868, Martinelli's was a hard cider company for its first fifty years, selling cider throughout California, winning awards, and adopting the Gold Medal moniker after winning at the 1890 State Fair. California's young male demographic continued to swill cider and most any other alcohol throughout the end of the nineteenth century. Prohibition threatened to send the company to disaster, but Stephen's son, Stephen Jr., together with a professor at the University of California, Berkeley, adopted a method for fresh juice pasteurization, ensuring the business's continuity.

As California grew, so did Martinelli's. After the repeal of Prohibition, alcoholic cider was reintroduced, but declining sales saw it discontinued in 1977. Increased competition from juice made from Chinese concentrates pushed the company to innovate their products. Cranberry-flavored apple juice was followed by grape, peach, and mango, and they reintroduced their hard cider in 2017. Still made from Newtown Pippin and naturally sparkling, the cider captures a vision of the past and nods to the future of the valley.

Orchards in the Pajaro Valley are planted on seedling rootstocks spaced thirty feet apart from one another, forming a blanket grid across the hillsides—a patchwork of different planting styles, varieties, and sizes and the antithesis of the tidy rows of small trees that have come to dominate the fruit-growing world. In the heart of Steinbeck country, Pajaro moves slowly. In many commercial apple-growing regions, trees are replaced after their yields begin to decline, which takes several decades on the East Coast. But in the Pajaro Valley, trees are removed only when they fall down.

In the 1960s and '70s, the valley was dotted with packing houses that selected the finest of the crop for the regional grocery stores and retailers, but this era drew to a close with the ascendancy of Washington State fruit and the rise of high-density orchards in the San Joaquin Valley. With the fresh market all but dried up, orchards had little recourse but to turn to juice.

Martinelli's continued using fresh apples, buying an ever-increasing share of the valley's fruit, even as many of their competitors switched to concentrates. With few other markets available, Santa Cruz growers interplanted Red Delicious and Mutsu between the towering Newtown Pippin trees in an effort to increase their yields.

Jake Mann is a fifth-generation orchardist in the Pajaro Valley. He returned to Five Mile Orchard with fresh eyes and a mind for innovation after a career in the Bay Area. As is common across the country, the family farm was costing more money than it was making. Mann touted the farm's Newtown Pippins and developed a network of more than a dozen California cidermakers who started buying his fruit.

The growing chorus of cidermakers brings specific needs to orchards. Looking to maintain the natural acidity in Newtown Pippins, Mikey Giugni of Scar of the Sea will often pick two weeks earlier than the former Martinelli's schedule dictated. Other cidermakers, like Eric and Katie Rider of Rider Ranch, delay harvest until the last possible window—often a month after Martinelli's harvest—in order to capture the unique texture, ripeness, and weight of Newtown Pippin juice. After their homemade cider won silver alongside professional cidermakers, the Riders decamped from San Jose for Santa Cruz County. The county allows wineries to open without additional local approval after state licensing, which has sparked considerable growth in the local cider community.

California's wine industry pervades Santa Cruz and has been a critical resource for cidermakers like Robby Honda at Tanuki Cider. Apples have been part of Honda's family for nearly a hundred years. His great-grandfather immigrated from Japan at the turn of the twentieth century, and his grandmother and mother were raised on the orchard he purchased in Sebastopol in Sonoma County. When 120,000 Japanese-Americans were evicted from their homes and lands during World War II, his great-grandparents and grandparents were among those interred. Because they owned land, however, unlike many of their fellow internees, they were able to return to their farm after the war to raise the next generation.

Newtown Pippin Revisited

From Santa Cruz to Oregon's Hood River, Newtown Pippin has found wide acclaim on the West Coast. As on the East Coast, the apple was originally grown for shipping and export, destined for European outposts and colonies in Asia and Australia. When grown in California, the Newtown Pippin makes distinctly different cider than its East Coast brethren.

CIDER PROFILE

In California, the fruit profile is riper, alcohols are higher, and the delicate spring herbs carry notes of sarsaparilla and chalk. Most notably, California Newtown Pippins are more tannic and bitter than those found on the East Coast.

Inspired by Michael Pollen's book *The Omnivore's Dilemma*, Honda moved from the suburbs to Santa Cruz, where he learned about the potential in value-added agricultural products. When he arrived in 2009, there were no commercial cideries in the city. By 2016, there were five. In a city where most wineries offer direct sales through tasting rooms, local retailers, and restaurants, cider was able to get an early foothold. While helping raise pigs and chickens at Fogline Farm, Honda made his first vintage of cider in 2014 with his brother, Brad, from century-old trees on the property. He started by using reliable yeast strains to test the market, but his focus is shifting to native fermentations with wild yeast. In a local-food-centric city like Santa Cruz, Honda's agricultural cider was a natural extension of the seasonal bounty: He delivered it to local restaurants along with flats of tomatoes.

Tanuki Cider nearly came crashing to an end before it had a chance to soar. At age thirty-three, Brad suddenly passed away in his sleep. Robby seriously considered folding the project, as the task of continuing seemed insurmountable through the staggering hardship. But through cider came creativity, inspiration, and community built around the memory of his brother and previous generations. Since 2016, Tanuki ciders have been made from a variety of heirloom and eating apples grown at Jake Mann's Five Mile Orchard, including Yellow Bellflower and Mutsu, that add aromatics and round out blends with the celebrated Newtown Pippin. Since Mann took over, he has introduced low-intervention practices in his orchards, using fewer sprays while pushing to decrease dependency on irrigation. Stressed trees grow deeper roots, and the vigor produces fruit of exceptional quality and creates sturdier trees to withstand a shifting and unpredictable climate.

Climate change is on the brain for orchardists across the Pajaro Valley. Droughts in 2014 and 2015 were devastating to many farmers during the warm winters, when trees did not get enough chill hours. Rather than the long-trusted Newtown Pippin, Martinelli's is encouraging growers to plant more warm-tolerant Mutsu. Reinvestment in new fruit is a difficult prospect for many orchards, as the economics makes it hard to justify ripping out whole blocks to replant with different apples. But orchards like Five Mile that are willing to work with the cider community are less beholden to Martinelli's demands.

Sonoma County

Orchards had been an essential part of Sonoma County's landscape for a century before the rise of grapes. The county's most famous apple resident has been the Gravenstein, which was first planted on a commercial scale in 1883. The apple's introduction is often erroneously traced to the Russian colony at Fort Ross, but there is little evidence to support that claim.

As in apple-growing regions across the country, Gravenstein's early success in Sonoma County would not last. Premiums for first-of-the-season apples and products like applesauce and dried apples were lost with the rise of globalized food and near year-round availability. Gravenstein's poor keeping quality could not compete with

Gravenstein and the Gravenstein Apple Fair

These pale yellow-green summer apples are high in sugar compared to many other early-ripening varieties. Dating back to before the seventeenth century, they were once popular in their possible home of Schleswig-Holstein (Denmark, then Germany, then split) and throughout the Baltic. But Russia, Italy, and Austria have all been speculated as the apple's birthplace. Gravenstein also formed the backbone of apple orchards in the seafaring outlets of Nova Scotia, where red-striped Gravensteins are the norm.

In the 1850s, Sonoma County Gravensteins were among the first fresh apples to hit the Bay Area each year in mid-August, weeks before apples from the Sierras or Santa Cruz, fetching them a high premium in gold rush towns. Like other early-ripening apples, Gravensteins do not keep as long, and as Sonoma's Gravenstein footprint grew, more processing infrastructure built up around it to handle the seasonal push. Over one hundred apple evaporators once scattered the valley, able to ship dried apples year-round throughout the Pacific and supplying American fleets and European colonial holdings in Asia. At the onset of World War II, Sonoma County had 13,875 acres of apples, with 9,750 of those planted to Gravenstein.

Although Gravensteins are the iconic apple of Sonoma County, they began to disappear at the end of the twentieth century. In 1973, drawing on the traditions of Sebastopol apple fairs that date back to 1910, Sonoma County Farm Trails began the Gravenstein Apple Fair as a way to draw attention to the culture and plight of the county's orchards. Cider has moved into the fair's spotlight in recent years, with a growing number of producers pouring cider made from apples grown in Sonoma County. Local cider guru Darlene Hayes oversees the cider wing of the festival, curating a selection of producers that best represent the diversity Sonoma County has to offer. Her efforts have pushed cider to the point where it now outsells both beer and wine at the fair.

CIDER PROFILE

Notes of citrus, jasmine, and bay leaf. Often slightly weighty, with bright acid and a honeyed, melon juice–like texture.

the packing operations growing in eastern Washington State. Over the ensuing decades, orchards struggled as more canneries and processors closed their doors, and when the bottom of the apple market dropped out in the 1980s, Sonoma County farmers were already looking toward other crops. There are now over sixty thousand acres of vineyards in Sonoma County, and grape growers can expect to receive ten times the price per ton for grapes that they would for apples. With rock-bottom prices, older, unprofitable orchards are continually uprooted for encroaching vineyards.

But apples are not entirely forgotten. In 2015, there were still 2,229 acres of orchard in Sonoma County, 704 of which were Gravenstein. It was in this climate that East Bay natives Ellen Cavalli and Scott Heath bought five acres along the famed Gravenstein Highway. They came to Sonoma after jump-starting their cider and fermentation curiosities in New Mexico. Drawn to Sebastopol by a need to reconnect with lost skills, the couple planted eighty trees and numerous cider varieties they got from Trees of Antiquity in 2011, unsure of what might take root in the historic apple region. They named the project Tilted Shed Ciderworks after one of the many decrepit buildings on their new homestead.

Word of Tilted Shed's ambition and intention spread and, before long, legends began filtering back to them about earlier generations of cidermakers in the Bay Area. Neil Collins of Trees of Antiquity became intrigued by their bittersweet selection and, in Tilted Shed's first year in business, helped them track down an orchard he had helped plant decades earlier. Now encased in poison oak and blackberries, the treasure trove included cider apples like Porter's Perfection, Yarlington Mill, and Roxbury Russet. The ten-acre orchard was planted in the late 1980s by a local couple who owned a bakery in town and wanted to explore more than sourdough fermentations. After carefully irrigating and growing their trees through the troublesome developmental years, they left California in 1991, and Sonoma County purchased the land but never developed it. Apple trees, a few rogue pear and quince trees, grapes, and a massive stand of chestnuts remained fallow until Cavalli and Heath began to beat back the competition and allowed the apples to shine.

Tilted Shed leased the land and transformed its apples under the name Lost Orchard Cider, a testament to the power of forlorn apples. Untreated and untended for nearly three decades, the fruit offers a glimpse at the complexities that might one day be possible for cider varieties in California. As Cavalli points out, the state is the size of Italy, and its terroir, climate, and apple-growing history are immensely varied. Cavalli's cider philosophy is evident in each bottle she produces, and it also shines through in *Malus,* her quarterly magazine edited by Darlene Hayes and inspired in equal parts by her decades as a book editor and by the lack of substantial conversation around the politics, economics, and sociopolitical realities that are deeply tied to apples and cider.

While Tilted Shed was the first producer of cider in Sonoma using all California apples, they were not the first cidery in town. The California Cider Company has been producing ACE Cider in Sebastopol along the Gravenstein Highway since 1993. From a small tasting room to a national brand, they have maintained popularity by blending globally sourced concentrates with creative flavors. Amid the growing wave of cider around them, ACE has begun to work with local farms on their path toward innovation.

Since Tilted Shed's initial influence, Sonoma County has seen tremendous growth in small agricultural cider, large-scale commercial cider, and cider that blurs the line. Jolie Devoto is from a family of apple growers. Her father Stan's orchard exceeds one hundred varieties and is synonymous with Sonoma County apples. In 2012, Devoto Cider was born, mostly from Gravensteins Jolie sourced from the family orchard. In 2014, she and partners launched Golden State Cider in cans, with the idea of producing cider year-round. Apples from large processors in the Pacific Northwest serve as a base for the hibiscus and ginger ciders that have taken the state by storm and become all but ubiquitous throughout the Bay Area.

Devoto's goal is to raise the profile of West Coast fruit and remain transparent about sourcing, which doubles as a celebration of other orchardists' efforts. A string of bad years for Sonoma apple growers from 2008 to 2012 left many farmers ripping trees out of the ground to make room for vineyards, but Devoto's apples remain part of Golden State Cider's harvest line, which focuses on apples like Gravenstein and Arkansas Black. Golden State's farm series is made from single orchards throughout California, including Five Mile, and brings some of the state's best fruit to new drinkers.

Sonoma's many forgotten small orchards enchant a host of different people. Ned Lawton bought five and a half acres half planted with apples in 2014 as a tool for preschools to make urban connections to a rural agricultural community through a program his wife, Michelle, had founded. When the opportunity to lease a three-acre orchard in Sebastopol arose, the Lawtons saw it as a means to broaden their program.

The project took on new legs with Sonoma County native Ryan Johnston. Johnston recalls seeing the orchards of his childhood bulldozed and was inspired to join the Lawtons when they launched Ethic Ciders to recontextualize farming and apples within Sonoma. Through cider dinners and pairings, Ethic's ciders have helped elevate not only apples but the codependency of the agricultural ecosystem, from field greens to salmon. Johnston champions the dry-farmed techniques that laid the foundation for Sonoma County's apple industry. While there are some cider-specific trees on the Sebastopol farm, they have yet to bear fruit. In the interim, vigorous fifty-year-old, organic, dry-farmed Golden Delicious trees provide the uniquely expressive juice base for Ethic.

Sonoma County has visible scars from the worst that climate change has wreaked. Years of drought led to devastating forest fires in the fall of 2017, followed by harrowing floods in the spring of 2019, and then the largest fires on record across the state in 2020. Orchards that were coated in ash were completely submerged two years later. The climate is getting more extreme, not just during cataclysms, but throughout the "new normal." Rainfall occurs with less frequency and unprecedented intensity, leaving soils supersaturated, causing erosion, and threatening soil health. Through new farm practices, Ethic Ciders hopes to be an agent of change in an old agricultural community fighting against the rise of unknown climate threats.

Not far from Sebastopol, in the Russian River valley, Darek Trowbridge's family has been involved in the region's grape-growing efforts since the end of the nineteenth century. Trowbridge makes wine under the label Old World Winery, but cider came to him through a friend, Troy Carter, who inspired him to collaborate on Troy Cider before his own Trowbridge Cider. At one remarkable site, an abandoned orchard had been overtaken by feral grape vines that stretched across the ground in a web of fruitful bounty. Grapes and apples were both picked, tread by foot, and pressed into a neon pink exuberant beverage that became one of Trowbridge's favorites of all time. The following year, when they returned to replicate the drink, a new driveway had been plowed through the old orchard. More Pinot Noir was not far behind.

Trowbridge is no stranger to unique agricultural creations. He is cultivating a large colony of mycelium, a fungus that increases biologic activity in the soil. By covering vineyards and orchards, Trowbridge's fungal threads improve soil health by trapping twice as much carbon in their fungal hug. He finds that vines and trees are healthier and stronger with the mycelium, producing fruit sooner and with more stability. Better roots and soil can hold water longer, helping plants through the worst of droughts, while being able to absorb the sheets of rain that can engulf large swaths every winter.

Trowbridge also farms California's only four acres of Abouriou, a nearly forgotten French Basque grape that was once common in Sonoma county's poly-variety vineyards. He runs a small household vineyard that is home to nearly a dozen varieties that were planted by his great-grandfather in 1890. Still, cider makes sense for Trowbridge. Its low alcohol content and carbonation are a great canvas for his natural style of winemaking, which captures the field and expresses its character in the bottle.

Mendocino and Humboldt Counties

North of Sonoma, orchards remain a landscape fixture throughout the maritime valleys of Mendocino and Humboldt Counties. The Gowan family has been growing apples here since 1876, along the Navarro River in Anderson Valley. At first, the small orchard sold apples to emerging cities along the county's coast, just ten miles away, via one switchback-riddled log road. As transportation networks into the valley improved, Gowan Orchards grew. Early in the twentieth century, locally dried apples made the long and arduous overland journey to Sonoma County for canning. After World War II, the farm made the leap into fresh fruit and started distributing throughout the growing cities of California.

Anderson Valley, famous for its Pinot Noir and sparkling wines, has been home to vineyards since the late nineteenth century. In 2014, after decades competing against the rising tide of wine and fresh fruit from the Northwest, Don and Sharon Gowan stepped back from fresh fruit and made a 130-acre bet on cider, hoping to capture the magic of their apples in bottles. Generations of variety selection equipped Gowan's Heirloom Ciders with apples that grow and taste great in their terroir. Now the Gowans are learning to pair their orchard savvy with fermentation techniques that can allow the fruit to truly sing. They proudly label their ciders as estate grown—a borrowed wine term—meaning that the fruit is grown, fermented, and bottled on their property. Each of their single-varietal ciders—Gravenstein, McIntosh, and Sierra Beauty—captures all of the fresh and delicate perfumes the varieties offer on their own. They are expanding their orchard with more cider-specific apples, adding a new layer to the Gowan orcharding legacy.

Heading north into Humboldt County, spruce, oak, and fir trees give way to towering redwoods. Some 270 miles north of San

Sierra Beauty

Sierra Beauty is a chance seedling that originated around 1870 outside the town of Oroville in the Sierra Nevada mountains. Its remarkable keeping ability and perfection in pie was not enough for it to overcome how difficult it was to grow, and it faded from orchards in Northern California. In the 1970s, the variety was written off as extinct when searches around its birthplace proved fruitless. The apple was "rediscovered" at the Gowans' roadside stand. It had been a family favorite since Don Gowan's great-great-grandfather planted trees in 1906, the year of California's great earthquake.

CIDER PROFILE

Fresh, exuberant pineapple aromas layered with apricots and aniseed.

Francisco, the area has always been a refuge, isolated by impassable mountains and thick forests. Pat Knittel returned to Humboldt County and her hometown of Arcata in 2014 after fifteen years working in wineries and labs in Napa and Sonoma. Intrigued by the possibility of cider, she adapted her background in site-specific Pinot Noir to local apples with Wrangletown Cider Company. Her orchard partners vary from small nurseries to century-old orchards filled with heirlooms that were planted to cater to growing markets in San Francisco and Eureka. These apples thrive in the cooler, wetter coastal climate and often produce leaner, lighter, and brighter ciders than their southern counterparts.

While Humboldt County has always shipped apples south to San Francisco, its challenging terrain and remoteness kept apples from becoming a substantial part of the county's economy. But generations later, apples have surfaced as an answer to the challenges faced by the county's most lucrative cash crop: marijuana.

Humboldt County is the tip of the Emerald Triangle, one of the most famed and expansive areas for marijuana cultivation in the country. Isolated and rugged terrain enabled multigenerational growers to evade law enforcement, but since legalization in 2016, the old model of farming in remote pockets is losing out against warehouse-grown hydroponics and massive acreage in the Sacramento Delta. As businesses of all shapes cope with declining sales, farmers are looking for other opportunities. Knittel reports that present and former marijuana growers are looking at cider apples as their next opportunity to compete—as they did with their marijuana—with the best in the world. One of the orchards she works with surrounds an existing marijuana plot, and each year the cider has distinctive herbal qualities.

Regardless of whether the merging of the two products becomes the norm, diversity in business is tantamount, especially in small towns where people are forced to wear many hats. Knittel has continued working with wine, under the North Story Wines label, and Wrangletown has largely been made possible because of her wine's success.

San Joaquin Valley and the Sierra Nevadas

Since the mid-nineteenth century, the alluvial plains through California's central valley have been the agricultural heartbeat of the United States. In the last decades of the twentieth century, the area's growers took a page from Washington State's high-density irrigated orchards and came to eclipse other parts of California in production.

Johann Smit first planted trees on his parents' dairy farm in the valley in the 1980s when he was uncertain about the future of dairy. Hidden Star Orchards began selling apples, cherries, and stone fruit from the hot central valley weeks before their counterparts in eastern Washington could get product on shelves.

This success is being challenged by climate change. Multiyear droughts are pushing wells deeper into the ground and turning neighbor against neighbor as the aquifers below them collapse. The warm climate, once a great asset in the global fruit market, is working against growers today who are perpetually spraying clay on the trees to prevent sun damage, which affects both the color and texture of the fruit.

Irregular and erratic harvests also take a toll on seasonal laborers, who have kept the industry afloat for decades. People are steering clear of increasingly unpredictable orchards and finding harvest work in berry fields. As labor scarcity and climate change squeeze the business, apples are being abandoned by growers in favor of almonds and walnuts—crops that require heavy irrigation and further strain the water supply—because they do not have the same labor demands and can easily be machine harvested.

For dedicated apple growers like Smit, warming and erratic weather means the future of apples is in the Sierra Nevadas. Smit's thirty-five-acre mountain orchard is at an elevation of 3,200 feet. His trees ripen nearly a full month later than his valley holdings, and he tolerates the perils of frost because of his dedication to apples and cider. Smit's parents, Dutch immigrants, inadvertently gave him first-hand experience watching their dairy business slowly implode and cautioned him against pushing efficiency over character and quality. For Smit, the future of agriculture rests on the belief that value-added products are a vital part of any small farm system.

This notion is shared among historic orchards east of Sacramento outside of Placerville, in an area aptly named Apple Hill. Remnants of Placerville's gold rush draw thousands of visitors every year for photo ops and apple pie. During the gold rush era, the high volcanic hillsides were the site of some of the earliest apple-growing experiments in the state. The mountains were home to Felix Gillet, whose work has continued on through "Amigo" Bob Cantisano, a descendant of the first Spanish settlers of San Francisco. He moved to the mountains in the 1970s to escape the confines of the city and embraced organic agriculture on his journey back to the land.

At one time, extensive water ditches ran the course of the mountains, capturing snowmelt for mining and irrigation. This fizzled out in the 1920s, when mining operations throughout the mountains were abandoned. Irrigation ditches that served mining and agriculture were diverted for hydroelectric plants, leaving many orchards to die in impending drought. Gold towns that once drew ambitious fortune-seekers were abandoned as the Great Depression sank in.

But while depression led to the demise of small orchards in the mountains, it did not spell the end for many trees. Cantisano discovered intact orchards up old logging roads, and in 2003, he started the Felix Gillet Institute, a nursery specializing in the revolutionary trees brought over by the French nursery tender in the nineteenth century, which were neglected and forgotten in the wild. Cantisano has propagated seventeen different tree species and forty-five apple varieties, mostly for other small-scale farmers who are increasingly interested in adding cider to their homesteads. For Cantisano, these old varieties that have proven their endurance may hold the key to farming in the Sierras as they are beset by climate change.

Devastating forest fires have become increasingly common throughout California. The 2017 Tubbs Fire in Sonoma and Napa was, at the time, the most destructive wildfire in California. That was surpassed the following year when the Camp Fire ravaged Butte County and wiped the town of Paradise from the map. At just over 1,700 feet in elevation, Paradise was an ideal place for apples and, before the housing boom in the late twentieth century, home to dozens of orchards. As the community was engulfed by fire in early November 2018, the flames bypassed the still-lush, irrigated orchard that belonged to the Noble family and had recently been harvested. While the trees were spared, the rest of the family's buildings and homes were consumed by fire. Since the fire, proposals to rebuild Paradise have included irrigated land—either as park or agriculture—as a deterrent for future disasters.

Ben Nielsen of Lassen Traditional Cidery has been working with Noble Orchards since he began fermenting commercially in 2015. In 2012, he followed his sister to Chico, at the base of the Sierra Nevadas, from Oregon, which was experiencing its own cider revival, to explore possibilities in Northern California. With a focus on fruit quality and heirloom varieties, Nielsen labels his ciders with the names of the fruit he sources from old mountain orchards surrounding the Sacramento Valley: Winesap, King David, Newtown Pippin, and Arkansas Black. In 2020 he released a Paradise Strong cider made entirely from the remaining Winesaps from Noble Orchards.

Most of the fruit that Nielsen works with comes from the American heirloom stock, but he and a few others also draw from a unique, methodical orchard just outside Yosemite National Park in Mariposa County, 230 miles south of Chico. Beth and Dave Lancaster tend to the only five acres of apple orchard in the county. As in other gold-driven communities, apples and agriculture supported the miners, but to a lesser extent in Mariposa. There were no irrigation ditches during the gold rush, so everything was either dry-farmed or packed in. Yosemite National Park has two remaining apple orchards that date back to its earliest European settlers, but none of the apples go to cider—or anything else. Weeks before they ripen, they are picked to deter bears.

In the mid-2000s, the Lancasters bought an old neglected orchard and bulldozed it to make way for replanting. They picked varieties based on research done at Washington State University's Mount Vernon extension to balance flavor against the threat of mountain frosts, planting American russets, crab apples, and European cider apples that would become the foundation of Sierra Cider.

When the Lancasters began their project, there were only three cideries in the state. The industry, like their orchard, was primed for its next step, and with their trees in full bearing, what began as a retirement project has outpaced them and their self-distributed local cider. While Yosemite Valley and the park have proven eager supporters, the couple has also begun to sell apples to other cidermakers, like Lassen.

Core Takeaways

California's cider community covers the full breadth of the state, from the arid Mexican border to the Pacific fog–flooded valleys and volcanic hillsides where fruit survived gold boom and bust. As California's cider community continues to spread and diversify, it becomes a closer reflection of the state's collective agricultural endeavors. In this state, farmers are being pushed to the limit by climate catastrophes. Fires and floods are simply the most visible expression of climate change, but apples and agriculture are increasingly under threat. Without serious examination of environmental, labor, or historic land use issues, agriculture in California remains on a knife's edge, but it can be a tool to heal a ravaged environment, to bring soils back to health and create systems that do not rely on exploitation. Cider in California—like cider everywhere—needs to be built on systems rooted in land stewardship and equity for all members of the community.

SOUTHERN CALIFORNIA

• **Location and Geography:** East of San Diego in Southern California, the town of Julian abuts the Mexican border in the Cuyamaca Mountains.

• **Soil:** Mostly granite, with some alluvial loams in the valleys.

• **Climate:** Arid climate, with early blooms and frosts challenging orchards in some locations. Santa Ana winds in the fall blow large amounts of dust into the orchards. USDA Hardiness Zone 8a–8b, with some orchards creeping into 10a.

• **Orchard Location:** Julian is a respite for urban Southern Californians looking for some cooler temperatures in the fall and snow in the winter. The orchards extend from Julian down to the Guatay and Descanso area, at an elevation of 3,700 to 5,000 feet. They are typically dry-farmed.

• **Orchard Type:** Orchards in Julian originally supplied the growing Southern California grocery markets, until they were supplanted by other fruits. Regional tourist boards promote Julian apple pies, but the apples used in them now typically come from elsewhere.

• **Significant Apple Varieties:** Golden Delicious, Winesap, Newtown Pippin, Jonathan, Black Twig, Granny Smith.

• **Cider Apple Plantings:** Limited to experimental plantings.

• **Producers to Visit:** Raging Cider and Mead Co. (San Marcos, CA), 101 Cider House (Los Angeles, CA).

CENTRAL COAST

- **Location and Geography:** Hundreds of miles of narrow coastal canyons and high-elevation mountains stretch from Santa Barbara roughly to Monterey Bay, all within range of the Pacific Ocean.
- **Soil:** Widely varied, as the river valley loads to mountains, with granite in the hills that morphs into sandstone and gravel in the valleys.
- **Climate:** Arid maritime climate, with high diurnal shift. USDA Hardiness Zone 8b–10a.
- **Orchard Location:** See Canyon, south of Saint Luis Obispo, is a unique coastal microclimate that's home to several farms. Apples were also once common at higher elevations in Paso Robles.
- **Orchard Type:** As in other parts of California, Paso Robles's orchards are being replaced with vineyards, while other orchards, like those in See Canyon, continue to sell mostly direct-to-consumer.
- **Significant Apple Varieties:** Gravenstein, Arkansas Black, Fuji, Gala, Rome Beauty, Jonathan.
- **Cider Apple Plantings:** A few experimental plantings, but nothing of size.
- **Producers to Visit:** Bristols Cider House (Atascadero, CA), Gopher Glen Organic Apple Farm (San Luis Obispo, CA), Mission Trail Cider House (Shandon, CA).

SANTA CRUZ

- **Location and Geography:** Along the north side of the Monterey Bay, the Santa Cruz Mountains span from Santa Cruz to the San Francisco Bay area to the north. A fertile strip of agricultural land runs between the mountains and the ocean.
- **Soil:** Very sandy loam.
- **Climate:** Arid, with heavy fog and high diurnal shift. USDA Hardiness Zone 9b–10b.
- **Orchard Location:** Most of the orchards run along the Pajaro Valley, a rich, well-drained agricultural valley. Many orchards are over one thousand feet above sea level.
- **Orchard Type:** Santa Cruz was a fruit-growing region since the mid-nineteenth century but, by the mid-twentieth century, orchards became primarily processing-focused, driven toward Martinelli's in Watsonville. Most of the trees are large standard trees with minimal irrigation.
- **Significant Apple Varieties:** Newtown Pippin, Mutsu, Yellow Bellflower, Hauer Pippin.
- **Cider Apple Plantings:** Newtown Pippin has gained a reputation as

an excellent cider apple. There are some new cider-specific varieties going in the ground, but most of the excitement is around existing heirloom trees.
- **Producers to Visit:** Santa Cruz Cider Company (Watsonville, CA).

SONOMA COUNTY

- **Location and Geography:** Sixty miles north of San Francisco, between Napa and the Pacific Ocean, Sonoma County is bisected by the Russian River and a series of other streams and valleys that wind toward the ocean.
- **Soil:** At elevation, soils are volcanic, but orchards thrive in the dark and sandy Goldridge loam along the course of the Russian River, left over from high sea levels. Soils have more clay near Sebastopol.
- **Climate:** Arid, with high diurnal shifts. Fog and marine influence play a large role in the climate of individual sites. USDA Hardiness Zone 9a–9b.
- **Orchard Location:** Most of the orchards are located along the famed Gravenstein Highway running from Santa Rosa toward Sebastopol. Old orchards can be found in the hills and flood plains of Sonoma.
- **Orchard Type:** Most of the orchards are large trees grown for processors. Manzana—the only remaining processor—is strictly organic, so most of the commercial orchards in the county are as well.
- **Significant Apple Varieties:** Gravenstein, Golden Delicious, Nehou, Wickson, Newtown Pippin, Jonathan, Transcendent Crab.
- **Cider Apple Plantings:** Local Gravensteins and other established heirloom apples have been co-opted for cidermaking, and a number of mature cider-intended orchards provide a strong base to local cideries.
- **Producers to Visit:** Tilted Shed Ciderworks (Windsor, CA), Golden State Cider (Sebastopol, CA), Horse and Plow Cider (Sebastopol, CA), Old World Winery (Fulton, CA).

MENDOCINO AND HUMBOLDT COUNTIES

- **Location and Geography:** Steep Redwood valleys and narrow, coastally influenced river valleys define the remote counties of Northern California.
- **Soil:** Alluvial gravel and clay soils along river valleys, with granite and uplifted sea beds at high elevation.
- **Climate:** Maritime arid, with heavy fog influences along the coastal waterways. Hotter and drier in inland valleys. USDA Hardiness Zone 9a–9b.

- **Orchard Location:** Most of the orchards lie in the well-drained valleys along the coast.
- **Orchard Type:** Fruit is grown primarily for the fresh market, both local and into the Bay Area.
- **Significant Apple Varieties:** Wickson, Pink Pearl, Jonathan, McIntosh, Sierra Beauty, Gravenstein, Hudson's Golden Gem.
- **Cider Apple Plantings:** Experimental orchards have thrived here for almost fifteen years, as different generations try their hand at growing unique fruits. New cider-specific orchards are coming to maturity in the next few years, but nothing of large scale.
- **Producers to Visit:** Wrangletown Cider Company and North Story Wines (Arcata, CA).

SAN JOAQUIN VALLEY AND THE SIERRA NEVADAS

- **Location and Geography:** High volcanic peaks run through the interior of California, above the great Central Valley.
- **Soil:** Granite and till and sediment from a series of complex uplift.
- **Climate:** Continental arid, with lots of snowmelt used as irrigation. USDA Hardiness Zone 8b–9b.
- **Orchard Location:** Apple Hill in Placerville, east of Sacramento, has the largest concentration of orchards, but small orchards exist at five hundred to five thousand feet in elevation throughout the mountains. While many are modern plantings, others date back to the time of the gold rush.
- **Orchard Types:** Most orchards, especially in Placerville, are focused on fresh market packing. Small orchards are mostly direct-to-consumer. The more feral orchards mostly feed deer.
- **Significant Apple Varieties:** Gala, Rome, Jonathan, Winesap, King David, Sierra Beauty, Autumn Strawberry, Reine des Reinettes, Rhode Island Greening, Golden Russet, Yarlington Mill.
- **Cider Apple Plantings:** Some of the larger orchards in Placerville are beginning to experiment with cider-specific plantings. The Felix Gillet Institute is helping many small-scale and homestead orchards get started with their cider plantings, as well.
- **Producers to Visit:** Lassen Traditional Cidery (Chico, CA), Sierra Cider (Mariposa, CA).

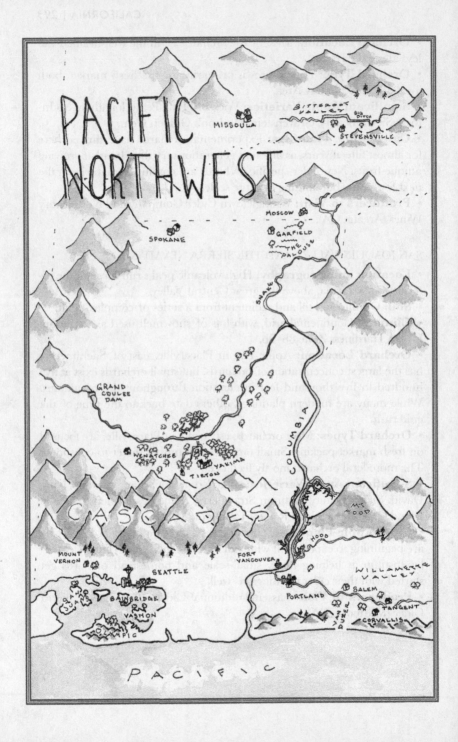

PACIFIC NORTHWEST

When the North American Plate began shifting westward two hundred million years ago, the western edge of North America started to expand, leaving room for mountains, plateaus, and the Cascade volcanoes to form. The greatest flow of lava in the history of North America created the Columbia River Gorge, opening a navigable, westward waterway that would bring settlers into the Pacific Northwest. Cataclysm shaped the landscape, and a series of Ice Age floods drained great inland seas. It formed canyons east of the Cascades and deposited the eroded topsoil of the Willamette Valley. Centuries later, when the river was dammed, it would create millions of gallons of irrigation for eastern Washington's dry desert climate and set a revolution in modern agriculture under way.

A merican missionaries and settlers began flooding into the Oregon Territory in the decades after Lewis and Clark's 1804–1806 expedition to the area. Russia and Spain had ceded their claims to the territory and, after 1818, it was under joint administration by the United States and Great Britain. By the early twentieth century, 250 years of colonization and apple growing throughout the country would reach a pinnacle in the Pacific Northwest.

Apples were introduced to the region in the 1820s at the forts of the British Hudson's Bay Company (HBC). Founded in 1670 to control the lucrative fur trade in Hudson Bay, the HBC was fundamental to the colonization of British North America and the development of Canada. James Bruce, the company's gardener, planted the first apple seeds in the Oregon Territory at Fort Vancouver, near the mouth of the Columbia River, in 1825.

The HBC planted orchards for sustenance and to establish trade with Indigenous communities. Orchards flourished throughout their forts as Euro-American missionaries, trappers, and families began arriving from points east with apples in tow, as they had for centuries. The difference in the Northwest, though, was that they landed on swaths of flat acreage with the means to irrigate it. Agriculture colleges and programs had been set up to investigate improvements to food production, which helped develop superior fruit, while improvements to technology and transportation got the fruit to market. A wealth of advancements found their foothold in the Pacific Northwest.

President James Polk pushed for westward expansion and control of the Oregon Territory in the 1840s. He was elected president after showing his earnest commitment to aggressively expanding the United States by campaigning on the slogan "Fifty-Four Forty or Fight," which referenced the proposed latitude line that might set the territory's boundaries. A dispute with Britain over the Oregon-California border was finally settled in 1846 with the Oregon Treaty, which created the modern boundary between the United States and Canada and transferred present-day Washington, Oregon, Idaho, and parts of Montana and Wyoming to the United States.

George Washington Bush, a free Black pioneer who was employed by the HBC as a trapper early in the 1820s, made fundamental contributions to the formation of what would become Washington State. After his stint with the HBC, Bush returned to Missouri to raise a family. In 1844, in an effort to escape racial prejudice there, Bush and four other families set out west for Oregon Territory along the Oregon Trail. But the territory's new boundaries were established in tandem with a series of Black exclusion laws to keep African Americans from settling. So Bush pushed north with his family into Puget Sound—a part of the territory that was still under British control and beyond reach of the racist laws—and established New Market (later renamed Tumwater), the first permanent settlement in what became Washington State. It was here that Bush staked a 640-acre claim, built the first gristmill and sawmill, and established a thriving farm and orchard—planted from seeds carried across the Oregon Trail—the bounty from which was always shared and vital in sustaining the town's growing community. When the Donation Land Claim Act came in 1850, entitling whites to land in the territory and attempting to keep Blacks out or invalidate their existing land claims, Bush's community sent a petition to Congress. Washington Territory split from Oregon in 1853, and members of the new territory's provisional government remembered Bush's generosity. In 1855, "An Act for the Relief of George Bush, of Thurston County, Washington Territory," was enacted, and the Bush family kept their land.

Other settlements first developed west of the Cascade Mountains: in the maritime climate of the Willamette Valley, in Oregon City, and downriver at Champoeg. Homesteaders planted seedling orchards from seeds they acquired at the HBC's Fort Vancouver, and the first commercial endeavor came in 1847. Horticulturist, abolitionist, and Quaker farmer Henderson Luelling set out west along the Oregon Trail from Salem, Iowa, with hundreds of young grafted apple trees. He arrived in what became Milwaukie, Oregon, partnered with William Meek—a fellow Iowan who traveled via wagon train with apple seeds and grafted trees—and established Oregon's first nursery. Luelling and Meek eventually sold fruit and trees locally, and at the peak of the gold rush in the San Francisco Bay, their apples sold for two dollars per pound, roughly sixty-five dollars in today's dollars. Fruit thieves were common, so apples were shipped in iron boxes.

More orchards and nurseries popped up throughout the Willamette Valley before the Civil War. Gravenstein, Blue Pearmain, Gloria Mundi, Red Astrachan, Esopus Spitzenburg, Baldwin, and Rhode Island Greening were all common varieties, heavily marketed and sold to California's surging gold rush population. None were as ambitious as Luelling and Meek. Their nursery grafted eighteen thousand trees in 1850. In 1851, Luelling traveled east to the orchards of Andrew Jackson Downing, along the Hudson River, in pursuit of Newtown Pippin. He returned via the Isthmus of Panama, reloaded with stock and ready for expansion. By 1853, Luelling and Meek were operating four locations.

To market this growing bounty of fruit, growers relied heavily on local publications. When it began in 1858, *Oregon Farmer* was loaded with columns and information about nurseries and fruit-growing. In one regard it provided growers a market, but it also led to local tree dealers acting as brokers between growers and nurseries, chipping away at grower profits. It dealt a fatal blow to Oregon's budding fruit industry—as did California's decade-long head start.

California's warmer climate, comparatively developed apple industry, and Bay Area ports got fruit to market nearly two months sooner and for higher premiums than the horticultural efforts in Oregon, which became a state in 1859. Oregon was able to market late-winter apples like Winesap and Newtown Pippin that outlasted California-grown apples, but the abundance of trees planted in haste by early settlers failed to find a local market as they came to bearing. Many of the trees brought to Oregon from California introduced fungus and pests to young orchards. Before rail transportation entered the state, more fruit ended up on the ground than in markets. Apples rotted on orchard floors and bred further insect and disease challenges. In many cases, acreage cleared for orchards was set to wheat or clover. Luelling and Meek, among others, moved south to California, in search of better opportunities in fruit and gold.

Hudson's Golden Gem

This conical russeted apple was found in a fence line in the early twentieth century in Tangent, Oregon, in the southern Willamette Valley. It quickly rose in popularity among commercial and home orchardists from the Redwoods of California through Puget Sound, before spreading across the country. One of the largest russeted apples, its skin, texture, and flavor resemble a Bosc pear, with slight nuttiness that carries through, fresh or fermented.

CIDER PROFILE

Sweet, floral, and spicy, with structured juice reminiscent of Golden Russet and pear.

Henry Miller and his son-in-law Joseph Lambert purchased the Luelling and Meek orchard in 1857. Miller had plum varieties brought from Ellwanger and Barry in Rochester, New York, and found success growing, drying, and canning an Italian prune variety. Seth Luelling, Henderson's brother, remained in Milwaukie, where he planted the first small plum orchard in Oregon just before the Civil War. By the time the Oregon and California Railroad was completed in 1887, finally bringing a larger market for Oregon's fruit, plums and prunes had largely replaced apples. Efforts to capture the nation's growing apple market shifted to Montana's Bitterroot Valley.

Western Montana became part of Washington Territory in 1853, when the region was divided from Oregon Territory. Traders and trappers had no intention of settling the region's inhospitable rocky landscape, which was home to roughly six thousand

Indigenous Peoples from about twelve tribes, including Salish, Koo-
tenai, Pend d'Oreille, and Nez Perce. The first European settlers
obliviously homogenized the entire Indigenous population and
began referring to them collectively as Flatheads. In the heart of the
Bitterroot Valley in 1841, Jesuit Father Pierre-Jean De Smet established Saint Mary's Mission and used agriculture and irrigation to
lure Indigenous Peoples onto settlements and farms and into
Christianity.

Flanked by the Bitterroot Mountains on the west and the less
imposing Sapphire Mountains on the east, the Bitterroot Valley
could be an agricultural oasis in the mountains. Irrigation was
required on the eastern, upper benchlands, but the west side of the
valley was fed by countless rivulets that emptied snowmelt into the
Bitterroot River. As a means to open land and draw white settlers,
Washington Territory Governor Isaac Stevens signed the Hell Gate
Treaty in 1855, which formed the Flathead Indian Reservation and
forced Indigenous Peoples onto it, ceding millions of acres to the
United States. In a similar fashion that would play out in the Plains
a decade later, American fences, farm endeavors, and hunting took
away Indigenous lands and food supplies, leaving Indigenous communities little choice but to sell their ravaged lands and relocate to
government-appointed reservations. Trains welcomed settlers,
Montana became a territory in 1864, and the entirety of the Bitterroot Valley—eight hundred square miles—was opened to settlement within ten years.

In 1866, traveling nursery representatives began convincing
Bitterroot farmers to plant apple trees. In 1871, the Vermont-born
Bass brothers—William and Dudley—planted Montana's first commercial orchard on their collective 320-acre homestead plot near
Stevensville, as orchards slowly and partially replaced wheat fields
and ranchland. The Bass brothers planted hardy Transcendent and
Hyslop Crabs and found success with McIntosh, as early September
frosts set the fruit's characteristic tartness. Markets developed
throughout the valley as the first rail line connected Grantsdale in

the south valley with Missoula, fifty miles to the north. Copper mines in nearby Butte drove the development of the state as they attempted to keep up with national demand for Thomas Edison's lightbulb, which used copper as a conductor.

Marcus Daly, an Irish-born American, arrived in the Bitterroot Valley in 1887, having already made a large fortune mining copper. He purchased thousands of acres in the valley, established Bitterroot Stock Farm, and developed preliminary ditch irrigation to support cultivation. By the 1890s, Daly's home of Missoula County had nearly ten thousand apple trees bearing fruit.

The first Pacific Northwest Fruit Fair was held in Stevensville in 1893, cementing local enthusiasm about the potential for fruit in the Bitterroot Valley. Montana's Board of Horticulture was formed, state funding poured in, and valley-based campaigns touting quality fruit reached a national audience. Daly's orchard grew to sixty-five thousand trees, while the Bitterroot Orchard Company, which formed in 1895, had close to fifty thousand. Nowhere else in the state had the soil conditions, moderate valley climate, and success with multiple varieties that the Bitterroot Valley did. Rome Beauty, Ben Davis, and Wealthy apples joined McIntosh and Alexander as premium market varieties for sale not only in the burgeoning mining state, but across the country.

Demand for water increased, and a series of land acts made irrigation a top priority. With twenty states' funding for irrigation solely in government hands after the Newlands Reclamation Act in 1902, for Montana that meant rapid and immense expansion of the flumes and canal systems Daly had put in place.

In 1898, agricultural workers began talking about the "Big Ditch," the 72-mile-long Bitterroot Irrigation District canal that would be completed in 1910. Early irrigation efforts supported farming on a local level, but the Big Ditch, as it remains locally known, was seen as a tool to transform the Bitterroot Valley into an agricultural paradise. Investors viewed the fruit industry as more profitable than wheat, and in 1905, valley production exceeded one hundred thousand boxes of apples, with nearly four hundred thousand trees on over three thousand acres.

Successful orchards were a sign of strong local and regional economies that stood the chance of attracting settlement and boosting prosperity within the state. At the turn of the century, conversations and efforts veered from home apple growing to commercial production. Samuel Dinsmore, a local Bitterroot entrepreneur and orchardist, picked up where Daly left off when he died in 1900. Copper mining companies deforested parts of the valley, and Dinsmore saw orchard potential in the cleared land. He partnered with Chicago financier W. I. Moody to buy valley benchlands and establish Como Orchard Company, named after Lake Como, which, when dammed, would supply large amounts of water for the Big Ditch.

Como Orchard Company commissioned young architect Frank Lloyd Wright to build a clubhouse and surrounding bungalows to attract investors to the company's vision and orchards. As outside investment came in, it proved there was national interest in Bitterroot Valley apples, spurring on the completion of the Big Ditch in 1910. From Lake Como in the western valley, the seventy-mile, steam-shovel-built ditch crossed the river and ran a northern course beyond Stevensville, providing irrigation to forty-five thousand acres.

Marketing shifted to a new realm. In the past, railroad and land companies had advertised to farmers and immigrants, who were invited to settle and cultivate land newly opened to transportation. But in the Bitterroot Valley, orchard companies did the developing. They divided land into smaller orchard tracts, and as companies planted trees in 1910 and 1911, they advertised their ready-made orchards to a targeted demographic. At the height of planting, the *Northwest Tribune* wrote, "Western Montana is now considered by eminent authority the logical fruit growing locality in the great Northwest."

Under the new model, farm experience was not required, and

Bitterroot orchard companies began marketing to Chicago-area professionals, professors, and students. They touted the valley's optimum climate for apples, its three hundred days of sun, spring rains, and lack of blizzards, frosts, diseases, and pests. The valley's rocky soils were flipped into a positive as the company convinced prospective investors that the rocks reflected the sun onto the apples, helping with ripeness. Here was a perfect summer getaway, and the start of seasonal and recreational tourism to the valley. The Como Orchard Company drew from an eastern elite population to develop a cosmopolitan farm community—a completely new concept. The company promoted the leisurely life of farming and even offered to farm the orchard with their own staff for the absentee owners, still promising sizeable returns.

Boxes of high-quality McIntosh apples shipped to Chicago and other U.S. cities, drawing investors to the Bitterroot Valley. But as towns and hotels sprang up around the boom, water became scarce. Landowners were unable to make continued payments to irrigate from the Big Ditch, and land use exceeded available irrigation. After nearly a decade of use, parts of the ditch required maintenance, but the Bitterroot Valley Irrigation Company lacked the funds to make improvements. Despite the company's early advertising claiming the valley was insect free, disease and pests chipped away at the young industry, as orchards were planted regardless of their long-term viability. By the start of World War I, the orchards of the Bitterroot Valley lay in ruin.

Irrigation efforts in Washington were proving to have more success. Between 1909 and 1919, the census reported an increase of three million bearing trees throughout the state. Washington's first generation of apple orchards was in the islands of Puget Sound, where moderate winters and mild summers gave favorite East Coast apples like Pound Sweet, Ashmead's Kernel, and Grimes Golden an ideal place to thrive. The San Juans in the northern sound were the center of production. In 1910, San Juan County claimed 76,731 trees and produced nearly a third of the state's total crop. Apples were shipped by boat to the ports of Bellingham, Tacoma, Victoria, and Seattle. But with increased irrigation in eastern Washington, by 1930, the entirety of western Washington was producing only 2 percent of the state's total crop.

Mission orchards in Washington Territory, Walla Walla, and near the Columbia, Clearwater, and Snake Rivers had utilized rudimentary irrigation. The first large-scale irrigation in the Columbia River basin was built in the Walla Walla River valley in 1859. As water became more accessible in central Washington, conflicts broke out between the newly arriving white settlers and Indigenous peoples.

Beginning in 1872, when the northerly and comparatively barren Colville Reservation was established, the territories' Native Americans were relocated from their land and forced into remote, homogeneous communities to make way for railroads and white settlement. A military post was established on the eastern border of the reservation, at the confluence of the Columbia and Spokane Rivers, and the Indigenous population was "kept in check" while Washington moved toward statehood.

By the turn of the twentieth century, Washington's population surpassed five hundred thousand, owing in large part to the completion of the Northern Pacific Railroad in 1883. Seven thousand miles of track connected Puget Sound with the Great Lakes, and it gave Washington growers access to Midwest and eastern markets in addition to those developing around Spokane, Seattle, and Tacoma. Farming became the dominant industry east of the Cascade Mountains in the Columbia River valley, and orchard crops were the leading pursuit.

One of the pioneers in Spokane-area orchards was Peter Barnabas Barrow, a man born into slavery in Virginia who escaped and fought with the Union Army before settling in Deer Park. In 1898, shortly after becoming the first Black landowner in the area, Barrow founded Deer Lake Irrigated Orchard Company, employed one hundred Black men, and shipped apples like Jonathan, Rome

Beauty, and Wagener nationwide via newly laid rail networks a few miles north in Loon Lake.

To appeal to customers in other parts of the country, Northwest apples were billed as consistently top quality. Growers in Washington and elsewhere began packing apples in smaller boxes that grocers from Denver to Charleston could easily unpack and display for their customers. Clever, fanciful designs and art began gracing the sides of these boxes to encourage the retailer to leave the fruit in its box, which worked as a vessel for advertisement, building brand recognition with consumers. Bright boxes of Washington apples paid for themselves because of the lack of waste further down the supply chain; within a few decades, wooden—and, ultimately cardboard—boxes became the industry standard throughout the country, entirely replacing barrels. National competition was no match for Washington, which by then had established itself as America's orchard.

Climates in eastern Washington mirrored the long, dry growing season in western Montana. What the Bitterroot River did for orchards in Montana, the Columbia River accomplished tenfold for Washington. As Montana's apple industry suffered in the 1920s and '30s, Washington, after righting its own wrongs from preliminary failures with irrigation and land speculation, became the leading producer of apples in the country, with 3.5 million acres of farmland being irrigated by 1928. Washington apples, grown with irrigation in a desert climate, came to market sooner than eastern fruit. More sun exposure, a longer season, and controlled irrigation combined to create the epitome of two centuries of apple growing throughout the country. Fruit was bigger, brighter, and crisper than ever.

Business was conducted at a scale the regional marketplace had never known. As part of his New Deal, President Franklin Roosevelt in 1933 authorized construction of the Grand Coulee Dam, ninety miles northwest of Spokane. When it was completed in 1942, it had used three times as much concrete as the Hoover Dam, ran a mile long, and stood over five hundred feet tall. The dam, which impounds the Columbia River, opened over one million acres to irrigation throughout central Washington. Farmers and communities no longer needed to establish themselves near water; water could now travel to them.

What unfolded in Washington is an amplified version of new orchard practices taking place at smaller scales throughout the country. Density of planting increased with the use of dwarfing rootstocks after World War II. From 1919 to 1961, the number of bearing trees in Washington went from 132,000 to 5.2 million. Into the twenty-first century, that number was seventy-five million, owing to the use of high-density planting on small rootstocks. Traditional, standard-sized tree orchards of yore usually maxed out at around fifty trees per acre. Under the new system, growers can fit a thousand trees per acre.

As Washington's fruit industry expanded, horticultural laws passed in 1915—and amended through the 1930s—were written to address national concerns with quality of fruit. Commissioners and inspectors were assigned to Washington's fruit industry, and they had the power to issue or revoke licenses and to "make, adopt, issue, and publish" at their will "rules and regulations governing the grading and packing of apples."

Modern Cidermakers and Apple Growers

Developments in technology, irrigation, and agriculture in the Pacific Northwest created an agricultural landscape that remains unsurpassed in the United States. Centuries of trial and error have given way to vastly irrigated deserts that produce some of the largest quantities of apples in the world.

The Pacific Northwest is also one of the most dynamic cider regions in the country, where small and large agriculture come together around growing cities seizing the opportunity. Portland and Seattle tout reputations as the first and second cider-drinking cities in the country, and approximately two hundred cideries dot the landscapes of Oregon, Washington, Idaho, and Montana. Nowhere else in the country has cider so deeply penetrated the public consciousness. It is available at nearly every bar, restaurant, and retailer, and thirsty enthusiasts can find everything from ghost pepper and marionberry ciders to varietal expressions of Yarlington Mill and Ashmead's Kernel. Northwest ciders are proof that there is no set formula for development and evolution. Cidermakers throughout the region take divergent paths and express their journeys through their products, markets, and communities.

THE CHARACTERISTICS OF PACIFIC NORTHWEST CIDER

Cider in the Northwest is overwhelmingly flavored, as berries, spices, and almost everything imaginable seem to be fair game for experimentation. With cull apples from the expansive orchards in eastern Washington, cidermakers have a near limitless supply of raw materials. In the shadow of these large orchards, many producers are making cider of unique potential and character. The region has a long history of growing European cider apples that bring tannin, weight, and concentration to many ciders of the Pacific Northwest.

Puget Sound

While the East Coast touts its four-centuries-old cider history, the more recent history of cider in the Northwest laid extensive groundwork for its current generation of cidermakers. European cider apples have been cultivated in the region since the 1980s, and they remain an important feature for nearly all estate cideries. New England's West County Cider and Farnum Hill Ciders have been growing cider apples and making cider at a large scale for longer, but they were preceded by an earlier generation of aspiring cidermakers in Puget Sound and the Willamette Valley. While these cideries no longer exist, they left behind a blueprint for contemporary cider culture. Before the focus shifted to eastern Washington, island orchards were a major supplier of apples to the cities of the sound. When people began looking at cider for the first time in the 1980s, they started from the sound rather than the high desert.

Cider Institute of North America

British native Peter Mitchell taught cidermaking in western England, and in 2003 he began coming to the States multiple times a year to teach his straightforward and scientific approach at Washington State University's research center in Mount Vernon.

Though Mitchell has since retired, the recently minted Cider Institute of North America has expanded his course across the country. CINA is a collaboration between industry leaders, Washington State University, Cornell University in New York, and Brock University in Ontario. It offers classes that equip the next generation of cidermakers with the techniques and knowledge that will help ensure success in the industry. As it expands its offerings and certifications, it also expands the flow of knowledge moving throughout the community and improves the quality of cider as a whole. Today a significant number of the cidermakers in North America have taken one of his classes.

The maritime climate and late cool spring of Puget Sound mimics Normandy, France, the ancestral home of many cider apples. For this reason, people began experimenting with cider apples in the 1970s and '80s. While living in Central Oregon, Nick and Carla Botner assembled over 4,500 varieties of apples in a large private collection on their farm. The trees helped shape the next forty years of cidermaking in Oregon and Washington, as professionals and amateurs alike collect scion wood from their orchard in search of special apples that would thrive in their own collections. Since the Botners' retirement, the Temperate Orchard Conservancy has continued care of the trees while preserving and expanding the collection, ensuring that the Botners' life work will be preserved for future generations.

Vashon Island lies between the Olympic Peninsula and Seattle, and despite being a short ferry ride from the heart of the city, it has remained a very rural community through environmental protection policies. Limited water resources have restricted development on the island, and the county's open space policies ensure that large parcels of land remain intact. Old rows of apples like King of Tompkins County can still be found along the shores of Vashon, like many of the other islands in Puget Sound.

Cider, once made by arriving New England farmers and refugees, was reintroduced commercially to Washington State on Vashon Island. Ron Irvine, former owner of Pike and Western Wine Shop in Seattle, began making cider in the 1970s from Cox's Orange Pippin grown in the Skagit Valley. On one of his trips north, Irvine learned about Dr. Robert Norton's research orchard at Washington State University (WSU) in Mount Vernon—the first cider apple research program in the United States, which Norton established with Gary Moulton and led from 1962 to 1992. While their research was driven by the booming apple orchards east of the Cascade Mountains, they also established an orchard with multiple varieties on different rootstock to see if the maritime cider apples of England and France would be suitable for the comparable Puget Sound.

Every year Irvine filled his car with fruit from Norton's WSU orchard, and he still recalls their intoxicating aromas on his drives back to Vashon. In 1989, he pressed, fermented, and began selling his cider, naming it Centennial for Washington's one hundred years of statehood. Irvine wanted to make single-varietal ciders that drew a comparison to the wines he sold at his store, but with WSU having only one or two trees of each of its forty varieties, he turned to the personal orchards of another WSU professor on Bainbridge Island for Kingston Black and Yarlington Mill.

In 1991, still making his annual pilgrimages to collect cider apples, Irvine sold his shop and moved to Vashon to work full time at his friend's Vashon Winery. He purchased the winery in 2000 and later became adjunct professor of oenology and grape growing at South Seattle College. At the winery, cider became less and less part of the conversation, relegated to festivals and gatherings rather than the tasting room.

Nevertheless, a growing communal interest in cider encouraged Irvine and others to start coming together in the late 1990s and early 2000s. Alan Foster of Oregon, Richard Anderson in the San Juan Islands, Drew Zimmerman in Mount Vernon, Vashon's Doug Tuma, and others formed the Northwest Cider Society (a precursor to the Northwest Cider Association). This vanguard of early cider professionals laid the foundation for the cider wave to come. Irvine still makes wine and cider at Vashon Winery, and as cider gains steam, he's been able to shift his fruit sourcing from WSU orchards to local Vashon growers.

In the three decades of cidermaking on Vashon, a new generation of orchardists and cidermakers has taken root. Wes and Laura Cherry of Dragon's Head Cider grow cider apples in thin glacial till soil that was once an extensive Japanese-American strawberry farm, until Japanese internment. With thirty acres in the center of Vashon, Dragon's Head is the largest farm on the island, and their orchard is loaded with late-blooming European cider apples. These varieties are well suited for Puget Sound, because they bloom in large part after the constant spring rains that can hinder pollination.

Instead of threats from early blooms and frost, the biggest orchard issue throughout the sound is anthracnose, a deadly canker disease endemic to western Washington. Found in nearly 90 percent of the region's apple trees, it kills 3 to 5 percent of Dragon Head's trees annually. Dead trees are often replaced with Kingston Black, a bittersharp apple that is highly susceptible to fire blight when grown on the Atlantic coast. But in Puget Sound, cool springtime temperatures have historically meant the disease is nonexistent. Kingston Black's midnight-black bark and fingerlike branches make it easily distinguishable within a row of other varieties, and the tree's success in the orchard has been met with drinkers who are beginning to ask for it by name. Wes Cherry quips that even if they produced five times as much of their single-varietal Kingston Black cider, they would still sell out. Their customers are increasingly educated, with the conversation evolving from asking for sweet cider, to dry cider, and on to single varieties.

Puget Spice Crab

This tiny red crab apple was part of a disease-resistant trial born from two conventional eating apples. Propagated by WSU professor Bob Norton, these cherry-size apples pack a punch and are loaded with sugar, acid, and tannin. Chemistry-wise, WSU reports that the apple closely resembles Kingston Black, but without all of the growing challenges and difficulties.

CIDER PROFILE

Greengage plums, tarragon, and dogwood backed by high acid and high tannin.

Education can be a powerful tool when explaining unusual tannic ciders and trying to provide context for cider drinkers. This lesson has been learned many times over by Jim Gerlach and Cheryl Lubbert of Nashi Orchards, also on Vashon Island. Nashi's perspective on orcharding comes from its collection of perry and Asian pears that were planted in a mix of pea gravel, sand, and glacial moraine debris in the 1970s. The fruit was planted as a hobby project by a local horticulturist interested in hybridizing Asian and European pears. Nashi's signature Asian perries are unique in the country and increasingly enjoyed by Seattle consumers, but it took years of education to explain the differences between perry and pear cider: that perry is made from pears, whereas pear cider is cider flavored with pears. Nashi's pears are concentrated, rich, and flavorful, worlds apart from the common, waterlogged Asian pears found in grocery stores.

With access to feral apples on Vashon, Nashi developed what it calls a cider collaborative. People bring Gerlach and Lubbert their crops from fifty-year-old trees, and a portion of the proceeds from their cider—called *issho ni*, which means "together" in Japanese—goes to a local nonprofit land trust that helps preserve the island's open space. By harvesting fruit that would otherwise fall to the ground and rot, Nashi's cider project is a step toward eliminating pest pressures on the island and building strength in the local economy.

Vashon CiderFest

Vashon CiderFest stands out among the many cider gatherings and festivals in the Pacific Northwest. Festival growers are encouraged to bring island-grown apples to a community press for their own experimentation and consumption. Unlike most cider events, Vashon CiderFest is limited to ciders made from 100 percent apples and pears, to the exclusion of bulk juice coming from other parts of the state. Alongside apple crisp, cider-braised lamb tacos, and wonderful Washington cider, Bob Norton, who started the Vashon Island Fruit Club, can be found hunched over a table identifying piles of apples brought to him by the island's residents.

An important early member of the Northwest Cider Society was Richard Anderson, a retired Boeing systems analyst. In 1996, he transformed his family's apple orchard in the San Juan Islands into Westcott Bay Cider, Washington's first commercial estate cidery. The archipelago of the San Juan Islands, sandwiched between the United States and Canada, was home to a burgeoning apple industry at the end of the nineteenth century. Westcott Bay's dry cider, released in 1999, was based on fifteen different apples, the majority of which were European varieties like Yarlington Mill and Kingston Black, and a few multipurpose varieties like Golden Russet and Cox's Orange Pippin. Their current product line has expanded to three ciders—Traditional Very Dry, Traditional Dry, and Traditional Medium Sweet—all very different drinking experiences even though the only variance is the amount of sugar added at bottling. All fifteen varieties still go into every bottle.

In 2010, Anderson was joined by Hawk and Suzy Pingree, and they expanded to distillation under the name San Juan Island Distillery. Their spirits soon outpaced the production from the orchard, and the distillery decided to source brandy apples from elsewhere while they continued to use their estate apples for cider. Utilizing the bounty and diversity of their island, they craft terroir-driven spirits with foraged local products like Salish juniper, sea beans, madrone bark, and camas root. In total they produce fourteen distinct gins in addition to their brandies, liqueurs, pommeaus, and ciders.

Across the sound from the San Juan Islands, in a small clearing of otherwise dense pine forests in the northeast corner of the Olympic Peninsula, is Alpenfire Cider. Steve "Bear" and Nancy Bishop purchased an old logging plot filled with downed trees and logging chains to build their homestead orchard. They mound dirt around the rows and trunks because of the limited topsoil, and they farm a certified organic orchard with few pests or disease pressures. Bear, a retired firefighter, practices flame weeding to cripple the weeds and dried leaves that are harbingers of pests. He outfits apple tree trunks with fire shell skirts that protect them when he takes a propane torch to unwanted grasses. The process keeps unhealthy insects at bay and adds to the organic matter in the soil.

Alpenfire's orchard was planted in 2003, and Nancy credits much of her foundational knowledge to Peter Mitchell's first class the same year. In the years since, the Olympic Peninsula has evolved from an outdoor hiking and biking destination into one for culinary tourism. Alpenfire's estate orchard is mostly European cider apples, but the Bishops also source heirloom fruit from throughout the region. Most of their six-thousand-gallon production is sold out of their small tasting room as people from Seattle make the trek across the Sound.

Hidden Rose
(aka Airlie Red Flesh and Mountain Rose)

A chance seedling discovered in 1960 in Airlie, Oregon, in the western Willamette Valley, this is one of the most visually striking apples grown today. Neon-green skin reminiscent of Granny Smith contains brilliant, crimson flesh. The fruit remained a local oddity for the first few decades until it was trademarked under the name Hidden Rose. The trademark comes with a strict guideline for ripeness, color, and size. Many of these pristine apples are exported to Japan, where they fetch sky-high prices. Since the cost of trademark is prohibitive to many growers, Hidden Rose can also be found under the name Airlie Red Flesh or, in Hood River, Mountain Rose.

CIDER PROFILE

Cranberry, rose petals, and watermelon. Low in tannin and high in acid. Excellent natural rosé cider.

Eight miles south of Alpenfire, in the Chimacum Valley, Finnriver Farm and Cidery is reaching a wider market while simultaneously focusing on sustainability. With more than seventy-five employees, Finnriver is the leading employer in Chimacum and is becoming an agent for rural development. To support this agricultural community, Finnriver relies on organic apples from eastern Washington for their perpetual bestsellers, lavender black currant and habanero cider, whose additional ingredients are all sourced locally.

Finnriver was started by Crystie and Keith Kisler and Eric Jorgensen, three environmental educators who purchased a two-acre blueberry farm, hoping to bridge conversations about nature and conservation with agriculture. Keith began making cider with fruit from old trees on the property after trying a neighbor's made with that same fruit. An eager local market, largely informed by the region's craft beer industry, took to the new offering immediately, and the cidery soon outgrew their own trees and began reaching out toward eastern Washington to supply the growing demand.

But the trio retained their desire to grow fruit on their own farm. In 2011, they transplanted a mature orchard that was going to be uprooted near Mount Vernon to their home farm. It has grown under the care of Cameron Denning to just shy of ten acres with 5,700 trees and more than twenty-two varieties. Chimacum is former dairy country, and the trees grow vigorously in the peat soils high in organic matter. While rainforest lies just ninety miles to the west, their small trees east of the mountains are reliant on irrigation and constant upkeep to make it through the year. Denning is interplanting with larger drought-tolerant trees, hoping to create an orchard environment that can meet oncoming climate change.

Finnriver also sources organic juice from eastern Washington; indeed, the meteoric rise of cider across the Northwest has largely been enabled by the incredible abundance of apples in the eastern part of the state. In 2013, Seattle Cider Company was created as a sister company to Two Beers Brewing Company, tapping into local resources to create a cider that appealed to new consumers. With no other cidery in the city limits, Seattle Cider branded itself after the aspirational lifestyle of the Pacific Northwest, featuring snow-capped peaks and evergreen trees on its cans. It expanded into sixteen states with sixteen-ounce cans and a story of apples making the 120-mile trek across the mountains to its urban operation. Innovation and freshness were important to their brand, so Seattle Cider Company installed a window into their production room where guests could watch herbs and fruit being prepared and integrated into particular ciders.

With access to an ample supply of on-demand juice, urban cideries continue to pop up across the Pacific Northwest. America's urbanization was one of the contributing factors to cider's demise in the mid-nineteenth century, but today, urban markets—and people traveling from them to rural cideries and orchards—are the very things enabling its growth.

Portland, Oregon, is often cited as the most cider-centric city in the country. More than a dozen cideries operate within the city limits and produce cider in every conceivable style, appealing to a wide range of palates and occasions. But while commercial cider has been made in Portland since 1992 by McMenamins, the industry remains shadowed by the city's hundred-plus breweries.

Portland's beer culture is diverse. New England, West Coast, and Brut IPAs share tap space at bars and restaurants with world-class pilsners and English milds. Into this space stepped the mail order–ordained Reverend Nat West, proclaimer of the cider revival. West took his amateur home cidermaking commercial in 2013 under the label Reverend Nat's Hard Cider. His first cider on the market, inspired by what he loved to drink and thought the city of Portland wanted, was one-third naturally fermented French bittersweet with two-thirds Newtown Pippin. Sales were modest, but when his second cider, Hallelujah Hopricot—made with apricot juice, Belgian saison yeast, cascade hops, and witbier aromatics—began outpacing it in sales, he never looked back.

West has not made his original cider in years, while Hallelujah Hopricot has become an integral part of his portfolio of convention-breaking ciders. Led by beer yeast, West has pushed past cider adjuncts and into formulating cider recipes that are more about process and technique than flavor-of-the-month. Process-driven ciders involve constant experimentation, often using blending, hops, fruit, and even coffee, less in an attempt to mimic flavors and more to push the limits of Portland's most curious drinkers. A former homebrewer, West's ability to speak beer allows him to fit seamlessly into festivals, collaborations, and the greater beverage community of Portland. His coveted tent-series ciders draw lines from around the region as people pay up to sixty dollars for one-of-a-kind bottles.

Reverend Nat ciders lie at the intersection of the Pacific Northwest's unique culture, knowledge, market, and access to resources. West proposes that, like European cider cultures, Northwest cider is an ongoing relationship between resources and demand. The rise and preeminence of adjunct cider in this part of the country is driven by the massive supply of apples and juice that is immediately available. In a town where monthly innovation and development drive taproom sales, the juice of eastern Washington provides an ideal medium for exploration.

Hood River, Oregon

Hood River, sixty miles east of Portland, runs from the high peaks of the Cascades into the Columbia River Gorge at close to sea level. The gorge was carved by the Missoula floods, when glacial lakes broke free as their thawing ice dam gave way. Millions of cubic feet of water were sent coursing down the Columbia Basin, carving many of the channels and canyons of eastern Washington and the four-thousand-foot deep Columbia River Gorge.

The Hood River Valley's volcanic alluvial soils have been irrigated from mountain runoff since the end of the nineteenth century. The three hundred or so orchards in the valley today cover fifteen thousand acres, and while the area is the largest pear-growing region in the country, apples have had their place for more than a century. Newtown Pippin, grown for fresh eating, processing, and export, was the preeminent apple for most of the twentieth century.

Before cidermakers created a new market for Newtown Pippin, many older trees were uprooted in the early 2000s in favor of Granny Smith, which processors preferred for its slightly superior keeping qualities.

Randy Kiyokawa is a third-generation orchardist in the upper Hood River Valley. At nearly two thousand feet in elevation, his is one of the last orchards in the region to harvest each year. At the peak of the Alar crisis in the early 1990s, when conventional chemical farming was linked to cancer and drove the American public from apples, a desperate Kiyokawa began selling apples out of his driveway for five cents a pound—which was still more than the large local packers were paying. While U-Pick orchards have been a staple of the Midwest and East Coast orchards, they arrived later to the Northwest because it remained profitable longer to grow for packing houses and processors. In 2000, Kiyokawa was the first to introduce the farm practice to the Hood River. He was able to keep every cent and grow his orchard from forty-five acres to well over a hundred, and from 5 varieties to more than 120.

Northwest Cider Association

The Northwest Cider Association has its roots in the Northwest Cider Society. What began as a casual gathering has become a regional initiative to bring together producers for the common cause of promoting cider and making it more accessible. Festivals, cider weeks, and successes with new marketing channels have encouraged a new wave of drinkers and cidermakers, as the association works to build common ground among different cider styles, scales of operation, and locations to improve cider's presence in the world.

Reverend Nat was the first cidermaker to reach out to Kiyokawa for cider apples, and Portland Cider Company began buying his coveted fruit as well. In 2013, Kiyokawa dabbled in European cider apples, planting Yarlington Mill and Dabinett, but their low prices have led him to graft over them in favor of apples for his U-Pick and farmers' market customers.

Back in Portland, Abram Goldman-Armstrong's Cider Riot! has split itself to reach a wider audience. One side of the cidery draws inspiration from the region's craft beer industry, focusing on fast fermentations using ale yeast and tankers of Hood River juice. The product is easy to make regularly and so brings in regular profit, which provides the means for the second side of the label. That side makes cider from bittersweet and bittersharp apples that are pressed and fermented slowly on site. New cideries and cidermakers in the Northwest often start along the same path as Cider Riot!, with plans for a dual-label business. But the "cash-flow cider," as Goldman-Armstrong calls the regularly produced cider, often becomes the driving force, because it sells quickly and easily and has a cheaper cost of production.

Willamette Valley, Oregon

In 1989, when Goldman-Armstrong was still in high school, he helped Alan Foster plant his cider orchard in the northern Willamette Valley. Foster, another early member of the Northwest Cider Society, accompanied Ron Irvine on a sponsored trip to England and France to learn about the European culture of cider apples. Foster's White Oak Cider, which operated from 1994 to 2004, was the first commercial cidery in Oregon, and it utilized the bittersweet and bittersharp apples that he planted with Goldman-Armstrong. Straining to sell cider, and with two daughters on their way to college, Foster ripped out half his orchard and planted Pinot Noir for local wineries. But he still sells the remaining apples to Goldman-Armstrong for Cider Riot!

Ciderkin

Cider apples have a lot of give, even after they have been squeezed dry. Ciderkin is lightly alcoholic (3 percent ABV) and made by rehydrating apple pomace with water, allowing it to ferment, then pressing it again. A little sour, a little funky, and remarkably refreshing, ciderkin is thirst quenching and easy drinking. Reverend Nat makes an excellent version from White Oak's spent English bittersharps.

While Foster was the first commercial planter of cider apples in the Willamette Valley, he is part of a longer tradition of innovation in the area. The patchwork valley was once home to an array of crops, including apple and pear orchards, but few remain, as growers fell victim to economies of scale. In their stead are hazelnut orchards and the less glamorous grass seed, the region's largest cash crop. The several hundred acres of fruit orchard left between Portland in the north and Eugene in the south are shrinking every year.

In the early 2000s, Kevin Zielinski of E. Z. Orchards was approached by a winemaker friend with the prospect of growing cider apples. Zielinski's family has been farming in the Willamette Valley since 1929. After multiple generations of cultural swings and technological improvements, the family is accustomed to adjusting to the agricultural market. With a handshake customer in place to buy the cider fruit when the trees were ready, Zielinksi set out planting a large collection of bittersweet and tannic apples. By the time the trees were bearing fruit, the handshake friend had moved to California, leaving Zielinski with a massive quantity of high-quality cider apples.

As a fruit grower, Zielinski had fermentation experience limited to a single annual barrel of Pinot Noir for personal use. He developed E. Z. Orchards Cidre from his newly bearing trees, using equipment at local wineries. Zielinski, working largely outside the cider conventions prescribed by Peter Mitchell, developed his own unique style of cidermaking, adapting keeving and other natural fermentation styles to create a mouth-filling cider low in alcohol and high in character. Utilizing French bittersweets in addition to some nearly century-old Rome Beauty and Jonathan apples, his naturally sparkling kegs, which were barreled while the cider was still fermenting and thereby naturally carbonated, were ahead of their time when he launched them in 2015.

West of E. Z. Orchards, along the foothills of the Coast Range that divides the fertile valley from the foggy, cold Pacific Ocean, Dan Rinke and Kim Hamblin's Roshambo ArtFarm is a radically different orchard. The farm lies in the Van Duzer Corridor, a break in the Coast Range that allows the cold Pacific air to slip into the valley, making the farm one of the coolest spots in the Willamette Valley. Born out of Rinke's day job as the viticulturist at Johan Vineyards, their label Art+Science Cider and Wine was founded from foraged apples as their experimental orchards came into fruition. Unlike in the Northeast, feral apples are a rare occurrence along the Pacific Coasts, but Hamblin supported the early vintages of cider by raiding old homesteads around the valley.

Built into the contours of the land, Roshambo's eighty-five varieties and seedling orchard—both biodynamic—are an experiment to understand how to improve farming on a small scale. They let their seedlings struggle through loving neglect, in order to weed out apples that cannot survive natural challenges, including the herds of elk that migrate through the orchards. Hamblin's vision for the orchard is as a natural part of the landscape, not a dominant force over it.

While Art+Science looks to tap into a developing culture of natural wine with its cider, it was an ode to past arts that seeded one of the most important players in the Northwest cider scene. When Roger Mansfield, a former litigator from San Francisco, began selling cider at the Oregon Shakespeare Festival in Ashland, he hoped the ciders from his Traditional Company would capitalize on the

Elizabethan connection between cider and Shakespeare. In 2002, he went to England to study cidermaking with Peter Mitchell and returned to his production space in southern Oregon with a shipping container full of equipment to grow the business.

When Mansfield was ready to retire, he passed his cidery on to Nick Gunn and Mimi Casteel. The pair had begun planting cider apples in 2002 on swampy land ill suited for grapes on Casteel's family's vineyard outside of Salem. They moved Mansfield's cidery to Salem, renamed the company Wandering Aengus Ciderworks, and initially stuck to their modest production of three hundred cases. They opened a tasting room and began selling 750-milliliter bottles priced at fifteen to twenty dollars, earning acclaim for their Wickson and Golden Russet ciders but struggling nonetheless as they ramped up production by a factor of ten.

In 2009, Wandering Aengus partnered with James Kohn and flipped the cider script. Cider at this point in the Northwest fell into two camps: small estate cideries like Wandering Aengus and larger operations (most of which now cease to exist) that based their product on imported concentrates. Aengus, with their Anthem line of ciders, and Crispin Cider Company in California were the first cideries to tap into the vast supply of cull apples in neighboring Washington, grown not for cider but for fresh eating. This departure from their estate ciders allowed them to sell their products on store shelves around the country, because Anthem ciders could be priced like beer rather than wine.

The ability to use Washington's excess apples for cider came about because of the changing varieties in orchards. Once-popular Red Delicious loses its acidity in storage, and its juice, while satisfactory for fresh consumption, can be inconsistent over the course of a year. So orchards throughout eastern Washington and Oregon began converting to Gala, Fuji, and acid-rich Granny Smith. These apples store better and are more desirable in the market—and consequently better for cider.

With growing demand from the cider community, large fruit-processing companies like Hood River Juice Company and FruitSmart in Yakima began adapting their practices, building custom blends for individual cidermakers. Having access to tankers of juice coming in near limitless supply has allowed Northwest cider to grow at unprecedented rates, but it comes with its own set of challenges. Hood River Juice Company's presses crush three tons of fruit in a single press, which is delivered in 5,500-gallon tankers—an enormous quantity for most small cideries.

Not every cidermaker is able, or desires, to make the leap into handling the large volume accessible in the Northwest. Mobile presses have been the norm for decades in Europe and have only recently gained popularity in North America. Mechanical engineer Ryal Schallenberger was the first to import a mobile press from Canada to the United States, for the 2015 harvest. Schallenberger's Northwest Mobile Juicing acts as a bridge across the industry, connecting orchardists with cidermakers. Schallenberger uses his diverse connections to help with everything from sourcing to the various nuances of certain blends. He works with over sixty-five cidermakers stretching from Washington to Colorado and into his home base in Montana.

In 2010, Dave Takush, Lee Larson, and Aaron Sarnoff-Wood returned from abroad to start 2 Towns Ciderhouse in Corvallis, Oregon. Their first batch of cider was made in part with rhubarb from a friend's father's rhubarb patch. They upgraded their production space from a two-car garage and soon became one of the largest cideries in the Northwest. The old rhubarb patch no longer produces enough to supply their current needs but, as luck and local infrastructure would have it, 2 Towns has ended up next to Stahlbush Island Farms, one of the largest sustainable berry growers and processors in the country. They contract millions of pounds of Oregon-grown marionberries for their new bestseller, Made Marion. Tapping into the Northwest's vast agricultural network enables

2 Towns and other Northwest cidermakers to grow while maintaining the integrity of their product, without having to compromise on inferior substitutes.

Central Washington

Expansive, high-density, irrigated orchards in Washington State have been the proverbial bogeyman throughout this cider journey. They grow fruit to precision and transformed apples from a fleeting delight, consumed in season or squirrelled away by devotees, into a perpetually available foodstuff. In the 1950s, boxes of high-desert apples began to compete with historic apple growers from Maine to Chihuahua, Mexico, who felt the pressure from the growing warehouses and supply lines along the Columbia River. In many ways, eastern Washington growers represent the culmination of a nation's orchard history. Most of the orchards here are located in the foothills of the Cascade Mountains and feed off the Columbia River basin, and their crops represent over half the apples grown in the United States. As of 2017, the state of Washington reported nearly 180,000 acres of apples and an estimated 126,000,000 trees grown across nine counties abutting the Cascades.

The Cascade Mountains create a rain shadow over the foothills to their east. Rugged, desertlike landscape is brought to life through irrigation from the Columbia River, fed from snowmelt from the Cascade and Rocky Mountains. Mountain winds, desert sun, and an extreme diurnal shift between daytime and nighttime temperatures aid in the development of shiny ripe fruit, with peak sugars and acid that form the sweet crunch that has epitomized Washington apples. While global warming is making apples increasingly difficult to grow in many parts of the country, growers in eastern Washington have had record years. Between 2012 and 2018, four years saw production numbers in the top five of all time, though how long apples can continue to soak in the increased sun and heat remains to be seen.

Billions of apples grown here each year are geared toward the fresh market, and massive packing houses dwarf operations anywhere else in the country. Large farms stretch over thousands of acres to supply the world with apples. In decades past, Yakima and Wenatchee were filled with small farmers who fueled the local packing houses, but the apple business has changed. For years, apples like Red and Golden Delicious dominated the international market, but today, the trend favors an ever-innovating selection of club and proprietary apples like Envy, Cosmic Crisp, Kanzi, and Pacific Rose. These varieties are developed by Washington State University, which sells the rights to growers on a pay-to-play basis. The practice comes with high costs but equally high returns. Apples stay popular for a couple of years before commercial farmers invest in the next great apple, and small farmers are simply not able to compete at that pace. They are increasingly being consolidated and integrated into large corporate farms.

Faced with bleak prospects, multigenerational farmer Tim Larsen began experimenting with cider, hoping for a different path for the sixty acres his family has farmed since the 1940s. He did early trials with dreadful blends of their Red and Golden Delicious, until a local winemaker introduced him to cider apples. When Larsen and Peter Ringsrud, his father-in-law, planted a test block of cider apples in 2003, they were told they had planted maritime apples that would never work in the arid Wenatchee Valley. Not every variety survived the cold winters or heat of summer, but many proved to thrive in America's modern fruit basket.

Cider apples challenge every norm that fruit growers in eastern Washington hold dear. Packing houses largely dictate the harvest schedule and make decisions based on logistics and predicted—not actual—ripeness. Red Delicious was the dominant apple in Washington not because it was delicious or nutritious per se, but because of its logistical flexibility. The hardy apple could sit in storage almost indefinitely and retain its value awaiting shipment. Cider apples offer growers no such luxuries. Their value is in their flavor and juice quality, both of which can deteriorate if stored too long. But cider apples are becoming a larger part of the conversation among growers large and small. Small growers like Larsen, who launched Snowdrift Cider Co. in 2008, are looking for viability through diversity, while some larger operations—facing the reality that people can consume only so many apples each year—are looking to increase their business through cider.

A number of years after Snowdrift launched, Larsen was introduced to unique red-fleshed apples with cranberry- and watermelon-like sensations that challenged the usual milky-white expectations for apples. The cultivars—close descendants of varieties from Kazakhstan—were brought to Washington in the hope that they could be sold as fresh eating apples. They were not. Larsen agreed to take an unspecified amount of the apples, expecting four or five bins, and was surprised when forty bins arrived on his loading dock. While none of the apples have names, collectively they are known as RedWave. The brilliant cider drawn from these apples is a stark ruby color loaded with fresh berry aromas and an acid profile unlike anything else on today's market. It complements the rest of Snowdrift's ciders, which are all backed by round tannins and depth. The apples also form the backbone of ANXO's rosé and rojo ciders in Washington, DC.

Because decisions made in the orchard are not realized for years, and trying to meet future demands involves a lot of gambling, Larsen laments that he has no idea if, in five years, he will need the five acres of Dabinett he recently planted. Just because he can grow the raw materials does not mean that he will have an avenue or customer base to sell the cider. It is important, then, for orchards growing specialized apples at scale to be able to market the fruit to a variety of cidermakers.

By the same token, the supply chain for excess Red Delicious and Gala has allowed parts of the cider community to grow exponentially. Near limitless supplies of juice are ideal for adjunct labels looking for a well-balanced base that is available throughout the year. Sourcing cider-specific apples in this sea of oversupply, on the other hand, can be financially and logistically challenging. Large agriculture in eastern Washington is not equipped for the annual ballet of harvest, sales, and logistics that sends Yarlington Mill and Kingston Black to cideries across the region. To better manage this process, Larsen paired up with cider industry vet Caitlin Braam to form The Source, to collaboratively market and sell apples and juice from five different orchards. By taking a page out of the efficiency books of their larger neighbors, The Source aims to bring cider with character, including their own Yonder Cider, to drinkers around the country.

Harmony Orchards is another contributor to eastern Washington's growing crop of cider apples. With four hundred acres, Craig and Sharon Campbell did not start looking at cider until 2008, when they planted their first test blocks of cider fruit. Located outside Yakima in Tieton, roughly one hundred miles south of Wenatchee in the center of the country's largest hop farms, their season is a bit longer and warmer than their northern counterparts. The comparable warmth, coupled with their experience of successfully growing cherries and apricots, gave them confidence in their ability to grow cider apples despite a number of uncertainties.

Fifty acres of estate cider apples provide Tieton Cider Works with some excellent bottlings of Ashmead's Kernel and a keeved perry, but most of their harvest is sold to other cidermakers across the country. Tieton cidermaker Marcus Robert, who also sells grapes from his family's farm to winemakers, says winemakers and cidermakers have very different expectations for the fruit they are purchasing. Grapes are generally contracted on a long-term basis that comes with strict yield limits and desired sugar levels. For apples, there are no such guarantees. Yields and sugars can vary dramatically year to year, far more so than with grapes, making people hesitant to sign long-term contracts. Instead, most fruit is presold by midsummer based on estimates—which, as the case proved in 2018, can be misleading and leave cidermakers short on the apples they desired.

Apple growing in eastern Washington has changed dramatically since the first irrigation projects brought water to the desert. In the early part of the twentieth century, migrant workers fleeing the worst of the Dust Bowl from Arkansas, Oklahoma, and the Midwest made up the bulk of the orchard workforce. After World War II, that labor was replaced by Mexican families who worked their way north with the seasons through California and into Washington. With a quickly industrializing, sustainable form of modern agriculture developing in central Washington, many of these families stayed. Today, migrant labor has shifted to guest workers with H-2A visas. Farmers recruit mostly men from towns across Mexico and Central America every year with the promise of lucrative pay for the season.

Farmworkers' Rights and Protections

Orcharding is very labor-intensive. From winter pruning through late summer and fall harvest, it takes a lot of work to put fruit on the table. Historically and today, agricultural workers have been systematically marginalized and exploited. Farmworkers were excluded from large parts of the New Deal legislation, including the National Labor Relations Act (NLRA) of 1935 that created broader recognition for unions and the Fair Labors Standards Act (FLSA) of 1938 that created federal minimum wage, overtime, unemployment insurance, and record-keeping requirements. The exclusion of farmworkers from these protections and programs was done at the behest of southern politicians in order to maintain the former plantation owners' class control over their once-enslaved workforce.

Agricultural workers were not included in FLSA until 1966, and they are still left out of overtime provisions. Small farms are even allowed to pay less than minimum wage. Later legislation, in the 1970s and '80s, implemented regulations with regard to safety, housing, and transparency, but not enough to bring farmworkers on par with the workforce.

H-2A workers make up a large portion of the country's orchard workers. They are afforded higher pay and better benefits and protections than the migrant workers of the past, but issues persist. Guest worker programs can be inaccessible for smaller growers and, in a market driven by lowering production costs, there is little left for workers. Movements to expand protections have been met by fear of increased food prices and farms being unable to absorb the added expense. The contemporary food system has been built on cheap labor, and any attack on that threatens to undermine an already shaky system.

In 2020, COVID-19 shed a frightening light on the plight of many workers who were deemed essential for the safety of the country, but were barely able to get proper protective equipment despite the pandemic.

The expansive orchards of Washington require consistently growing profits and optimization, but most of the work for apple and tree fruit is still done by hand. Washington's orchards have had a difficult time finding enough workers to fulfill their needs, with labor shortages fueled by changing immigration and guest worker policies. With fewer workers, wages could go up until supply meets the demand, but pressure from the international market and investors has farms looking for other options. Dr. Carol Miles, at WSU in Mount Vernon, is researching methods of sustaining orchards in a future faced with labor shortages.

In Europe, machine harvesting is the norm for cider fruit, which is dislodged from the tree (usually shaken) and then collected by an oversized sweeper that picks up the fruit and readies it for the press. Because of bruising and damage that may occur during the process, fruit is pressed shortly thereafter. Unfortunately, these implements are not feasible in the United States, since fruit comes into contact with the ground, raising *E. coli* fears. Even though 100 percent of harmful pathogens are killed during alcoholic fermentation, the issue remains at the forefront of regulators' minds. Miles's project aims to better understand how to grow trees for mechanized harvesting and to develop systems of handling and processing that will keep orchards viable in the future.

Montana and the Rocky Mountain Foothills

Orchards in Montana's Bitterroot Valley never emerged from under the shadow of the Great Depression, but their contributions enabled agriculture to grow throughout the valley. Large irrigation projects from a century ago remain a crucial part of the region's agriculture, but cows, hay, and hemp have largely replaced apples as the crops of choice. Remaining agriculture is being slowly swallowed up by hobby farms and vacation homes and, in a way, finally fulfilling the dreams of the valley's early investors.

Unlike those in Washington and Oregon, Bitterroot orchards are measured in dozens of acres, not hundreds, and the fruit serves the local communities rather than being shipped from coast to coast. The valley's growing season is short but intense, with the sun rising before five o'clock in the morning and holding in the sky past ten o'clock at night. This pushes sugars and acid through the roof. Despite significant snowmelt runoff in spring, the valley—which receives only thirteen inches of rain a year, all of which comes in the spring and makes fire blight a dire threat—is dependent on irrigation.

Lee McAlpine came to Darby as part of the United States Forestry Service, to manage parts of the Bitterroot National Forest. In 2007, after years of tinkering in her cellar and orchard as an amateur cidermaker, McAlpine launched Montana CiderWorks, the first commercial cidery in the state. Her first orchard was devastated in 2010 by an out-of-control brushfire, but McAlpine was able to tap into local resources to assemble unique ciders that fulfilled the agricultural promise of the Bitterroot Valley—the same one sold to the hopeful and speculative at the turn of the twentieth century. From McAlpine's early success, others have begun to reach into the agricultural potential of the Bitterroot Valley for a future with cider.

Michael Billingsley started working north of the valley outside the Flathead Indian Reservation in Paradise, Montana, where a fluke microclimate has enabled the state's only peach orchard to thrive. From Paradise, he succumbed to the intrigue, history, and excitement of fruit growing in the Bitterroot, where century-old McIntosh trees can still be found. Billingsley started Western Cider in 2012 with Matthew LaRubbio, and the two are trialing fifty varieties to better understand what they can do in the valley.

Bitterroot's current apple pioneers are acutely aware of the mistakes that led to the region's orchard bust at the turn of the century, from lack of communication to poorly suited apples and ignorance toward pests and disease. Today, Montana's agricultural research station, at the southern Bitterroot in Corvallis, has cold-hardy rootstocks and variety trials under way.

Small home orchards, old and new, dot the river valleys and foothills in the northern Rocky Mountains. With the apple belt of Yakima and Wenatchee three hours away, Rick Hasting has drawn upon these smaller orchards around Spokane, along the western slope of the Rockies. Tired of his desk job, Hastings became interested in making cider after his beer-loving brother developed celiac disease. Spokane is filled with urban wineries, so Hastings went about recreating that tasting room experience with Liberty Ciderworks. He found the cider apples he needed for Liberty while attending Peter Mitchell's course at Mount Vernon. In a slide presentation, he saw someone wearing a sweatshirt from Bishop's Orchards in Garfield, Washington. Hastings went home and gave them a call.

Bishop's had planted European cider apples years before, fifty miles south of Spokane, and was more interested in growing them than fermenting them. On the flip side, Steury Orchards, twenty miles east of Bishops, in Idaho, was planted with the intention of making cider. Tim Steury wanted to recreate the cider he drank in France with his wife, Diane Noel, who is from Normandy. Liberty works with both orchards, and each exists on the legacy of the Palouse Loess's history of growing apples north of the Snake River.

Idared

Developed by the University of Idaho Agricultural Experiment Station in Moscow and released in 1942, this apple takes its name from Idaho Red, even though it is often multicolored. Popular in midcentury orchards, it quickly became a favorite in cool climates for pies, sauce, and fresh eating as well as for its storage capabilities. While not the most characterful variety, it is an important blending apple for cidermakers across the country, who love it for its fruit-forward aromas and firm acid backbone.

CIDER PROFILE

Subtle aromas of pear and green bean. Ability to blend with even the most tannic and wild ciders.

The Palouse Loess is a distinct geographic and agricultural region defined by soil made up of windblown Ice Age sediment that reaches over 240 feet deep. Two land-grant universities opened there at the end of the nineteenth century, helping shape agriculture in the region. The area is more noted for lentils and wheat, with orchards relegated to small farms like Steury and Bishop's, but apples from the Palouse Loess are distinctive. Golden Russets and Kingston Black sourced from Palouse orchards often have 20 to 30 percent higher sugar than their Puget Sound counterparts.

In an effort to utilize the full richness of the area's terroir, Hastings began sourcing crab apples from orchards larger than his partners' in the Palouse. Crabs like Dolgo and Manchurian can be found scattered in the rows of Washington's orchards as pollinators for other trees. In the past, these apples were rarely harvested because of the logistical challenge of picking a few rogue trees among hundreds of tons of Fuji and Granny Smith apples.

Nearly impossible to press, cherry-sized Manchurians yield incredibly tannic, acidic, and sweet cider. Because of their high tannin and low pH, they are also very hard to ferment. Liberty's Manchurian Crabapple SV Cider is blended with a small amount of McIntosh and Cortland to aid with the fermentation. Manchurians naturally keeve, meaning they never ferment fully dry and often exceed 12 percent ABV. While Hastings's other ciders use native yeast, the Manchurian needs the strength and virility of commercial yeast. The final product is reminiscent of port, even though it is not fortified. At 12.5 percent ABV and 20 grams of sugar, the punchy cider is ruby colored with aromas of red plums, currants, and dusty red clay.

Core Takeaways

Cider in the Pacific Northwest is hard to fit in a box. For every large cider company tapping into the oversupply from eastern Washington, there are dozens of boutique estate cideries, urban taprooms, and everything in between. The Northwest is blessed with numerous resources from the rich wine and beer infrastructure and culture that help cidermakers not only produce but also talk about and sell their products. The region also has a bounty of explorable raw materials, and creativity in using them is supported by producers and drinkers who come from a tradition of spurning convention. Oregon was once considered marginal for Pinot Noir, and citrusy, hoppy West Coast IPA was thought to be improper, but both beverages have emerged to become mainstays of the local and national markets. These successes pave a hopeful path for the future of cider in the region.

PUGET SOUND

• **Location and Geography:** West of the Cascade Mountains, Puget Sound is filled with deep waterways and hundreds of islands.

• **Soil:** Diverse soils, including lots of clay, sand, and silty loam, with many exposed or deposited by glaciers.

• **Climate:** Moderate maritime climate, with mild winters and summers. While often thought of as a rainy climate, it is dry throughout most of the growing season, especially in the San Juan Islands and Olympic Peninsula. USDA Hardiness Zone 8a–9a.

• **Orchard Location:** Old orchards can be found throughout the islands, where they once served urban markets before the rise of irrigated eastern Washington after World War II.

• **Orchard Type:** Small orchards still thrive throughout the region; the Skagit Valley, in the northern sound by Mount Vernon, maintains a small but fading core of commercial apple growers.

• **Significant Apple Varieties:** Jonagold, Kingston Black, Yarlington Mill, Dabinett, Hewe's Crab, Puget Spice Crab, Jonathan, Redfield.

• **Cider Apple Plantings:** Cider apples have been grown for decades, and estate cideries are numerous. Other growers have actively embraced and begun replanting with cider in mind.

• **Producers to Visit:** Dragon's Head Cider (Vashon, WA), Nashi Orchards (Vashon, WA), Alpenfire Cider (Port Townsend, WA), Westcott Bay Cider (Friday Harbor, WA), Finnriver Farm and Cidery (Chimacum, WA).

HOOD RIVER, OREGON

• **Location and Geography:** Sixty miles east of Portland, the Hood River descends from Mount Hood, an active volcano, and flows into the Columbia River Gorge.

• **Soil:** Alluvial, sandy loam deposited from centuries of erosion from the active volcano.

- **Climate:** Maritime, with supplemented irrigation from snowmelt and rivers. The area is very windy, as the air travels from the high pressure of the desert to the low pressure of the Pacific Ocean through the narrow gorge. USDA Hardiness Zone 7b–8a
- **Orchard Location:** The orchards are located in the sandy volcanic soils along the river, from 500 to 1,740 feet in elevation.
- **Orchard Type:** Most of the apples go to the fresh or export market, while a few orchards have begun direct-to-consumer sales. Processing—especially juice—remains an important part of the industry. Hood River grows nearly ten times as many pears as apples.
- **Significant Apple Varieties:** Newtown Pippin, Red Delicious, Gala, Granny Smith, Golden Delicious, Hudson's Golden Gem, Hidden Rose (aka Airlie Red Flesh and Mountain Rose), Pink Lady (aka Cripps Pink), Ashmead's Kernel.
- **Cider Apple Plantings:** Growers are more likely to grow heirloom apples for farmers' markets and retail sales, with any excess being utilized by cidermakers.
- **Producers to Visit:** Runcible Cider (Mosier, OR), Hiyu Wine Farm (Hood River, OR).

WILLAMETTE VALLEY, OREGON

- **Location and Geography:** South of Portland, extending 150 miles to Eugene, the valley is centered on the Willamette River, running between the Cascades to the east and the Coastal Mountains to the west. Rich, deep farmland in the valley is flanked by vineyards on the western slopes and foothills.
- **Soil:** Very deep, silty loam deposited by the cataclysmic Missoula floods, which brought topsoil from eastern Washington on its way toward the ocean. Hills are a mix between sandstone and basalt.
- **Climate:** Moderate arid climate, with little rain during the summer months. It is cooler in the north close to the Columbia River and in the middle section adjacent to the Van Duzer Corridor—a break in the coastal range that allows cooler maritime air to seep into the valley. USDA Hardiness Zone 8a.
- **Orchard Location:** Orchards thrive in the deep, well-drained soils of the valley floor and alongside vineyards in the western foothills.
- **Orchard Type:** Once home to many apple and pear orchards, the area is now focused on other crops as apples become ascendant elsewhere. Those orchards that remain grow mostly for direct-to-consumer and fresh markets.

- **Significant Apple Varieties:** Hudson's Golden Gem, Dabinett, Kingston Black, Rome Beauty, Jonathan, Muscadet de Lense, Somerset Redstreak, Golden Russet, Wickson.
- **Cider Apple Plantings:** While the number of orchards in the area is dwindling, many of the new orchards going in the ground have an eye toward cider. The existing winery infrastructure and market has been an excellent launching point for many producers.
- **Producers to Visit:** Art+Science Cider and Wine (Sheridan, OR), Bauman's Farm and Garden (Gervais, OR), 2 Towns Ciderhouse (Corvallis, OR).

CENTRAL WASHINGTON

- **Location and Geography:** The eastern foothills and ridge of the Cascade Mountains.
- **Soil:** Alluvial and porous soils carved out by cataclysmic flooding during earlier Ice Ages.
- **Climate:** High desert, arid continental climate, with little precipitation throughout the year, making the area heavily dependent on irrigation. USDA Hardiness Zone 6a–7a.
- **Orchard Location:** Most of the orchards are found in the Wenatchee and Yakima Valleys, in the foothills above the valley floor, taking advantage of air drainage.
- **Orchard Type:** Large orchards here grow the majority of the apples in the United States. Most are geared toward large packing operations to supply grocery stores nationwide.
- **Significant Apple Varieties:** Gala, Fuji, Pink Lady (aka Cripps Pink), Red Delicious, Granny Smith, Yarlington Mill, RedWave, Manchurian Crab, Columbia Crab, Pink Pearl.
- **Cider Apple Plantings:** An increasing amount of orchard is being converted for cider purposes. Cider varieties have been grown here—first experimentally and then commercially—for several years. Growers of all sizes are looking to expand the diversity of their businesses with cider apples.
- **Producers to Visit:** Snowdrift Cider Co. (East Wenatchee, WA), Tieton Cider Works (Yakima, WA).

MONTANA AND THE ROCKY MOUNTAIN FOOTHILLS

- **Location and Geography:** Western Montana and southern Idaho, into far eastern Washington.
- **Soil:** Alluvial deposits of loam and clay along the Bitterroot Valley, with windblown loess in the Palouse in southeastern Washington.

- **Climate:** Arid continental climate with often erratic winter weather. USDA Hardiness Zone 4a–5a.
- **Orchard Location:** The Bitterroot Valley was briefly a large producer of apples, and some of those orchards remain. Small orchards can still be found in the river valleys of Idaho and Washington, but they are mostly homestead plantings.
- **Orchard Type:** The remaining orchards in Montana are mostly focused on growing fruit for fresh markets and direct-to-consumer. Smaller orchards are mostly for local use and markets. There is some renewed interest in commercial juice production.
- **Significant Apple Varieties:** McIntosh, Golden Russet, Porter's Perfection, Wickson, Manchurian Crab, Jonathan, Gravenstein, Winesap.
- **Cider Apple Plantings**: Cider-specific apples have been grown for quite a while on a small scale, and midsized growers have taken interest because of the growing market for cider. Estate cideries are growing considerably.
- **Producers to Visit:** Liberty Ciderworks (Spokane, WA), Western Cider (Missoula, MT).

AND SO . . .

Following the trajectory of cider in the United States offers an opportunity to understand the human condition and our relationship with nature, food, agriculture, government, and one another. These things are inherently bound together, looped into the history of the United States. Cider's differences around the country are expressions not only of the different terroirs, but of the settlement patterns, customs, and commerce that followed the European colonization of North America. Cider embodies the best and worst of America's history and agricultural practices.

The beverage, like humans' waltz through time, is a liminal journey inevitably subject to human decision. Ciders made on the East and West Coasts—and in all points between—are representative of the histories that precede them. In New York and New England, regions that have significantly longer histories than elsewhere in the country, there is an abundance of heirloom apples and legacy orchards, while in the Midwest, large orchards producing fruit grown for factories have been redirected toward cider. Throughout the country, cidermakers have become stewards of this old fruit and the systems put in place to sustain and ferment it. In some cases, with new technologies, their markets have gone national, but cider is historically built on local customs, traditions, and expectations.

As the country transitioned from singular Euro-Christian

cultures to diverse and increasingly global collections of people, orchards became an extension of the nation's struggle for homogeneity. Western settlement into the early twentieth century coincided with improved orcharding methods. Most cider from the region today reflects this, and showcases the agricultural infrastructure put in place generations ago.

This complex narrative is more than can fit on a label, and it leads to the simplification of large concepts into dualities. Cider's most significant conundrum lies in the human interest to label and define things, to form two-sided arguments or categories. Black or white. Good or bad. Sweet or dry. Cidermakers are often split into two camps: those who make cider year-round from concentrate or bulk juice and those who make it once a year, during fall harvest when nature provides the fruit. But cider is not that simple: it is a diverse, dynamic, and layered product. There is no single voice or path being forged in cidermaking today. Even for the well informed, the breadth of contemporary cider makes it nearly impossible to keep up with innovation, styles, and techniques. Simply summarizing the nearly one thousand cidermakers in this country does them all a disservice, failing to highlight the unique perspectives of the environments they were born from.

In the modern market, with access to seemingly endless knowledge, resources, and agricultural diversity, cider cannot be framed as a singular beverage. It is multifaceted; it tells a story while tasting great. This complex identity needs to acknowledge the foundations on which it is built. Cider drinkers and makers alike skew heavily white because of these foundations. There is an omnipresent relationship between products born from white-owned land and the resulting market. But, because of the apple's bipartisan role in the journey from fledgling nation to global powerhouse, cider has the potential to reach people even if they do not identify with U-Pick orchards, let alone old notions of Manifest Destiny. Simplified, idealized stories of cider's glory days fail to capture the complexity of the beverage, while alienating many potential cider devotees.

As the twenty-first century unfolds, and we labor to build new narratives around a historical product, a generation of drinkers, producers, consumers, and farmers all face tough, often contrary decisions about the future of society and the planet. The role of agriculture in our society has shifted dramatically since the last time cider enjoyed marginal popularity. The abuse of natural, agricultural, and human resources into the early twentieth century exacerbated the Great Depression and directly led to today's consolidated agricultural system, with large enterprises built on exploitation.

Agriculture, though, has the power to heal the land, create opportunities, and foster a national dialogue. Cider's growth can be fueled by its ability to connect with people across demographics ready to take up new challenges. Communities that have been overlooked through the consolidation of a national supply chain can now raise a glass filled with cider. Instead of attempting to reshape cider's narrative for an inclusive audience in ten, twenty, or fifty years, we can—and should—get there right now. Although cider came to America from western Europe, where the culture has existed, thrived, and been ingrained in local communities for centuries, U.S. history had a different plan for the beverage and its fruit. As we come to understand that complex and multifaceted history, we find ourselves in a position today to restitch cider and apple culture into the fabric of the country.

ACKNOWLEDGMENTS

We would like to acknowledge the fact that most of the land on which contemporary cider is being produced was first stewarded by Indigenous Peoples, the country's original champions of agriculture.

This book was born from a conversation early in 2018 and a friendship that precedes that. It is a collaboration, and, like cider, it is the result of two or more people or groups coming together to execute and celebrate a vision. It would not have been possible in three years (or ever) to put these ideas to paper if not for the stoic guidance and clear vision of Emily Hartley, who, with true grace, shaped many meandering thoughts into a cohesive read. Dana Murphy, our agent, was always there to help steer us through the process. So many people worked on this book that, in some instances, introductions were never made. We are grateful for their help, too.

We conducted over 120 interviews in person and over the phone. Many conversations averaged an hour, but some chats were longer, like the one with Steve Wood of Poverty Lane Orchards and Farnum Hill Ciders in New Hampshire. We caught him in the dead of winter, a somewhat dormant time for trees and cidermakers alike. He had to hang up once when his dog, Newton, ran off. But he called back and gave us nearly four hours of his time. So did Dan Bussey, in Iowa, who spent twenty years writing *The Illustrated History of Apples in the United States and Canada*. We are indebted to John

Bunker, Judith Maloney, Ellen Cavalli, Darlene Hayes, and the late Lee Calhoun, who have taken the work of previous generations and polished it with fresh hands so that the modern world may see it anew. Through opening their hearts, homes, and libraries to us, we were drawn up from the depths of digital rabbit holes back into the realm of human light.

The authors are fond of the eureka moments and countless phone calls, texts, and emails between each other, the strange places they slept while reporting parts of the book (from cabins in the backwoods of Maine to tents in Sonoma County orchards), and they are grateful to share with you the collaborative result of their friendship.

Craig is indebted to his mom and dad, his brothers Phil and Todd, and his close college buds Chris, Dan, Sean, and Jer. He is who he is in part because of them, but he got the apple bug from Pucci, and this book journey will forever be one of the great pleasures of his life. For that he is grateful to Pucci in ways words cannot express. None of this was possible, though, without his wife, Jenny, whose giggle, companionship, and unwavering support for everything he does make the largest tasks seem small and each day a profound joy. If not for Jean and Jon, his in-laws, his life would have a great void.

Dan would like to thank his wife, Lucy, and their daughter, Sylvie, who was born during the writing of this book. Also to Ben Sandler, Jennifer Lim, and Sabine Hrechdakian, the three people who first showed him what cider was and what it could be, thank you. Wassail was something special.

INDEX

ABOUT THE AUTHORS

DAN PUCCI is one of the nation's leading cider experts. He was the founding beverage director at Wassail, New York City's first cider bar and restaurant, and has since traveled the country in a continued pursuit of cider education, awareness, and research. He is a partner in Wallabout Hospitality, a New York City–based consulting and hospitality company.

Instagram: @danpucci

Syracuse native CRAIG CAVALLO anchored in New York City for thirteen years, working in restaurants and then writing for *Saveur*. His work has been published in *Condé Nast Traveler*, *GQ*, *New York* magazine's *Grub Street*, *Thrillist*, and *Vice Munchies*. He left New York City for the Hudson Valley, and when he's not at Golden Russet Cafe and Grocery, the café that he owns and operates with his wife, Jenny, he can be found picking fence line apples and dabbling in his own cellar cider experiments.

Instagram: @seecavallo

ABOUT THE TYPE

This book was set in Baskerville, a typeface designed by John Baskerville (1706–75), an amateur printer and typefounder, and cut for him by John Handy in 1750. The type became popular again when the Lanston Monotype Corporation of London revived the classic roman face in 1923. The Mergenthaler Linotype Company in England and the United States cut a version of Baskerville in 1931, making it one of the most widely used typefaces today.